Real Estate Rookie

# REAL ESTATE ROOKIE

## 90 DAYS
### TO YOUR FIRST INVESTMENT

# ASHLEY KEHR

**BiggerPockets**®
PUBLISHING
Denver, Colorado

# Praise for *Real Estate Rookie*

"Fun, easy to read, and insanely thorough, this book will become a bible for a generation of up-and-coming real estate investors!"

**—Brandon Turner, Best-selling author of *The Book on Rental Property Investing***

"Every new investor MUST read this book. Real estate can be one of the best ways to achieve finical freedom, but you can only get there by taking the right steps. Ashley walks you navigates you through these you through the basics of real estate investing to get you going on your financial journey."

**—James Dainard, Managing Partner at Heaton Dainard Real Estate and co-host of the *On The Market* podcast**

"Nothing is more daunting than embarking on a career in a new domain without a formal education, mentorship, know-how, or a roadmap—yet this is commonly the case for new real estate investors. Ashley's book is *exactly* what I'd recommend for the rookie investor. It demystifies a complex industry and provides a clear framework for building the tools you need for long-term success. This book will provide the perfect jumpstart for the self-starter!"

**—Leka Devatha, President of Rehabit Homes**

**Real Estate Rookie: 90 Days to Your First Investment**
Ashley Kehr

Published by BiggerPockets Publishing LLC, Denver, CO
Copyright © 2023 by Ashley Kehr
All rights reserved.

**Publisher's Cataloging-in-Publication Data**
Names: Kehr, Ashley, author.
Title: Real estate rookie : 90 days to your first investment / by Ashley Kehr.
Description: Includes bibliographical references. | Denver, CO: BiggerPockets Publishing, 2023.
Identifiers: LCCN: 2022947438 | ISBN: 9781947200845 (paperback) | 9781947200852 (ebook)
Subjects: LCSH Real estate investment--United States. | Real estate business--United States. | Personal Finance. | Investing. | BISAC BUSINESS & ECONOMICS / Real Estate / General | BUSINESS & ECONOMICS / Investments & Securities / Real Estate | BUSINESS & ECONOMICS / Personal Finance / Investing | BUSINESS & ECONOMICS / Real Estate / Buying & Selling Homes
Classification: LCC HD1382.5 .K84 2023 | DDC 332.63/24--dc23

**Printed on recycled paper in Canada**
MBP 10 9 8 7 6 5 4 3 2 1

# DEDICATION

For Mr. Emerling

# TABLE OF CONTENTS

# INTRODUCTION

## My Rookie Start

Everyone who tries something new starts out as a rookie. That's the truth. Even though I have bought, sold, owned, and managed a large real estate portfolio and now help others get started in real estate, I began the race at the starting line like everyone else. To prove it, here is my Real Estate Rookie origin story.

First, let me begin by telling you that there is nothing special about me or my ability to achieve success. In school, I worked hard to receive average grades. I went to college, but I didn't excel there right away. In fact, I failed an accounting class—and I was an accounting major! I transferred to a different university and eventually graduated with a degree in public accounting and finance.

See? Nothing remarkable so far.

After college, I started working for a public accounting firm, one I had interned for while still in school. I couldn't wait for the day when I'd receive my first full-time salary offer. I was ready to finally be paid the big bucks. But, to make a long story short, when that long-awaited offer came, I was super disappointed.

The dollar amount shocked me. It was so low! When I finally held everything I had been working for in my hands, I was left feeling less than satisfied. I remember talking with another employee and sharing my disappointment. She was the youngest partner at the firm, a successful woman I admired immensely. Through her, I learned that even the partners (the top dogs at the firm) didn't make "great money," even after years of hard work and long hours. That moment was one I'll never forget. I didn't want to be her. I didn't want what she had. I wanted more.

But I didn't know what else to do. While I didn't love my line of work, I still had the idea in my head that a job was a job. A job was a necessity. So I swallowed my pride and frustration, and I stayed.

I worked at the firm for about six months. During that time, I started studying for my CPA exam and took the first of the four required tests. I failed. I was so embarrassed. Maybe I wasn't good at being an accountant; maybe I had wasted my degree; maybe I would be broke forever. When tax season came around, each day became more painful than the last. I didn't want to go to work. Even though I'd worked so hard to arrive at this destination, I wanted out. The thought of spending the rest of my life like this killed me. I wanted to go somewhere else. To do something else.

I talked with my husband, and his blunt answer was, "Well, if you want to be a barefoot stay-at-home mom on the farm, I think it would be great if you quit." I put in my two weeks' notice, and a week later found out I was pregnant. It seemed meant to be.

After six weeks as a pregnant stay-at-home soon-to-be mom, I was approached by a family friend to help him organize his business. It was a part-time position where I could work at home and make my own hours. I wasn't really good at doing nothing, so this seemed like a good solution. The "organize" part of the job ended up being managing a forty-unit apartment complex. Without even knowing what a property manager was, all of a sudden, I was one. I was shown my setup—a small office with no windows or AC, a drawer full of keys, and a box full of leases. In that little office, I started a property management company and grew the courage to start investing myself (after I had my *aha* moment).

This *aha* moment came from working for this investor. Not only did I see firsthand the properties and businesses he owned, but he also let me assist and learn along the way. When I first started, he was acquiring a new business, purchased in *cash*. I couldn't comprehend how someone could just have that much cash laying around, but I learned quickly that it wasn't just sitting in piles around his house. Instead, he showed me how to help him refinance one of his apartment complexes that had appreciated in value. He took a new mortgage on the property and used the money he'd gained in new equity to purchase the business. The apartment complex's rental income was paying the mortgage, and he was using the funds from the refinance to buy this new business that would generate more income for him. My mind went a mile a minute. It would have taken me years—maybe decades—to earn and save enough cash to buy a business, and here this investor was leveraging money into more money, into more money again!

At the closing table, he let me write out the checks. It was more money than I ever thought I would write a check for. The impact this moment had on me can't be understated—I realized both that I wanted to be the one signing those checks one day and that it might genuinely be possible for me. Over the next few months, I talked with his son about investing in real estate with me. Within a year, we pulled the trigger and bought our first duplex. That was just the beginning, but I had my work cut out for me.

Four years later, in 2018, I was thirty, married with three kids, living in the dream house my husband and I built—and I was $169,000 in debt. This debt was from a line of credit, farm equipment, student loans, and our vehicles, and the monthly payments amounted to $3,712. I wish this was a dramatic rags-to-riches story for your entertainment, but it's not. Each month, we paid our bills. We didn't struggle, but we didn't thrive. I was making around $35,000 a year at my W-2 and my husband's farm income averaged around $60,000 a year. We had less than $5,000 in savings.

It all seemed normal until I found Dave Ramsey and his sometimes-divisive debt-free plan. He inspired me to get out of personal debt. I started taking all of my cash flow from the small rental portfolio I'd built up and paying off our personal debt. We did it in two and a half years. I honestly don't know if we could have done it without my rental portfolio. There are so many opinions on whether you should get out of debt before investing or if you should just dive in. I'm not going to give you a single answer on that—I believe you should choose what's right for you. For us, paying down debt and investing simultaneously was the best option.

The answer for me to start thriving in life, as you can probably guess by the title of this book, was real estate. Since that first property purchase in 2014, finding BiggerPockets in 2017 (when I tripled my portfolio thanks to the resources I found there), and getting out of personal debt, I have completely transformed my life. I went from stability to building wealth, and I saw some of the most growth in my personal development. Having something you are passionate and excited about can be transformative. At first, I wanted to buy investment property because I wanted to be wealthy. I wanted the extra income. I wanted to get out from under our debt and to be work-optional. But once I was investing, I realized how much I wanted to be spontaneous. I wanted to be secure *and* have time freedom. Real estate got me there. Once I defined my "why" (living spontaneously and not being bound to a job or set income), I became even more motivated and focused.

In less than a decade, I have created two property management companies, opened a wine and liquor store, built a portfolio of over thirty units in residential and commercial real estate, and embarked on many other random business ventures. This will probably be the hardest paragraph I have to write in the book, because it's where I'm supposed to highlight my accomplishments so you know I'm legit and should listen to me. The truth is, I've had just as many failures as I have had successes. Nobody's perfect, and so much of life is an experiment. I made my fair share of mistakes along the way. In this book, I want to share with you both my successes and pitfalls; armed with both pieces, you can be more successful and reach your goals even more quickly than I did (with less trial and error than it took me). The "why" I started with all those years ago has shifted and pivoted. But the beauty of real estate is that it is a vehicle that can help you arrive at your dream destination or reach your next milestone, no matter what your goal may be.

## About This Book

If it's all right with you, let's skip to the good stuff: I'm going to tell you how to become a Real Estate Rookie by getting your first—or next—deal.

To the outsider, real estate can look confusing. And it's true that there are many moving parts, some of which go unseen, especially if you don't know what to look for. But don't worry. In this book, I will walk you through the entire process, step by step. In fact, each step will get its own chapter. Before we go any further, I want to give you a rundown of where we are headed. Through this abbreviated version of our journey, you'll learn what lies ahead on the Real Estate Rookie roadmap.

You may already have questions popping up in your mind. That's good. You can use the double-entry journal I've provided at **www.biggerpockets .com/rookiebonus** to write them down. Emptying your brain of these questions rather than forcing yourself to hold and remember them while you also try to take in new information will help you learn more successfully. As you learn the answers, fill them in.

# Chapter 1: Goal Setting

How are you supposed to know how to arrive if you don't know where you want to go? In this opening chapter, I'll present a variety of tips and tools to help you set goals and align them with your investing journey.

# Chapter 2: Real Estate Investing Strategies

This chapter is all about learning your options. Once you know what types of investments are out there, you can pick the opportunities that best match your skill set, goals, and lifestyle.

# Chapter 3: Building a Business

It's important to treat your real estate investing like a business rather than a hobby, so I'll give you step-by-step instructions on how to set up your business so that it can take you to where you want to go.

# Chapter 4: Partnerships

Perhaps the best news about this entire process is that you don't have to do it alone if you don't want to. This chapter will teach you how to create real estate partnerships that will boost your success.

# Chapter 5: Financing

It's all about the money, right? To find success in real estate, you first must learn how to grow with the money you have. This chapter will help you think about (intelligently) leveraging your current assets in order to grow and scale your real estate business.

# Chapter 6: Market Analysis

Learn how to maximize your time as a rookie real estate professional by analyzing the best potential markets for you. In this chapter, you'll find my list of sixteen questions to help you better understand a selling area and the potential it holds.

## Chapter 7: Deal Analysis

There are all sorts of important aspects to consider when analyzing a deal, and this chapter lays them all out for you in the form of checklists, sample formulas, and reports.

## Chapter 8: Building Your Team

Building a functional and efficient team can skyrocket your real estate success and earning potential. In this chapter, I'll lay out the potential team members you can invite to join you on your journey, as well as their roles in the process. I'll even assist you with where you can find new team members!

## Chapter 9: Making an Offer

You've found your market and have a team in place. You have secured financing and are confident you've found a property you want to purchase. It's time to make an offer! In this chapter, I'll cover important considerations for the buyer and seller, negotiation tips, what to do if there are multiple offers, and my favorite ways to present an offer.

## Chapter 10: Under Contract

You've got your first property under contract. Everyone has agreed upon the purchase price and terms . . . but the work is not done. Now what? In this chapter, I share checklists and advice for navigating the finalization of funds, conducting the inspection, and setting up utilities.

## Chapter 11: After Closing

You have a property! Congratulations. Pop the champagne and then read this chapter to learn about your responsibilities as a property owner, as well as how you can get started on renting out or flipping the property.

## Chapter 12: Automation and Software

Now that we've talked about the entire process, let's look at how we can make it as smooth and easy as possible. To adequately grow and scale your business, automation and software implementation are key. I will walk you through some of the available options and share how you can choose the best tools for you and your business.

## Chapter 13: Motivation and Inspiration

Even though I achieved my real estate success in a short period of time, it can feel like a long road. To truly be successful, you need to stick with it. In this final chapter, I share some of my favorite ways to stay motivated and inspired, as well as stories from some real-life rookie rock stars.

In short, by reading this book, you're going to learn how to make your dreams come true. I realize that sounds like a big promise, but I can assure you that if you are willing to put in the work, it *can* and *will* happen for you. Trust me. I'm walking, talking proof.

I like to think about real estate as a puzzle. The pieces you need to put together are time, money, experience, and security. As you read this book and embark on your real estate journey, you'll learn where and when to place these pieces and how to put them all together to form your picture-perfect career and lifestyle.

When I purchased my first investment property, I was an absolute rookie. I had never bought or sold any type of real estate. At the time, I was living in my husband's grandma's old farmhouse for free. I didn't even have experience getting a mortgage. You guys, I didn't even know a real estate agent was a free service to me as a buyer. I was such a *rookie*!

Although I found my way on my own, you don't have to. I don't want you to feel as lost as I did. I want to help you! If you're taking the time to read this book, then you're on the right track. Investing in yourself is the first step toward success. I am thrilled you have chosen me to help you get your first (or next) deal done.

Your new life is out there, waiting for you to make it happen. Are you ready, rookie? Me too.

**Let's go.**

# Chapter 1

# GOAL SETTING

## Why Set Goals?

The very first step in your whole real estate plan is to make a goal. It's difficult to arrive at a destination when you don't know what that destination is. How will you know if you've reached your version of success if you don't first define it?

Some of you might be wondering why you can't just try your best and see what happens. The answer is, of course you could. But I'm guessing you didn't pick up this book to become a real estate investor of mediocre proportions. Even if you don't have mogul-sized dreams, you likely want to succeed, and do so as efficiently as possible. Without a goal, that probably won't happen.

The world is full of distractions. Once you open your eyes to the entrepreneurial opportunities available to you, chances are pretty good that you'll see many ideas that look appealing. These new opportunities fall into one of two categories: distractions or room for growth. It will be important to learn how to differentiate between the two and pick out only the best options (for you).

Shiny-object syndrome is real! I have it. I know it can be fun to daydream and wonder "what if." But chasing after each and every bright idea can slow you down. In order to efficiently and effectively reach your desired destination, you need to have a focal point to keep you on track and moving forward. Navigating through all of the choices life throws at you can be hard. Who wouldn't want to open a coffee shop, pimp out an RV and travel cross-country as a full-time vlogger, or finally launch that start-up business with your best friend? All of those things sound like a blast! And they have oh so much potential for profit. Why not do all of them?

(That was a rhetorical question—I'm going to tell you why not.)

It can be easy to fall away from your first intentions. But if you have a specific goal, you can lay out a plan that keeps you on the path to success.

## Setting Your First Goal

Tarl Yarber, an investor out of Seattle, once said to me, "You wouldn't hire a contractor that had a *dream* of building your home. You would hire one who had a *plan*." The ideal builder would have drawings, a skilled team of laborers, and a system to implement the completion of your project. This is how you should design your goals.

Your goal (your dream) needs to have a plan in place. You need to ask yourself, "What are the action steps that will get me from where I am to where I want to be?"

Start with a goal and reverse-engineer it. Work backward. Let's say that within five years, you want to earn $5,000 in cash flow a month.

How many units does that require? If you can net $200 a month from a property in your market, you would need to obtain twenty-five properties (or units) to reach your goal. Essentially, you'd need to purchase five properties every year, for five years.

From there, we can break it down to monthly, weekly, and daily action items. These items could range from calling lenders to getting preapproved for a loan to reaching out to three private lenders a week to analyzing one deal a day. As we go through the book, you will fine-tune these action items, but for now, a good place to start is to think of one task you can do monthly, one task you can do weekly, and one task you can do daily.

For example, once a month, you could analyze a new market or neighborhood. Once a week, you could submit an offer, and once a day, analyze a deal. It sounds good in theory, but to make it happen, you will want to assign yourself action items to complete and track these items. Write things down. Set deadlines and lay out specific instructions. The more detailed you are in your plan, the easier it will be to implement it.

This book is subtitled "90 Days to Your First Deal." Some of you will be able to accomplish the goals in that amount of time, but there's nothing wrong with choosing a different timeline. You'll hear me say it a hundred times in this book, but do what works for you. Just know that it is possible to get your first deal in ninety days . . . if you stay focused and motivated, and, most importantly, take action!

Before we go too far, you need to accomplish that very first step. You need to write a goal.

Close your eyes and picture your desired destination. What do you want to accomplish in the next ninety days? Is it to own your first investment property? Is it to make $15,000 off a house flip? Do you want to have a team in place?

Believe it or not, there is such a thing as a bad goal. I don't mean a goal that is unethical or illegal (although those certainly do exist); a goal can be bad by being ineffective.

If you simply said, "I want my first rental property," and left it at that, I would consider that a bad goal. The problem with this goal is that it's too broad. It is hard to plan for something that isn't specific.

Let's go back to Tarl's reference, and I'll show you what I mean. If you had a floor plan and budget for a house you'd like built, wouldn't that make it easier than just saying, "I want a house"? By not specifying your wants and needs, you are making it harder to control your outcome. Could you imagine trying to build a house when you have no idea what it should look like? What materials should you use? What color pallets should you pull from? Where would you even begin? It would be a disaster, and also highly unlikely that the end result would be one you desire.

The more dialed in your goal is, the better you will be able to create a plan and build out your action items and, thus, the more likely you will be to reach success.

Framing goal setting this way means you could want to run a company that buys multimillion-dollar commercial buildings or you could want to live on the beach and work four hours a week. Both are options: It all depends on *your* vision, *your* lifestyle wishes, and *your* goals.

Typically, there are two different kinds of people.

**Type #1:** This kind of person thinks it's easy to identify what they want out of life, but they struggle to figure out how to get there.

**Type #2:** This kind of person knows what they have to do, but not what they want. They can accomplish tasks, but they can't identify the end goal or their desired destination.

Which type of person are you? (Neither is bad, and you might be a mix of both.) For example, you may have an idea of what you want to gain from investing in real estate and know a couple of actionable steps to get there. The issue is that your plan is a little fuzzy. It's not clearly defined and written out. Or perhaps you know exactly the lifestyle you want to live. You have it all perfectly designed, right down to the paint color on the wall of your villa in the mountains. But you aren't sure which task on your list to tackle first.

That's okay. As you read through this book, you will be able to fine-tune your goal and put the pieces together to get there. Right now, you just need to write something down.

What do you want your real estate investing to help you gain? If you are really stuck for ideas, ask some friends or family members. In a perfect world, what would your life look like? What would you spend your time doing? What kinds of things and experiences would you spend your time and money on? Write down their answers. Write down your answers. Ask yourself these questions before you go to sleep and let your subconscious come up with the answers. Or try spending some time with the questions on the goal-tracking worksheet I've made for you at ***www.biggerpockets .com/rookiebonus***. Once you have your ideal lifestyle and goals in mind, write them down. Post them where you can see them each day. My friends Tyler and Zosia Madden have large sticky notes right on the wall in their dining room! The main point I hoped you've picked up by now is: MAKE A GOAL.

Analysis paralysis happens when you spend so much time researching and analyzing a situation or problem that you prevent yourself from taking any real action. It can be a big problem and happens without your notice or consent, so be aware! This goal-setting step is crucial, but it's not set in stone. Don't dwell on it so long that you stop yourself from moving forward on your real estate journey and getting to the real work. You don't want to be a Real Estate Rookie forever!

I want you to feel excited every day to work on your action items and to reach your goal. Your goal should motivate you, it should drive you, and it should give you endurance. Dig down deep and figure out what you want out of life. Real estate provides the opportunity to create the lifestyle you want. Focus on the lifestyle you desire, and then we can build your real estate investing plan around that.

## SMART Goals

Enough talking theoretically. Let's take some action. You may have heard of SMART goals. SMART is an acronym that is used to guide the development of measurable goals. It's a framework that helps users identify and achieve good goals. Your task is to create a goal in which each objective is:

- Specific
- Measurable
- Achievable
- Relevant
- Time-oriented

For example, earlier I told you that stating, "I want to own my first rental property," isn't a great goal. But it could be. Let's apply the S.M.A.R.T. goal strategy. If instead you said, "Through working in real estate I want to create $250 of additional cash flow each month so I can pay off my car loan by the end of the year," that would be SMART!

- **Specific:** pay off car loan
- **Measurable:** $250 cash flow
- **Achievable:** dollar amount is totally achievable
- **Relevant:** through real estate
- **Time-oriented:** by the end of the year

Once you have your SMART goal, you can take it to the next level with the additional acronym of MINS, otherwise known as the Most Important Next Step. What action, however small, can you take to get the ball rolling? What can you do after that to increase the distance or speed your business ball will roll?

Go on, step away from this book. Do a little dreaming. Search your soul. Envision the life you want to live. What is a weight on your shoulders? Is it missing your kid's games? Not being able to afford bills? Can't support your parents? What do you want and what do you want to change in your life? Then legitimately write down your goal. By putting these pieces on paper, you will gain two things: direction and motivation. With these two forces propelling your efforts, good things will happen!

Seriously, go ahead and write your goal down. I'll wait. I promise. Afterward, come back and we'll move on together.

Got it? Good. You are one step further down the road and just a little bit less of a rookie. But we have a long way to go. Goals are great, but on their own, they aren't enough. There are a few things you can do to make the most of your goal.

Note that I'm not saying you *have* to do all of these things. Everyone has their own toolbox of strategies that work well for them. Right now, I want to offer up a few that have worked for me and could work for you.

## The Rookie's Toolbox

### Intention Journal

Technically, the definition of "intention" is similar to "goal," but I perceive it as the feeling behind a goal. Intention is more about the emotion tied to the goal than the steps to achieve it. An intention is less specific than a goal, but once made, it can support a person's progress. "Intentions help create more clarity and confidence around goals and connect us to the present moment," says Liv Bowser, founder of the mental-fitness company Liberate.

An intention journal is a tool you can use to record and reflect on your goal-related intentions. By taking time to focus on your intentions, you are communicating to your brain that this goal is important. It is worth your time and worth your energy.

How about some scientific support? According to biologist Dr. Bruce Lipton, "The power of intention has the ability to literally change the shape of our brains. This process is known as neuroplasticity—the brain's soft and interchangeable potential, stimulated through repetition of a particular behavior. In the context of intention setting, neural pathways are the trail to self-optimizing behaviors. The more we repeat a positive intention or general positive behavior, the more likely our brain is to reorganize its neurons in our favor. Through cultivating healthy intentions, we are now learning that we have the power to shape our brains in more adaptive and beneficial ways."[1] Isn't that amazing?

Recording your thoughts about your intentions can also help you identify when your feelings about your goals shift, perhaps signaling a breakthrough or a desire to go in a new direction. Being aware of your own journey on the road to real estate success can help you celebrate mini milestones, identify (and prevent future) negative experiences, pivot in real time, and more.

There is no wrong way to intention journal. Highly recommend checking out Brandon Turner's Intention Journal found in the BiggerPockets bookstore. You can jot down a bulleted list of intentions, free-write in paragraph style about your personal reflections, or sketch out your ideas with pictures. Try out a few times of day and methods to discover what works best for you. It could be at the beginning or end of the day. It could be daily, midweek, or the last thing you do before you shut down for the weekend. This activity could be a quick five-minute bulleted list or a solid half hour of reflection. Creating a habit that is enjoyable and beneficial is the surefire way to continue this habit. Just make sure this isn't a waste of time or something you are using to put off actually buying real estate.

## Time Blocking

Do you know where your time really goes each day? Do you ever find yourself reaching the end of a day (or week) thinking, "Gosh, I felt busy, but what did I actually get done?" You aren't alone. If this is something you struggle with, the information that comes next is going to be helpful for you. Even if you think you do utilize time well, you might be surprised by what you find when you do a time study.

We all do things that waste time. Scrolling on social media, bingeing TV, and running to the grocery store multiple times a week instead of making one planned trip are common time wasters. What about tasks in our day that might not seem like time wasters, but are actually sucking up a huge chunk of our day, week, or month? What if you could be doing required tasks in a way that is more effective and efficient? These are great questions.

The first step in creating a productive work schedule is looking at how you use your time. The best way is through a time study. As you move through your day, carry a notebook or record a note in a phone app. Each

---

1   "The Powerful Science Behind Setting Intentions," Balance Festival, February 26, 2019, www.balance-festival.com/Journal/February-2019/The-Powerful-Science-Behind-Setting-Intentions.

time you do a task, change tasks, or switch a work location, write it down. Track your time as accurately as possible for at least a few days—you can get the best sense of where your time is going by tracking for two weeks. You can use a format like the following to help you keep track of your day. (You can find a downloadable version at **www.biggerpockets.com/ rookiebonus**.)

# Time Tracker

| DATE | DESCRIPTION | CLASS* | START TIME | END TIME | DURATION |
|------|-------------|--------|------------|----------|----------|
| | | | | | |
| | | | | | |
| | | | | | |
| | | | | | |
| | | | | | |
| | | | | | |
| | | | | | |
| | | | | | |
| | | | | | |
| | | | | | |
| | | | | | |

* **CLASS EXAMPLES:** Family, Work, Real Estate, Personal Development, Fitness, Lazy, Household, Etc.

Afterward, analyze your results. How much time did you spend on each task or category of tasks? Can you identify any time wasters or any areas you can tweak for improved productivity?

Here is a sample study so you can see this strategy in action.

# Time Tracker

| DATE | DESCRIPTION | CLASS | START TIME | END TIME | DURATION |
|------|-------------|-------|-----------|----------|----------|
| 1/1/23 | Wake up, shower, get ready | Routine | 6:00 a.m. | 6:30 a.m. | 30 min |
| 1/1/23 | Eat breakfast and read | Routine | 6:30 a.m. | 7:00 a.m. | 30 min |
| 1/1/23 | Clean up house while watching Netflix | Household | 7:00 a.m. | 8:00 a.m. | 1 hour |
| 1/1/23 | Phone calls | Work calls | 8:00 a.m. | 8:15 a.m. | 15 min |
| 1/1/23 | Run errands, pick up prescription, get mail from PO box | Errands | 8:15 a.m. | 9:30 a.m. | 1 hour 15 min |
| 1/1/23 | Get settled in office, talk with Liz | Transition | 9:30 a.m. | 10:30 a.m. | 1 hour |
| 1/1/23 | Open mail and sort, read emails and respond, start bookkeeping | Work | 10:30 a.m. | 12:15 p.m. | 1 hour 15 min |
| 1/1/23 | Pick up lunch, eat at desk while browsing www.biggerpockets.com | Routine | 12:15 p.m. | 1:00 p.m. | 45 min |
| 1/1/23 | Phone call with tenant and other calls to resolve issue | Work calls | 1:00 p.m. | 1:30 p.m. | 30 min |

| 1/1/23 | Desk work, finish bookkeeping, lease renewals | Work | 1:30 p.m. | 4:00 p.m. | 2 hours 30 min |
|--------|-----------------------------------------------|------|-----------|-----------|----------------|
| 1/1/23 | Drive home, stop for gas | Commute | 4:00 p.m. | 4:30 p.m. | 30 min |
| 1/1/23 | Get home, make dinner, scroll on social media | Routine | 4:30 p.m. | 6:00 p.m. | 1 hour 30 min |
| 1/1/23 | Eat dinner | Routine | 6:00 p.m. | 6:30 p.m. | 30 min |
| 1/1/23 | Scroll social media, Netflix, look at property listings | Lazy | 6:30 p.m. | 7:30 p.m. | 1 hour |
| 1/1/23 | Take a bath | Routine | 7:30 p.m. | 8:15 p.m. | 45 min |
| 1/1/23 | Browse the internet looking at new software | Soft work | 8:15 p.m. | 9:30 p.m. | 1 hour 15 min |
| 1/1/23 | Bed | Routine | 9:30 p.m. | | |

*End of day summary:*
45 min: Phone calls
2 hours 30 min: Social media
1 hour 30 min: Browse internet
1 hour: Getting settled
4 hours 30 min: Concentrated work

*Summary Report:*
- *Today I could have spent less time on the phone with tenants and other issues. I need to create a policy for this tenant issue to automate it.*
- *More focus on growing portfolio to reach my goal, maybe need to block more time on calendar to look at deals.*

In addition to identifying time wasters, a time study helps some people realize that they spend a lot of time transitioning back and forth, either physically traveling from one place to another or mentally switching between tasks.

If you can find a way to time block, doing related tasks during a specific and concentrated chunk of your day or week, then you can cut down on unnecessary drive time and heavy mental lifting. This will be extremely beneficial. Multitasking (or attempting to multitask) uses oxygenated glucose, which fuels your brain's ability to focus on a task. By focusing on important tasks in blocks of time rather than dipping into them randomly over the day, you can better use your physiological fuel resources that help you function. When you're interrupted, it takes twenty-three minutes on average to get back into the zone.[2]

Just think of all that time lost! Look at your time study and see how you can better line up your tasks and schedule your daily agenda to avoid this costly mistake.

## Accountability Partner

Later on in the book, we will talk about building your team and creating partnerships that foster success, but there is one person you need to get on board right away: an accountability partner. The best accountability partner is someone who knows you and your goals, and will keep you on track. Someone who will check in with you and ask you about your progress. Someone you trust. Someone who motivates you. Someone who understands why the highs are truly worth celebrating and why the lows are disappointing but are also lessons learned. Someone who will help you make your dream a reality.

Starting your investing journey can be lonely. The people currently in your life may not understand your new goals; they may challenge you on your choice to invest in real estate. There will be ups and downs on the journey, along with many questions. Having a friendly person in your corner as you navigate this journey will make all the difference.

I could talk to my parents about real estate until I'm blue in the face. While they'll always be supportive of me and my big dreams, they don't get as fired up about market analysis and low interest rates as I do. And that's okay. Not everyone has to be passionate about the same things. But I believe that if you want to stay committed to a goal, you need to have someone you can talk to who feels the same as you do.

Fortunately, there is a huge network of people online (this is where

---

2    Olivia Goldhill, "Neuroscientists Say Multitasking Literally Drains the Energy Reserves of Your Brain," *Quartz*, July 3, 2016, qz.com/722661/neuroscientists-say-multitasking-literally-drains-the-energy-reserves-of-your-brain/.

I'm to go against every mother's wisdom "of talking to strangers online") that you can connect with, even if you don't have anyone in your family or friend circle in the real estate game. BiggerPockets has over 2.5 million users; there are dozens of real estate investing Facebook groups, many of which have tens of thousands of members. The communities are out there. One year, as an April Fool's Day prank, BiggerPockets announced they'd created an online dating website for investors. I think most people were upset when they figured out it wasn't true!

Whether you connect with another investor online or at a local meetup, there can be opportunities and benefits for both of you. One of the hardest attributes to maintain in any endeavor is endurance—the endurance to stay motivated as you analyze deal after deal, make offers, go over budget on rehabs, and so on. This is when you can lean on an accountability partner the most, during the struggles, to make sure you don't give up. An accountability partner knows your goals and action plan. Their purpose is to keep you motivated and continuously working on your goal. This person will support and encourage you, but also push you. In return, you will reciprocate and provide the same to them.

When choosing an accountability partner, consider the following:

- Don't choose someone whose only role is a cheerleader. (Hint-hint—don't ask your mom.)
- Make sure the person has some understanding of real estate investing. Your accountability partnership can be even stronger if the person you choose has the same level (or higher) of real estate investment knowledge and experiences as you.
- Make sure both of you can make the time commitment necessary. There is nothing worse than a one-sided relationship.
- Keep in mind that an accountability partner doesn't have to be one person. You can put together a group. Again, just make sure everyone is committed.

Once you have found your person (or your people), set up a video call or an in-person meetup each month. When you first start out, it may be beneficial to do a couple of meetings within a short time to really get to know each other and hone in on each other's goals.

Remember, this is not a book club or friendship club. It's a success group. You want to lead each other, respect each other, and push each other. You want to hold each other responsible for completing action items.

Motivating each other as well as inspiring. If someone is falling behind and losing interest in their goal, then it is your responsibility to listen, attempt to understand, and then help them create a solution. There is nothing better than surrounding yourself with like-minded individuals who are hungry to succeed. Also, don't be afraid to throw a little healthy competition into the mix. For some, this can be extremely motivating (and fun!).

Not sure how to find one of these amazing accountability partners? I've got you covered. Try attending networking events and local meetups. You can also search the BiggerPockets forums, real estate Facebook groups, or find people by following hashtags on Instagram such as #BiggerPockets, #RealEstateRookie, #BuyAndHold, and #NewbieInvestor. There are more ways every year to connect with fellow investors online.

One of the first mastermind groups I participated in started through an Instagram direct message. (A mastermind group is usually a form of peer-to-peer coaching; accountability is a key part of this, but masterminds lean more heavily toward mentoring.) A now friend, @nerdsguidetofi, was looking for accountability partners and connected with each of us separately and then, once she was sure she wanted to work with us, brought all eight members together. Even though our mastermind group isn't meeting monthly anymore, we still have a direct message thread going where we can ask questions and connect.

My advice is not just to ask someone straight out, "Do you want to be my accountability partner?" Get to know them first. Make sure they are the right fit and that you can also provide value to them.

Your accountability partner should not only help you stay on track but also help you pivot when needed. Goal setting is a continuous process that will be reset and adjusted. Don't be intimidated. Stay focused. Don't beat yourself up. Treat this as a journey and understand you will make mistakes. Having an accountability partner to pick you up when times are low will definitely help.

# HOMEWORK

If you want to make this goal happen in ninety days (or happen at all!), you need to put this information into action. Here is the homework to get done before moving on to Chapter 2.

- Dream, journal, or reflect: What do you want your life to look like? How does real estate fit into your ideal lifestyle?

- Create a SMART goal that helps you move closer to the vision of your ideal life.

- Start your time tracker and complete each day for two weeks.

- Find your accountability partner or group and set up your first meeting.

**OKAY, YOU'VE GOT A GOAL.** You've got some strategies to help you stick to it. Now turn the page and learn about the many different ways you can go about achieving your goals in Chapter 2: Real Estate Investing Strategies.

# Chapter 2

# REAL ESTATE INVESTING STRATEGIES

## Vocabulary You'll Need to Know

**ASSET CLASS:** A grouping of investments that have similar characteristics, are subject to the same laws and regulations, and behave similarly to one another in the marketplace.

**BUY-AND-HOLD:** A long-term passive investment strategy that involves keeping a relatively stable portfolio over a significant period of time, regardless of short-term market fluctuations.

**REHAB:** Changing the look and/or structure of a building by removing current materials and replacing with new and upgraded materials to transform the property into a safe, functional, and cosmetically appealing property. This is used to add value to the property.

**SCALABLE:** Describes the ability of a company to sustain or better its performance in terms of profitability or efficiency when its sales volume increases.

# What Are You Working With?

One of the best things about real estate is that there are many ways you can make a profit. As a Real Estate Rookie, you might not be aware of all the options available to you. In this chapter, I will introduce you to a wide variety of strategies. In addition to this solid foundation, I will also give you the pros and cons of each strategy, as well as list additional resources where you can learn more. I want you to know that no matter your past or current circumstances, there is an opportunity for you to become a real estate investor. Hopefully after reading this chapter, you'll not only believe me but also have your personal path selected.

Before we dig into the plethora of options available to you, I want you to pull out a notebook and ask yourself this question: "What resources or knowledge do I have available already?"

Knowing what you have to work with will make picking the best option (for you) all that much easier. You might be sitting there thinking, "Ashley, I've got nothing! That's why I got this book—so I can learn how to make some money." I hear you, but I'm going to challenge you to think creatively about your current situation and not just about your current cash flow.

- Is your dad a contractor who can help you with a rehab project?
- Do you have ten, fifteen, or twenty hours a week to invest into this new business adventure?
- Do you have a lot of capital and can make cash offers quickly?
- Do you have an eye for design and making spaces look great?
- Do you have a mentor who is already experienced in an investing strategy and is willing to guide you?
- Do you have a passion for anything in particular?
- Do you have certain tasks and jobs that you love doing? Or ones that you dislike?
- Do any of your current skills at your current job correlate into real estate investing?

If you have resources available to you for a particular type of investment strategy, then I highly recommend taking full advantage of them. Passion projects are great too, but as a rookie investor, finding and building on success might be more important. Think about what you can most efficiently do first—you can tackle that pie-in-the-sky endeavor later on after you've built a strong foundation.

The investor I first worked for used the buy-and-hold strategy. I started with this strategy to build a strong foundation. I could build a buy-and-hold portfolio more quickly and more successfully because I had resources (a mentor willing to share knowledge) available to me. Now that I have income and have reached a level of financial stability, I am moving on to another strategy that is more exciting and interesting to me: campgrounds and cabins as short-term rentals. It would have taken me a lot longer to get to where I am today if I had just jumped in to these property types without knowledge, guidance, or resources.

As you read this chapter, think about the goals you made in Chapter 1. What strategy will take you down the path to achieve those goals, the life you want, and your legacy? I also want to remind you that the strategy you choose to start with does not have to be the strategy you stick with forever. Choosing one strategy and mastering it *first* will give you the opportunity *later* to pivot and explore other strategies.

## Put Your Blinders On

After you choose your strategy, know that it may be difficult to stay focused. Life moves fast and throws a lot of stuff your way. It can be challenging to keep your eyes on the prize, stay committed, and truly maintain forward movement on your goal-oriented course.

In Chapter 1, I mentioned shiny-object syndrome. In addition to the responsibilities in your life (e.g., family members, another job) the razzle-dazzle of other opportunities may catch your eye and try to pull you off course. You will inevitably listen to a podcast or read a book on a new subject or hear how much money your neighbor's cousin is making doing XYZ and say to yourself, "I want to do that!" The great part about being an investor is that it's highly probable that there will be a time in your career for you to explore these shiny objects. But that time is likely *later*. As a rookie, you should focus your energy and efforts on one strategy. This means putting blinders on.

Think about driving through Amish country and seeing one of those horse-pulled buggies. Their reins have large black circles attached that keep the horses' eyes focused straight ahead. Instead of looking at what is off to the side in their peripheral vision, the horse keeps moving, one foot in front of the other, only focused on what's in front of them.

You are like that horse. You need to get from the starting point to a destination. That destination is your goal from Chapter 1. Once you have reached that destination, feel free to reevaluate and decide if you want to continue with the same strategy or pivot in a new direction.

After all this time in real estate, I still struggle with shiny-object syndrome. I can't tell you how many different business models and strategies I have researched. New business ideas flow through my brain constantly! They can be sparked by anything. Any time I hear someone talk about their investing strategy, my brain runs a scenario as to how I can do that too. When I see a property, my mind starts thinking about the different ways I can create income off it—even if it's a business model that I would have to research and develop from the ground up! What can I say? I'm a dreamer.

At the end of the day, these ideas waste a lot of time and energy that could be put to better use focusing on and strengthening my current business model.

Over the years, I have made many shifts in my business and experimented with different strategies. When I first started out, though, I stuck to buying duplexes that needed slight rehab. I took on projects that only needed cosmetic repair—meaning surface updates such as paint, flooring, and new fixtures. I wasn't ripping apart walls or gutting the units. I never even broke into a wall until my twenty-fifth unit, and even then, when I did decide to take that step, it was with a partner who knew how to complete a full-gut rehab.

I can buy a duplex blindfolded in my market—sight unseen—and give you the numbers on the property off the top of my head. Can I do that with a self-storage facility in my area? Nope. (Though I am working on learning that niche market!)

Having mastered the buy-and-hold duplex arena of real estate, I spent the last full year really trying to hone in on what I wanted to do next. I've looked into campgrounds, mobile home parks, self-storage, and short-term rentals. They each have aspects that appeal to me. Part of my mission to diversify my portfolio has forced me to learn that I need to focus on one strategy to master next. If you want an update or would like to take a peek at how my strategies are pivoting in the world's ever-changing economy, check out my recent social media posts to learn about my current projects.

I want you to know that a lot of investors will only invest in one strategy for their lifetime. That is perfectly fine too! There is no right or wrong way. As I said at the beginning of the chapter, real estate is achievable for the masses because there are so many paths to success. It's all about choosing what works for you. As a rookie, now is your time to decide on one strategy and build your systems out for that strategy—the rest of your spectacular journey will unfold as you choose.

## Focus Four

Here are the four things I want you to have running through your head as you read over each strategy. We've talked about each one a little already, but as you move forward, keep these crucial questions top of mind. Maybe write your answers on a couple of sticky notes and use them as bookmarks.

1. What resources or connections do you have now that are an advantage to you?
2. What is your current goal?
3. How active/passive do you want to be in the present and the future?
4. What excites you?

That fourth question might not seem all that important, but without this piece, you are likely to fail. Every minute detail of the strategy you pick doesn't have to appeal to you, but if you cannot be excited about the process, it will be a slog and you'll be more likely to abandon your goals before achieving them.

## Real Estate Strategies

Many rookie investors start off thinking they know exactly what strategy they want to begin with, only to find once they sit down and review the pros and cons, it is not for them! This can occur after trying out the strategy too. Your personality, strengths and weaknesses, and drive will all play a part in the strategy that you select.

Here are the strategies we are going to review:

1. Long-term rentals
2. Short-term rentals
3. BRRRR
4. Turnkey
5. House hacking
6. Fix-and-flip
7. Wholesaling

## Long-Term Rentals

This is probably the first strategy people think of when they consider investing their money in real estate: purchasing property with the intent to rent it out to a tenant who will occupy the unit(s) for six months or longer. With this kind of investment, there is no immediate intent to sell the property. Instead, the idea is to maintain ownership of the property for a long period of time, making money off your tenants' rent (in the meantime) and eventually making money off the sale of the property (far in the future). There are both pros and cons when it comes to this strategy. Let's take a look at both.

First, the pros. Each month, you are receiving income from the rental—this income (after expenses) is called cash flow. The rental income is also taxed lower than earned income, such as W-2 income or self-employed business income, which means you get to keep more in your pocket. There's a reason that long-term rentals are the bread and butter of so many investors. Every market has renters seeking stable and secure housing; by providing that housing, you can have a cash flowing investment for life that can even be passed on to future family as generational wealth. By renting out a property over the course of many years, you are less vulnerable to the short-term fluctuations of the economy and the housing market. Long-term rental investors are in it for the long haul!

There are also other tax advantages like depreciation (the ability to deduct the cost of the property from your taxes over time). These are legal tax strategies that make owning a long-term rental beneficial. Additionally, long-term rentals have several options for management. You can self-manage to save money but give up time, or you can outsource the property management and make your investment more passive. With more software, apps, and technology being released every year, it has never been easier and more efficient to be a self-managing landlord. Lastly, there is also the opportunity to increase the value of your investment by remodeling or increasing the rent—value-add investors love long-term rentals for the ability to find undervalued properties that can be improved and rented out at market rate.

The disadvantage of this strategy is that your rental income isn't guaranteed. The steady stream of consistent cash flow can be great one year but can be in the negative next year when your boiler breaks and your tenant falls behind on rent. Just because a tenant stops paying rent doesn't mean the bills stop for your property. You still have to pay the mortgage, property taxes, maintenance expenses, and insurance. Your property is also in the hands of your tenant and how they care for it. The last thing you want is to remodel and update your property only to have a tenant's dog and children destroy the place. There is a lot to keep track of with long-term rentals, such as regulations and fair housing laws, maintenance, leases and turnover, insurance policies, and more. Major expenses *will* come up—you need to factor these into your numbers—there's the chance of evictions that can drag on and several other worst-case scenarios can happen and kill your cash flow. Even with the security deposit, damages or repairs can sometimes wipe out a huge chunk of the profit you made while renters were in place. The best thing about real estate is that there are ways to prepare and educate yourself so you can be proactive instead of reactive when these situations come up.

## Short-Term Rentals

A short-term rental, also known as a vacation rental, describes furnished, self-contained apartments, houses, or more unique properties (like cabins) that are rented for short periods of time, usually by the day or month. This is opposed to annual rentals in the unfurnished rental market. Short-term rentals are commonly listed on websites such as Airbnb or VRBO and are primarily marketed to vacationers. They're a hot-ticket item in the entrepreneurial and real estate world!

Short-term rentals are attractive because they give the option to have higher cash flow than long-term rentals. But be ready to work, because they are more of an active business than a passive one. As a short-term rental investor, you won't only be in the real estate world, but in the hospitality industry as well!

I currently have three short-term rentals. For two of them, I am renting apartments in an apartment complex, which my partner and I furnished and then listed on Airbnb. The crazy thing is, I am making money off these properties, even though I don't own them! This is called rental arbitrage. Rental arbitrage is when you sign a long-term lease to rent out a place, furnish it, and then list it on Airbnb, VRBO, and other sites as a nightly, weekly, or monthly rental. You do need to get the landlord's permission to do this, so be sure to ask before signing a lease. Of course, the downside to arbitrage is that you have no real ownership stake and it's likely not a long-term endeavor; the landlord can choose to not renew your lease. You also aren't getting the tax benefits that you would have owning real estate.

The more traditional and ubiquitous short-term rentals are when you own a property and offer it for stays that are shorter than thirty days. There are also medium-term rentals, where tenancy is longer than thirty days but either month-to-month or for short, time-bound stays (rarely longer than six months). These medium-term rentals are attractive to traveling nurses, construction workers, who are assigned to a new job for several months or even weeks, as well as a handful of other careers and industries where medium-term travel is the name of the game. They aren't staying long enough at the job site to rent and furnish a long-term rental before they are assigned to a new city. Similarly, medium-term leases are great for digital nomads and people needing temporary housing (e.g., new to the city, displaced by renovations). Some investors have pivoted their short-term rentals to the medium-term strategy in response to policy changes (more on that in a moment).

Let's break down the pros and cons of short-term rentals.

The two major wins for short-term rentals are the increased potential for high earnings and the flexibility. Think about it: You could make $1,500 a month renting a place out to a tenant, or you could make $1,500 a week off someone's vacation! Since the property is furnished and offered for a short amount of time, you are getting a higher rate per night than you do for someone who rents a property for a whole year. While you can command a much higher rate for vacation and short-term leases, there is also more work and greater expenses associated with operating a short-term rental than a long-term rental. However, that higher income is definitely a pro!

Another great thing is that you get to pick how often you use a vacation property for income generation and how often you get to use it yourself. I love the idea of purchasing a property in a market that I would want to vacation in, renting it out for X number of years to pay the property off, and then enjoying it with my family while owning it free and clear! That's the exciting part about short-term rentals to me, although some investors prefer to keep their feelings out of it. I also really enjoy the process of designing and furnishing the property, as well as the management flex-ibility—like with a long-term rental, you can manage it from afar or hire a property management company that specializes in vacation rentals.

Sounds pretty good, right? I agree, but there are a few drawbacks to consider as well. It can be a lot to manage a short-term rental property. Rather than the yearly (or less frequent) turnover process you go through with a long-term rental, you are required to find "tenants" over and over and over—if you want to make money, at least. I recommend checking out Hospitable and Hostfully to automate and streamline your booking process, but there are many more apps. It's also important to acknowledge that short-term rental management is a hospitality business. There is a lot more hands-on involvement, and you are responsible for keeping people happy—they're on vacation, after all.

Another thing to watch out for is local laws, regulations, and HOA (homeowners association) rules. There can be extensive fees to host a short-term rental, such as lodging taxes (again, you're now in the hospitality business!). Because of limited housing supply and high prices in some markets, local laws can have strict limitations on the number of short-term rental operators there can be, where vacation rentals can be located, and who can or can't rent out properties in the short term. For example, Denver, Colorado—location of BiggerPockets HQ—only allows licenses for people who are renting out their primary residence, but many of the suburbs of Denver have looser policies. The members of an HOA are allowed to change the rules any time they choose. The lesson here? Research the market you're interested in, because if things don't go well, you might lose your opportunity to continue this kind of real estate investment.

Avery Carl, who literally wrote the book on short-term rentals,[3] once told me that she is actually attracted to markets that already have strict short-term rentals laws in place. This reduces the risk that the laws will change. For example, in Joshua Tree, California, there were few short-term rental laws, which made it seem like a great market for investors. However, in 2022, a new law was put in place limiting investors to one vacation rental in that market per person. Everybody with rentals was grandfathered in, but they couldn't purchase any new ones. Investors there needed to pivot into a different market or a different strategy in that market.

Finally, there can be additional and ongoing costs when running a short-term rental. Things like cleaning crew fees, insurance, utilities, and property management can eat into your profits. Your desired passivity is something to consider when thinking about this real estate investment option.

To learn more about short-term rentals, the best place to start is The

---

**3** *Short-Term Rental, Long-Term Wealth: Your Guide to Analyzing, Buying, and Managing Vacation Properties* by Avery Carl. Buy it at www.biggerpockets.com/strbook.

Real Estate Robinsons YouTube channel,[4] where Tony and Sara Robinson share everything there is to know about getting started with this strategy. Tony is also my cohost on the *Real Estate Rookie Podcast*, for those avid listeners who not only care for our boring banter but also can vouch for Tony's extensive knowledge on short term rentals.

## BRRRR

Have you heard of BRRRR? Does it mean it's cold out? Where I live in New York, it definitely is. But in the real estate world, it's a term that has been coined by the *BiggerPockets Real Estate Podcast* hosts David Greene and Brandon Turner.

BRRRR is an acronym that stands for Buy, Rehab, Rent, Refinance, and Repeat. These represent the steps you can take as you invest in a rental property. Basically, an investor buys a fixer-upper using short-term funds (oftentimes cash, hard money, private money, or other creative means, all of which we'll talk about in Chapter 5), fixes it up, rents it out, and then seeks a new long-term loan to pay off the old short-term loan. Let's break down each step of BRRRR and then look at the pros and cons of the strategy as a whole.

**Buy:** The first step is to purchase a property. Your target property will be below market value because it's in need of repair. Because you'll be conducting a rehab, you need to factor in the cost of renovations as well as the ARV (after-repair value) of the property to ensure you're getting a good deal. Which means not overspending on the rehab to where you are spending more than what it will be worth.

**Rehab:** Next, you want to be able to do a few projects on the property to increase the value. This may be as simple as adding a few cosmetic updates or completing a full-gut rehab. Cosmetic updates can include changing carpet to vinyl plank, painting the walls, or changing out light fixtures. A full-gut rehab entails ripping apart the building down to the studs and building it back from there. And, of course, there is every level of rehab in between those two options. There is a full spectrum of possibilities when you use the word "rehab," so know that you can find value to add anywhere in between these presented extremes.

**Rent:** Once the property is renovated and cleaned, you can rent it out. After screening the applicants that reach out to you, select one and

---

4  www.youtube.com/c/therealestaterobinsons

draw up a lease agreement for them to rent the unit. Each month, collect the rent from your tenants to pay expenses and create some cash flow!

**Refinance:** Now that the property has been renovated and upgraded with rental income, the bank can do an appraisal to determine the new value of the property. The bank will then loan you money based on the appraisal value of the property. It is common that a bank will lend you 70 to 80 percent of the appraised value. This is your cash-out refinance. With the money the bank loans you, you can pay back what you borrowed either from yourself or someone else (a person or a bank) to purchase the property. This refinance will free up more than just the short-term capital that was used to initially buy the property, allowing the investor to have some cash to purchase another property.

Let's look at an example to help make this concept clearer.

Say you purchased a piece of property for $100,000 and then put in $20,000 worth of renovations and upgrades. When it is reappraised, the property is worth $180,000! Based on the new appraisal value, a bank will loan you 80 percent of its new value. Eighty percent of $180,000 is $144,000, allowing you to pay back the original $100,000 purchase price as well as the $20,000 you spent on rehab. You can now use the remaining $22,000 to pay for another property, or you could choose not to take the higher loan amount and just leave the equity in the property. A key factor as you make this decision would be your property cash flow—the refinance often leads to a higher mortgage payment. The higher your mortgage the less cash flow is left.

**Repeat:** Finally, it's time to start at the beginning and do it all over again. And again. And again. The "repeat" process of the BRRRR strategy is taking the original funding of $100,000—and the $20,000 of rehab funding that your new loan just paid back, whether to yourself or to another private lender—and using it to purchase the next property!

Let's talk about the pros and cons.

Starting with the drawbacks: It's important to know that most lenders make you wait three to twelve months (which is sometimes called a "seasoning period") before you can refinance a property. Ask lenders before purchasing so you know what their seasoning period is, if any. Another aspect of BRRRR that could be seen as a negative is that it involves rehab. Renovation-averse investors or cash-strapped investors might have a tougher time with completing a project like this. Finally, in an inflationary market where costs are rising, it can be harder to keep your project under budget, which can make investing in this kind of property feel intimidating to some rookies.

Don't let these cons overwhelm you. There are plenty of good things about BRRRRs too! First, it's scalable, meaning you have the ability to grow your business and profit through the volume of properties you work with. Not only that, it is one of the best returns on investments you can get in real estate these days and a great way to benefit from forced appreciation while still earning cash flow. With a BRRRR, your cash works for you. You can get much of the money you put into the property back through the refinance, meaning you can turn around and BRRRR another property. You can continue to reuse the same purchasing power and not continually have to save up.

## Turnkey

A turnkey property is a fully renovated home or apartment building that an investor can purchase and immediately rent out. Turnkey properties can often be purchased with tenants in the unit and property management in place.

There are both pros and cons to using the turnkey strategy. With a turnkey property, there is no rehab required, meaning you'll have a quick turnaround when it comes to collecting on your investment. Oftentimes, a turnkey property will also come with tenants and a property management company already in place. This isn't always the case, but sometimes it is! Personally, I think turnkeys are a great investment for rookies because they are a convenient option for someone with little to no time to put into the property.

However, it's not all easy-peasy. For this strategy, you will have to be trusting since you don't have a checks and balances system. Let me explain. If you go with a turnkey company that is selling you the house, they have likely been in charge of the *entire process*—they rehabbed it, they selected the tenant, and they are the property manager. In this type of situation, you don't have a third party involved who really knows if there are any issues. For example, what if there was something done incorrectly during the rehab or cheap materials were used for plumbing? If the tenant later complains of this issue to the property manager, they could sweep it under the rug to protect themselves. If you use a property manager who didn't sell you the house, they are likely going to be more transparent when communicating issues and bringing them to your attention.

The good news is you can mitigate your risk by vetting the turnkey company that is managing the property you plan to buy. There are plenty of bad companies in the turnkey game, but also plenty of good ones! Ask other investors for referrals.

When vetting a turnkey company, don't rely on the turnkey provider to give you references, because they will likely send you only people they know will give a good recommendation. Instead, ask the turnkey company for locations of their sold properties, then search for the owners and contact them directly. Remember as well that if the turnkey's management company has property listings up for rent, you already have the address! All you need to do is find the owner's contact information. You can use free websites such as the county GIS (geographic information system) mapping system to find the owner. Plainly put: Google the property address with your county's name. If you use software such as PropStream or Privy, you can find the owner's address. Sometimes just a simple Whitepages search online will give you a telephone number. Calling is much faster than waiting for someone to return a response by letter, but if you can't find a number, don't worry. Mailing them a letter is always an option too. Once you find a person who bought a house from the turnkey company, you can ask them about their experience and if they would recommend working with this company.

Finally, it is important to keep in mind that turnkeys do not earn you the return on investment that you may earn with other strategies, simply because it is a more passive investment. Because there is a company involved also looking to make a profit, you are giving up more profit than if you would have done the work yourself. If you want to maximize your profit, this is not the strategy for you. However, if you are looking for an investment that is less time intensive and are willing to give up some return for minimal work, then this would be a great strategy to start with.

## House Hacking

This is my favorite one for new investors! I wish I could have house hacked. The goal is to have all (or most of) your mortgage paid for by renting part of it out to someone else. Not having to pay for living expenses can be a huge savings, which in return can be used to invest in another property.

I helped my sister buy her first house hack when she turned 21. My sister graduated college in May, started her first job in August, and closed on her first house in October—not a bad start to her grown-up life! And it was all made possible by house hacking. Here's how it worked out.

My sister's job is two minutes away from one of my other rentals. I was eager to buy another property and I loved the area, partially because it had really appreciated over the last couple of years. The house we looked at had already been on the market for over ninety days. The issue was that both tenants were on long-term leases with low rents, so it wasn't an appealing option when it was first listed and I'd originally seen it. Other investors must have agreed, because it wasn't selling.

When we looked at the property a second time, several months later, (now that my sister was interested), we learned that the lower unit would terminate their lease early if the property sold. This gave my sister the opportunity to make it her primary residence and get an FHA (Federal Housing Administration) loan. I'll teach you more about this soon in the financing chapter, but just know that an FHA loan requires a low down payment amount and also comes with a low interest rate. I told my sister that if she got the FHA loan, I would gift her the money she needed for the down payment, provided I could be 50 percent owner on the deed.

A lot of people told us that if I was on the deed I had to be on the mortgage. Not true. If my sister defaults, I obviously lose my interest in the house to the bank, but I don't have a personal responsibility to the mortgage.

After we closed and the inherited tenants left, we did some cosmetic updates and raised the rent. My sister now pays $45 a month toward her mortgage ( which includes escrow, property taxes and insurance in the payment)—the rest is covered by the tenants in the other half of the house. When my sister decides to move out and we rent both units, we will split the cash flow and, in the future, split the proceeds from the sale.

Moral of the story? My sister was able to buy a house with no money out of her pocket and I was able to invest in a house with only a 3.5 percent down payment instead of a 20 percent down payment. If you are looking for an out-of-the-box way to finance a property or to help someone (who you really trust) get into real estate, this might be an option.

I said house hacking is my favorite, so, for me, the pros definitely out-weigh the cons. One big benefit is that it builds more wealth than other alternatives such as renting a home or traditional homeownership with a mortgage. Over the long term, a house hacker has exponentially more wealth *earned* from the property—wealth that can then be reinvested.

By renting, you are spending earned income that you never see a return on. By owning (but not house hacking), you gain equity over time but not income to pay down your mortgage. House hacking is the perfect entry into real estate investing that also supercharges your wealth. Another pro is that you benefit from owner-occupant financing, which usually has lower interest rates and lower down payment requirements.

In the best-case scenarios, house hacking allows people to live completely free or for a very low cost compared to renting or paying the mortgage in full (even in expensive areas!) or generate income through home ownership. Also, you'll learn a lot about the process of property ownership and rentals, because you'll be living it day in and day out. The best part is that you'll be able to invest your money in something else (another property, maybe?) because you aren't having to pay your full mortgage or rent.

> Did you know that the majority of Americans spend 30 percent of their income on housing? If you house hack and live for free, that's 30 percent of your income back in your pocket (not including what you were already saving). This situation makes it much easier to save enough for another investment. Think of how hard you'd have to work to get a 30 percent raise at your job!

Despite being one of my favorite strategies, there are some things you need to consider before taking on a house hack. House hackers are essentially landlords who are living at one of their rentals. Usually, a landlord has some distance between themselves and their tenants, but in this situation, that's not the case. You are literally living in the same house, which makes it super easy for your tenant to access you with their requests and complaints. In order to make this strategy work, you must be willing to tolerate this arrangement of close proximity and potential sacrifice or compromise your personal comforts to make the situation work.

## Fix-and-Flip

"Fix-and-flip" is a term coined for properties that need a lot of rehab work to make them appealing to buyers. For this strategy, real estate investors will buy the property, renovate it, and resell the property for a profit.

Are you an HGTV or A&E property show junkie? Do you love watching people take dirty, old houses and shine them up into something fabulous? First of all, I want you to know that while these TV shows are extremely entertaining, they are pretty unrealistic. Still, I love when I get to see how much the property cost, how much the investors put into it for renovations, how much they sold it for, and then, the best part, the bottom line: how much money they made in the end. If you love this concept and, like me, get all fired up about the idea of taking a distressed property and making it beautiful, then the fix-and-flip strategy might be the best one for you.

Flipping a property is a great way to build capital. It is common for investors to simultaneously flip houses and build a rental portfolio. Flipping houses is an active investment strategy, so be ready to put in some sweat equity if you choose to go down this road.

Rehab is a great fear of many investors. I often hear my Real Estate Rookie Bootcamp participants say, "I don't know anything about construction!" "What if there is mold in the walls!" Trust me, I know that scary things can happen in this line of work. Here's what I want you to do. Think of your greatest fear during a rehab. What is that worst case scenario? Now, if that scary thing actually happened, what would be the solution? If you knew you could fix the issue, would you not be afraid anymore? Would you get out of your analysis paralysis? The easiest way to fix a problem is with money. The second easiest is to find a partner who knows how to be proactive but can also be reactive if necessary.

To really illustrate this real estate investment strategy, I want to show you an example with actual numbers. This is a property I fix-and-flipped with the help of experienced flipper James Dainard.

## Direct Costs

Let's look at the direct costs first. Here are the things I needed to pay for up front.

| | |
|---|---|
| Purchase price | $740,000 |
| Estimated rehab costs | $110,000 |
| Loan points (1.5%) | $10,837 |
| Loan fees | $1,700 |
| Interest payments (over 6 months) | $23,833 |
| Real estate taxes (over 6 months) | $2,700 |

| | |
|---|---|
| Insurance (for 6 months) | $500 |
| Utilities (for 6 months) | $1,200 |
| Staging | $3,500 |
| **TOTAL DIRECT COSTS** | **$894,270** |

# Selling Price

You don't want to just look at what this is going to cost you. That would be scary and perhaps make you shy away from giving this strategy a try. You also need to think about the selling price. For this property, the estimated selling price is $1,050,000. This price is based on looking at comparable properties that have sold (not what they are listed at or pending at). These properties are comparable in square footage, same market, bed/bath count and finishes.

# Selling Costs

There are also costs associated with selling a property. Here's what those ran me for this property.

| | |
|---|---|
| Realtor commission (6%) | $63,000 |
| Tax 1.78% | $18,690 |
| **TOTAL SELLING COSTS** | **$81,690** |

# Profits

In the end, it cost $171,770 out of pocket in cash, required a loan of $722,500, and took six months to complete renovations. Once you subtract both the direct and selling costs, this property left me with a profit of $74,040! Not too shabby, especially when you look at the cash-on-cash return, which was 43 percent. We will talk about this more later on, but this is the percentage of money you make compared to the cash you invested into the deal. In this case it is 43 percent of the amount we invested into the deal.

James Dainard and I recorded the whole flip process, which you can watch on YouTube!

Now that you've seen the numbers, let's talk about the pros and cons. The obvious benefit of a fix-and-flip is the income that you can generate. A successful flip can profit you a lot of cash upfront instead of a buy-and-hold where you have steady income over time.

While the benefits of the fix-and-flip can be lucrative, I want you to know that you will work hard to earn every penny of it, often working at a single project for a few months. To take on an investment like this, you will have to be responsible for a timely and on-budget renovation, which is no small deed! This process will involve interacting with many others including bankers, contractors, skilled laborers (like plumbers and electricians), and buyers and/or real estate agents. This strategy requires vision, organization, and discipline. But if you can pull it all together, the payout will be worth it.

As for the cons of this strategy, the first is that you don't receive the tax benefits of holding onto a property like a rental. Your flip income is taxed as earned income and not rental income. You are also at the mercy of the market when listing your property; the market can change drastically between when you purchase a flip and when you sell it, which can impact your bottom line. There is no way to predict exactly where the market will be when you sell your house, so you can only do your best guess. Hopefully, it is more than what you projected! A lot of flippers saw massive, unexpected gains in 2021, only to find the late-2022 market to be commanding lower sale prices compared to the boom of the previous year.

Remember, no one is holding your feet to the fire on any of these investment strategies. The beauty with each and every one of them is that you get to pick! You can pick the size of a house as well as the amount and type of renovations that need to be done. If you are nervous, start small. Then, as your confidence grows, you can expand your options and workload as you choose.

## Wholesaling

Just like flipping, wholesaling is a great way to build capital for your real estate investing. However, unlike a fix-and-flip, the wholesaling strategy requires using little to none of your own money up front. Real estate wholesaling involves finding a person who no longer needs their property (or one of their properties) and is unwilling or unable to invest the time and effort required to prepare it for a sale. There could be many reasons they want to sell. Wholesalers offer the sellers a quick close by having cash buyers on hand instead of the seller having to put their property on the market and deal with a different type of buyer. By taking on this type of real estate investment, you earn revenue through a wholesaling fee attached to the transaction of the property sale. Wholesalers typically calculate their fee based on the purchase price, rehab cost, and what the after-repair value of the rehabbed home would be. They typically leave a 25 percent equity margin for the end buyer to profit. From there, they reverse-engineer the fee to charge. For example, if a property is under contract for $55,000 and rehab costs are $12,000 and the ARV (after-repair value) will be $100,000, the wholesaler computes that the end buyer must be $75,000 into the property in order to achieve the 25 percent equity.

The wholesaler can work backward from there: $75,000 (equity margin) − $12,000 (rehab) − $55,000 (purchase price) = $67,000. This leaves room for an $8,000 assignment fee to be charged by the wholesaler ($75,000 − $67,000). In this wholesaling scenario, the flipper is making the profit they want, the wholesaler makes a good fee, and the seller is getting rid of a house quick and easy—everyone is happy.

Perhaps the most exciting news about this strategy is that it's possible to do it with no money out of pocket! Isabelle Zukowski, who was on *Real Estate Rookie* episode 79, has successfully wholesaled without paying any money out of her pocket for business expenses. I think she is a great example that having no money isn't an excuse to not get started in real estate. Did I mention she is also a full-time college student?

Anybody over the age of 25 . . . does this make you cringe and wish that you would have spent your time wholesaling deals in between college classes? (I am definitely raising my hand!) You can learn more about Isabelle and how she made this strategy work for her by listening to the full episode here.

The con of this strategy can be the time it takes to find the deals, although there are many ways to source wholesale deals. This is an active investment. Wholesaling is a job consisting of finding property owners, negotiating deals, and finding investors to buy the properties you get under contract.

Like flipping, wholesaling is generally an active strategy—when you don't have a project in the works, you aren't getting paid. You also don't own any of the houses you wholesale; you're simply connecting a buyer and seller. This means no tax advantages either. However, wholesaling is a fantastic way for rookie investors to earn cash, learn the ins and outs of real estate, and build rewarding connections.

 **WARNING!** Government employees cannot accept paid referrals. Protect yourself and your people by following all the rules and regulations.

## Asset Classes

Just like there are different types of real estate strategies, there are different types of properties you can work with within each strategy. Knowing the type of property you'd like to work with can help you narrow down your top-choice strategy, so let's spend a little time looking at the different asset classes.

### Residential

Residential properties refers to property zoned specifically for living or dwelling for individuals or households; residential-class properties can range from stand-alone single-family dwellings to large, multiunit apartment buildings. One reason I love single-family homes is because the tenant can take care of all utilities, landscaping, and snowplowing (if applicable). There are also no disputes between multiple tenants, which can save a property manager a bunch of headaches! With multifamily residences, you have fewer overhead expenses with more units under one roof. A property is considered multifamily if it has two or more units. As a heads up, know that for units with two to four units, you will be able to get residential loans, but for anything above, you will have to get a commercial loan. If you are flipping or wholesaling, you may have a larger buyer pool choosing single-family homes.

The management of multifamily and single-family homes is very different. Knowing these differences up front will help you decide which kind of property you'd like to purchase. I can't stress enough: You are building the life you desire. Don't take on a project or property style that sounds unappealing to you! For example, multifamily units have common areas that need to be maintained and that hold the potential for tenant disputes. There are more regulations that need to be followed for multifamily units, especially as you get into the larger complexes.

## Commercial

You can find a lot of diversity, even within one asset class. This is absolutely true for commercial real estate. This class includes industrial (factories and manufacturing spaces), office spaces, and retail (plazas, malls, and individual storefronts). There are also mixed-use properties, meaning buildings that host more than one asset class. It is common to find buildings with commercial real estate on the first floor and residential on the second floor. For example, I have a building with two retail spaces on the first floor and two residential on the second floor. I opened a liquor store in one of the commercial spaces. Instead of paying rent to someone else, I had the business pay rent to me!

## Specialty

First up, campgrounds. Campgrounds can be seasonal rentals, daily rentals, or a mix of both. Purchase to the level of your willingness (and the amount of time you want to participate in campground life). Some will have amenities and some will have nothing but a spot for your tent. Your income is generated by campers paying rent to use the campsites or cabins. Some things to think about: How much do you want to manage? How much maintenance are you willing to handle? How active or passive do you want to be? Can you outsource? Always keep in mind the lifestyle you are trying to build as you make decisions along the way.

Mobile home parks are another good option, and their modern counterpart, tiny home parks, are becoming increasingly popular! If you are a BiggerPockets groupie like me, you have probably heard Brandon Turner talk about his company Open Door Capital and how they started sweeping up mobile home parks rapidly over a short period of time. Mobile home parks are often classified as "recession-proof investing" since they are affordable housing. Mobile home parks can be operated in a variety of models. The first way has you, as the owner, rent out only the land, and tenants own the mobile homes they have on the lot. This way you have no maintenance on the mobile homes and you don't have to worry about renting them. If a tenant decides to leave, it is their responsibility to take their mobile home with them or to sell it. The second option is to own the mobile homes and have the tenants rent the homes that sit on the lot from you. The rent you charge will obviously be more than if you are only renting them just the lot, but you will have more expenses to cover necessary repairs and maintenance on the mobile homes. Additionally, there are some parks that use a hybrid model, where some mobile homes may be owned by the tenants and some are owned by the property owner.

If you'd rather house stuff than people, self-storage units might be a good fit for you. I mean, hey, coffee tables and couches don't make a lot of demands, do they? This can range from small storage units to large storage for massive vehicles like boats and motor homes. There are some storage facilities that are simply a lot where you park your car or RV, and then there are climate-controlled self-storage units with electric outlets. My friend A. J. Osborne, aka the self-storage king, once had a person build a house inside his storage unit! Even though you aren't dealing with people living in the units legally, you are still in a customer service–based business. There is still involvement with people. Self-storage presents a wide range of opportunities, and unlike some of the more popular strategies, this might be one you hadn't heard about or considered before. I would encourage you to take the time to think about it and perhaps do a little more research, because it definitely has the potential to be a great real estate investment.

## Vacant Land

Hey, they aren't making more of it! Purchasing vacant land and letting it appreciate over time could be a great long-term play. Land flipping or wholesaling is very common too. For example, a developer may put some site work into the property, such as a roadway and utilities, and then sell it. Alternatively, wholesalers might get the raw land at a discount and then sell it to developers.

One other common land-flipping technique is to sell it to hunters. Some of the large land brokers will purchase land and turn it into a hunting paradise. They do this by putting food plots and tree stands on the properties. I once spent a day with a broker touring properties and learned all about this. It was so interesting. (Especially to my business partner, who is way more into hunting than me!) There are also investors in the Amish community near me who purchase raw land, build a wood shed or cabin on the property, and then sell it to the city folk to come and get back to their country roots. The options are literally limitless!

# Time to Make a Decision

Okay, so there you have it! Seven different real estate investment strategies and three different property asset classes. Did I overwhelm you with all of the choices? Did a couple of them excite you? Can you already name some you have no interest in? This is what I love about real estate investing—there are so many options!

I know it's a lot to think about and process. Instead of thinking about all the options, look at one at a time. Examine each opportunity and gauge your reaction individually. Don't worry if you don't have a clear-cut answer right away. This is a big decision. Look back at the notes you took while reading, as well as your answers to each of those "focus four" questions. Talk to another investor who is investing in the strategy you are interested in. Sleep on it and plan out the logistics.

# HOMEWORK

Choose your real estate investment strategy and write out why you think this is the best choice for you and your goals. Also reflect on how this strategy will fit your current lifestyle while leading you toward the lifestyle you want to eventually live!

Writing is a good way to process information, as well as to document the thoughts and ideas you are having now. It's also fun to revisit these writings later to both see your progress and review your original intentions. If you really hate writing, try sending yourself a voice note. It will accomplish the same goals! Personally, a white board always helps me plan out my thoughts; I then keep the board in a location where I see it every day, such as in my living room, so that my goals are always top of mind.

Then, when you think you've identified the right real estate investment strategy for *you*, turn the page and head on to Chapter 3: Building a Business.

# Chapter 3

# BUILDING A BUSINESS

## Vocabulary You'll Need to Know

**BALANCE SHEET:** A summary of the financial balances of an individual or organization.

**LLC:** Limited liability company. An LLC is one type of legal entity that can be formed to own and operate a business.

**PRINCIPAL PAYMENT:** Money paid to a lender that decreases the balance of the original loan amount that was borrowed.

**INTEREST PAYMENT:** Money paid to a lender that does not decrease the balance of the loan but is rather a percentage of earned interest based on the loan amount.

**PASSIVE INCOME:** Revenue that is generated from little or no work by the investor.

**PROFIT AND LOSS STATEMENT:** A report that shows the income that was received (such as rental income) and the breakdown of the expenses or costs within a given time frame, including property taxes, insurance, and utilities.

**PROPERTY MANAGEMENT:** The daily oversight and operation of a rental property including collecting rent, leasing units, regulating tenant/landlord and fair housing laws, processing evictions, communicating with tenants and vendors, and coordinating repairs and maintenance.

**SCOPE OF WORK:** A detailed list of the work to be performed by a contractor on your property.

**UMBRELLA INSURANCE:** A policy that provides extra liability protection in the event you are sued. This policy will pay out after your homeowner's policy coverage. The policy will pay for attorney fees and costs associated with a lawsuit up to the amount of your coverage.

B uilding a business is a big deal, and it differs from having a side hustle or hobby. It's definitely not easy, but picking a strategy best suited to your situation and personal strengths can go a long way in paving a more successful path. Hopefully, with the help of Chapter 2, you've done that. Now it's time to take the next step: building a business around your chosen strategy.

It's now time for you to figure out if you want to continue as a solopreneur in this endeavor or if it might be smarter (and better for your wallet long term) to outsource some of the tasks involved in real estate.

In this chapter, we are going to talk about LLCs, taxes, levels of passivity, and the benefits and costs of outsourcing. By the time you reach the end of this chapter, you'll not only have your strategy picked out but you'll also have a business plan built around it, so that when we reach Chapter 4, you'll be ready to make some moves and take action.

## LLC or Sole Proprietorship

One of the most common questions I see posted by rookie investors in the BiggerPockets forums is "Do I need an LLC?" This question appears many different ways and can also sound like:

- "Do I need to put my property in an LLC?"
- "Do I need an LLC to collect rent?"
- "Do I need an LLC for liability protection?"
- "Do I need an LLC for tax purposes?"

First things first: Let's start with what an LLC is. LLC stands for limited liability company. An LLC is one type of legal entity that can be formed to own and operate a business. LLCs are a popular option because they are easier and cheaper to form than other options, yet they still provide the same liability protection as a corporation. The main reason an investor would choose an LLC is for asset protection. Simply put, having an LLC protects your personal assets. For example, if you have an LLC and someone falls down the stairs in your rental property and decides to sue you, it would be hard for them to come after your personal residence or other assets in your personal name, such as your car (or, if you are cool like me, your motorcycle).

As of right now, you're probably thinking, "Well, why wouldn't I want asset protection, Ashley? I don't see why I shouldn't form an LLC!" And that's a good point.

First of all, LLCs cost money to start up.

Here are some of the associated costs where I invest, in the state of New York. Other locations may have varying requirements or fees.

- $200 filing fee when you start the LLC
- Newspaper publication stating you started an LLC, in two different newspapers. I usually hire out a service that does this for me. They charge $285.
- Operating agreement, which an attorney can draw up for you. Most likely your attorney would charge a fee for this, estimated around $200.

All in all, LLC have different start-up costs, depending on your location. In New York, it costs approximately $685, but in California, the filing fee alone is $800. Some states also have a yearly fee. If yours does, you'll need to add on an annual payment fee to the equation. You can check online to see your state's initial filing fee and if they require an additional annual fee.[5]

**MONEY-SAVING TIP!** Whenever you need a legal document drawn up, ask your attorney if they will provide you with a draft copy. This way you can plug in information prior to submitting it to them, without having to pay them to create a brand-new document every time. You can use this money-saving

---

5 I recommend www.worldpopulationreview.com/state-rankings/llc-cost-by-state.

strategy for lease agreements, operating agreements, buy/sell agreements, and other legal contracts. After you fill in the blanks, I suggest you have your attorney do a quick review just to double-check your information. In addition to saving you money, this tip can save you time by not having to wait for your attorney to get this step done, allowing you to move forward (and make money) faster!

When you are starting a business of any kind, it's very easy for people to throw money around. Everything feels like a *need*, when it might really be a *want*. Which category does an LLC fall into for you? Let's dig a little deeper to help you figure it out.

One of the most important reasons people decide against an LLC is because of the financing options available to them when putting the property into their personal name. When approaching a bank for financing, there are two departments: residential and commercial. When you're purchasing an investment property, you can receive lending from either category, but there are some limitations.

On the residential side, you can usually get better interest rates along with a longer fixed-rate term. For example, you can get a mortgage interest rate fixed at 5 percent over thirty years. On the commercial side, the interest rates are usually a little higher and only fixed for five to ten years, after which the interest rate adjusts with current market rates. That's definitely a risk. If rates increase over the next five years, your mortgage payment will increase after the five years is up. This could really hurt your cash flow and is why most investors prefer to lock into a long-term interest rate, especially because, recently, interest rates have been at historical lows (though they are now on the rise as of summer 2022).

Here's the issue: Most often, a bank will only loan to you on the residential side if you put the property in your personal name and *not* an LLC. I have found one bank that would do it, but the interest rate was 7.35 percent at a time when market rates were around 4 percent. There was no value to this except that the interest rate was fixed for twenty years, allowing me to control my costs more. The main reason investors opt out of an LLC for properties that are four units or fewer is because they want to take advantage of the residential loan options. Getting a low interest rate and having it fixed for thirty years can give you a higher cash flow than a commercial loan that may only amortize (reduce or get paid off with regular payments of principal and interest) over fifteen years. Since the repayment period is shorter, your monthly payments will be higher to pay it back in the shorter time frame.

All right. Protecting your personal assets versus getting a better interest rate on your loan. Which of the two do you want to prioritize? It's a hard choice, I know. Let's look at a few other factors that might help sway your decision.

## LLCs and Taxes

Let's talk taxes. A common misconception is that you need an LLC to deduct expenses against your rental income. This is not the case. Even if the property is in your personal name, you can still deduct business expenses related to the property. However, if you do decide to have an LLC, it can be taxed as a "pass-through entity," meaning you are only taxed once. This is the same as if you kept the property in your personal name. Corporations, on the other hand, can be double-taxed on your personal tax return and your business tax return. LLCs and corporations have different legal requirements, record keeping, liabilities, structures, and tax ramifications, but the most obvious difference between the two is that an LLC is owned by individual owners and a corporation is owned by shareholders.

The benefit is that the LLC income is taxed as personal income to you. If your income tax bracket is 22 percent, then you are taxed 22 percent on the profit from your LLC. If your profit, after all expenses are paid, was $100,000, then you would owe $22,000 in taxes. Keep in mind that this doesn't account for tax credits and other deductions that you may be eligible for. We are just using this as a rough example. Your actual tax liability could be a lot lower due to the power of tax advantages available for real estate.

Now let's take it the other way. If your entity is a corporation, then the profit is taxed at 21 percent. (This is the corporate income tax rate as of 2021.) As the owner, if you take any distributions from the company (often called withdrawals, aka pulling cash out of the business to use for personal expenses), you are then taxed again on that dollar amount. That means if you withdraw $50,000 over the course of the year, you would pay 21 percent tax on that from the corporate income and would then pay another 22 percent on your personal income taxes (assuming from our first example that is the tax bracket you are in).

So, in terms of tax savings, an LLC looks pretty good! However, before you jump into an LLC, I want to make sure you understand how to properly run your LLC like a business. You might be thinking, "Ashley. I'm serious about this! I'll run it like a business!" And that's great, but running a business is about more than mindset. In order to run an LLC, there are specific requirements. The LLC must:

- Have its own bank account (no commingling of business and personal funds).
- Keep proper bookkeeping records.
- Maintain meetings and minutes according to state rules.

If you don't treat the LLC as a business and maintain the proper separation between your personal and business accounts, your personal assets could be left up for grabs.

If you decide to not go the LLC route, umbrella insurance is another option. The main reason most people select an LLC is because they want liability protection. If they are sued because of something that happens with the investment property, they don't want their house and personal assets to be at risk. Umbrella insurance may provide coverage when your policy limits are exhausted, including claims liability coverage on rental units you own (like, among other things: bodily injury, property damage, false arrest, libel, and slander). This won't stop someone from going after your personal assets, but the large amount of money the insurance company would pay out may deter someone from bothering.

Reach out to your insurance agent and learn what exactly an umbrella policy could do for you and if it provides the right level of protection. I am a huge believer in going the route that helps me sleep at night and not necessarily the route with the greatest return or profit. Think about that before you choose an option that you might not feel secure with. If you currently rent and your only asset is your bike, you may not need a lot of liability protection. But if you own your personal residence free and clear, you may want to make sure that it is protected.

To summarize, let's look at the questions you should be answering before diving into an LLC:

- What are the costs associated with an LLC in the state you are filing in?
- How does having an LLC affect what you pay for bookkeeping and tax prep?
- How do you want to finance the property?
- Can you commit to running your LLC like a business?
- What kind of liability protection will help you sleep at night?

I know that some of you just want me to tell you what to do. You see me as the expert (thank you!) but, really and truly, this is a personal decision you need to make based on your personal circumstances. However, I will give you one more piece of advice.

If you are doing a partnership on a property, I always recommend an LLC. To me, that is a no-brainer. You don't want to be personally liable for something that your partner may have been at fault for. The same goes the other way; you want your partner to be protected from your mistakes too. After all, you are a rookie. Mistakes are bound to happen, although hopefully none that get you sued! An LLC can help you limit the damage and effects of your amateur mistakes if they do occur. Can you imagine if a mistake you made caused your partner to lose their family home and life savings because you didn't have any kind of liability protection in place and their personal assets were up for grabs?

I'll also say that I recommend, in addition to talking to your insurance agent, that you reach out to your accountant and attorney to help you decide what is the best route. Unlike you, they aren't rookies. They've seen a few things and can make some solid recommendations based on their clients' and customers' past real estate experiences based on your state laws and regulations for LLCs and the tax consequences.

After partnering on several properties, I decided to purchase some properties on my own with no partners. I bought them in my personal name. Later, as my portfolio grew, I put them into an LLC. Here's how it worked.

I purchased my first couple of properties in my personal name because I wanted to capitalize on the residential-financing option. The banks I was using would only give a thirty-year fixed-rate loan at a lower interest rate if I went with a residential loan. Again, a commercial loan would only be fixed for five or ten years, and the interest rate wouldn't be as low. I didn't want to risk interest rates increasing in five or ten years, so I wanted to lock in my rate for thirty years.

As my net worth grew and I had more assets that would be open to liability, I decided to "quitclaim deed" the properties into an LLC. To "quitclaim deed" means to sign the deed over to someone, in this case my LLC, and accept the property as is with no new survey or title work. My LLC accepted it as a clean title since I already did that legwork when I purchased the property in my personal name.

There is one thing to be cautious of. Many mortgage documents state that if the property is sold, the mortgage is due in full. This is called the due-on-sale clause. Before I transferred ownership to my LLC, I made sure I had other options to pay off my mortgage.

You have to remember that banks are not in the business of foreclosing on houses. They are in the business of lending money and collecting interest over the life of a loan. I also did not sell the property, and the LLC that is now stated on the deed has me as 100 percent owner. I did not decrease my ownership or take on partners. Lenders have caught on to this and most have updated their mortgage documents to allow the sale of property to an entity as long as the ownership interest is the same. For example, if I own the property personally as the 100 percent owner, then as long as I am the 100 percent owner of the LLC, there is no due-on-sale clause.

I kept making my timely payments. As long as you keep paying the bank, the due on sale clause may not be an issue. While this is only my personal experience, I have seen this topic come up many times in the BiggerPockets's forums and have yet to see anyone who had the due on sale clause called on them. Just in case, however, my advice would be to have an exit strategy available (such as a private money lender or another bank to refinance) if the due-on-sale clause is called on you. Think worst-case scenario: Could you refinance with another bank if the bank did exercise the due-on-sale clause? All in all, I like that my properties are now protected by an LLC, and they still have the thirty-year fixed-rate mortgage on them.

So, what do you think? Is an LLC for you or not? Before continuing with the rest of this chapter, add a note on your to-do list or calendar to make an appointment with your attorney or another trusted advisor. Consuming information is great, but only if you do something with it. Don't sit on this. Make a plan and take action so you can move forward in making your real estate dreams into reality.

That was a big topic, but it was an important one. Next, we can move on to building out the rest of your plan. To create a real estate reality that fits your life, you first need to decide how active or passive you'd like to be.

## What Is a Passive Investment?

A passive investment simply means you are making money without having to trade hours for dollars. You have either done the work up front and are now collecting from it, or you have money (and perhaps people) working for you to earn additional income.

Let's look at an opposite example first. A chiropractor needs to be at work to make money. They need to see patients in their office to help them and then collect payment from them. This is an active, involved career.

An example of a passive-income career is an author. Yes, it takes work to write a book! But each time the book is sold, the author does not need to be present (or even involved in the transaction) to earn money from it. People are buying the author's work (thus producing income for the author) while she sleeps, drives her kids to school, and goes on vacation.

There are many ways to make passive income. A few non–real estate examples include affiliate marketing, vending machines, digital download sales, and e-courses. If this topic is of interest to you, I highly recommend you check out the *BiggerPockets Money Podcast* for more ideas. Just don't let those shiny objects pull you away from the real estate goals you originally intended to achieve when you picked up this book!

Real estate is much the same way. You may have heard the term "mailbox money." It's a slang term for rent checks mailed to the landlord. It's money that just shows up every month! Pretty great, right? You put in energy and effort now, and then you continue to make money moving forward with little time invested. An example of particularly passive real estate investing is a syndication deal. In a syndication, someone else is acquiring the deal and managing the property, but investors like you are providing the funds. You have no duties or control over the operations. You are simply someone who gives money and gets a return on that investment. (At least, that is the hope that it turns into a positive investment.)

But that's just one strategy. In the real estate world, passive income can also come in a variety of ways. Some additional examples of investments that tend to be more passive are real estate investment trusts (REITs), private money lenders, and turnkey rental properties. And the possibilities don't stop there! You can make other real estate strategies passive by building a team (which we'll talk about in Chapter 8).

As a rental property owner, you have the option to be as involved as you would like to be in your investment. Some people choose to manage, and others choose to have property managers. Some people do their own rehab work and others contract it out. Some people do their own bookkeeping and accounting, while others hire a person to do it. The choices you make can drastically change how passive or active your real estate investment is. You will usually see a greater monetary return on your investment if you are an active investor, but remember, you also must consider the value of your time when playing an active role in your investment. Eventually, as you grow and scale, this will reverse. Building a team and hiring the best will bring you greater returns because you have more time to work *on* the business than *in* the business.

Personally, I started out extremely active. I did everything except maintenance. I acquired the properties, secured the financing, and lots more. I was working as a property manager and leasing agent (for another company) at the time, so why wouldn't I manage my own properties? I also did the bookkeeping for several entities and had those skills, so I decided to use those with my own properties as well.

After a while, I learned that if I really wanted to grow and scale, I would have to start outsourcing. At one point I was managing one hundred residential units and ten commercial units all on my own. I started with a part-time employee opening the mail, entering payables, and showing apartments. It was a small step toward taking tasks off my plate, but it helped a lot. Eventually, I gave up the property management completely for both myself and the investor I was working for. It freed up a lot of my time and was worth the property management fee to get some time back to focus on investing.

When you are deciding whether to do something yourself or outsource it, take into account your own capabilities. Oftentimes, this boils down to how much time you have (even more than your personal skill set and the amount of money you have available). Right now, you might have the time, the knowledge, and the hustle to acquire and manage your investment properties. But that doesn't mean you will want to do everything yourself forever. Think about now, but never lose sight of the long term. I like to have options, especially the option to be as passive or as active as I would like. Don't be fooled. There is no one right answer. The answer is what works for you!

## To Outsource or Not to Outsource? That is the Question.

When you think about choosing to complete a task yourself or to outsource it, there are many factors to consider. You'll hear different people preach their opinions on this. My advice is to listen to what they have to say, but, ultimately, you need to figure out what will suit you. This is *your* life and *your* business.

There are two important questions to ask yourself as we go over the information in this section.

**1.** Will I be good at this task?

**2.** Will I enjoy this task?

Part of the reason many people enter the real estate world is to create the life they want. Yes, we want to make money, but we are making money in service of the life we want. (If you are only wanting to make money for money's sake, you will find yourself very unfulfilled when you do get what you thought you wanted.) As you work to create wealth, you likely want to make it in a way that doesn't add an additional drain and strain on your life. If you wanted more of that, you'd stick to the job and life you are attempting to leave behind. This endeavor is meant to be different from those experiences. And to make it different, you might need to think a little differently.

One of my mentors encouraged me to look at the big picture. He told me that even if I am enjoying what I'm doing now, there is still a chance I could get burnt out in the future. Or, if another opportunity popped up, he wanted me to be in a position to take it if I wanted to. His point was that I should always leave my options open and be able to outsource. That way, I'll be able to pivot in a new direction rather than being locked into my current plan.

In this case, my mentor was talking about me doing rehab work myself. I was working on a house that needed new flooring. I was debating if I should tackle the work by myself or hire a contractor. There were lots of factors to consider—my time, my level of expertise, my budget, and the project timeline, just to name a few. My mentor wanted me to be able to make a choice that I felt good about and worked for me.

If I chose to do the floor myself, it would be cheaper, but it might also take longer and not look as great (since I am not a professional floor installer). By doing the floor myself to save money, I would also not be spending that time researching new properties, contacting buyers, or analyzing deals. At the end of the day, I chose to hire a contractor, and, let me tell you, I'm so happy I did. I know where my skill set lies, and the return on investment for my time and energy is much higher when I stick to real estate investing and let the contractors handle the rehab.

But that's me! This is about you. As you read through the three areas of business below (management, rehab, and accounting), think honestly about what you *can* and *want* to do and how taking on tasks (or leaving them to others) will impact the results of a project as well as your bottom-line earnings.

## Property Management

Property management is the daily oversight of a residential, commercial, or industrial property. Property managers take responsibility for the day-to-day repairs and ongoing maintenance, security, and upkeep of properties. Every real estate asset class needs managing in some respect, including apartment and condominium complexes, private home communities, shopping centers, and industrial parks. The main role of a property manager is to preserve the value of the properties while also generating income through rent collection. Plainly put, it's a job that varies in scope, depending on the size and age of the property.

If you have rental property, such as a residential unit, there are many things that need to be done to manage it. In particular, there are a lot of laws and regulations regarding rental property. If you plan to be a landlord who is also acting as the property manager, you need to know these. There are local housing organizations that offer free or low-cost classes on the state laws. If you are willing to do the research and stay up-to-date on the laws and regulations, then property management might be something you try to do on your own.

Housing Opportunities Made Equal (www.homeny.org) is the organization I learned from in Buffalo, New York, but a simple Google search should lead you to one in the area you will be investing in. Local laws cover the lease agreement and screening requirements, rent amounts, and the eviction process. Each state has different laws. Your county or city can also have different regulations. For example, some cities require landlords to register as landlords and pay yearly fees.

If you don't want to take the time to learn these laws and regulations, then it may be better for you to outsource this. Trust me. The last thing you want is to be sued by a tenant because you didn't follow the rules. Fair Housing Act violations are no joke! Don't be scared away, though—it's very doable to be a property manager and work another full-time job.

I enjoyed learning how to be a property manager. I also now enjoy having a property manager. I've talked to people who insist on learning how to do everything before they would consider outsourcing. This seems like a smart move to me, to an extent. It can be beneficial to know how tasks are completed and how things are run; knowing the ins and outs of your business can help you outsource more effectively and find the best-qualified people. But there are only so many hours in a day.

It's hard to know what you don't know. Perhaps take a class in property management or get your feet wet by reading *The Book on Managing Rental Properties* by Heather Turner and Brandon Turner. Then decide if this is an aspect of your business that you are going to be actively involved in or outsource.

## Rehab

Another common way people choose to save money when investing in real estate is by completing rehab on their own. If you are handy, sweat equity can be great. But know that it will take up your time. You have to decide what is more valuable to you right now—time or money?

In my early days, I took on a partner to learn how to do rehabs. I thought that if I was armed with this kind of knowledge and possessed DIY project skills, I would be a better investor. If I didn't have to pay someone else to do the job, then I'd be saving money. I soon found that it is more difficult (from a numbers standpoint) to factor in what your actual return is if you aren't accurately calculating how many hours you are putting into the project. Initially, I didn't treat the rehab I did on my properties like part of the business. Instead, it was something my business partner and I did in our free time to save money instead of hiring contractors.

Here are a few other considerations to think about when deciding if you want to do rehab work or outsource it.

- How large is your portfolio? Can you realistically keep up with all the projects that need to be done?
- How much time do you have to invest in your real estate business?
- Do you own the tools necessary to complete the jobs? Purchasing additional equipment will initially eat into your profits.
- Do you hold the necessary licenses to do certain rehab work (such as electrical and plumbing)?
- Do you have the money to complete the rehab job?

And one final question: *Will you get burned out?* Even if you love it now, that doesn't mean you will always enjoy it. People can love to do something, only to find the enjoyment fades once it becomes work and they *have* to do it. If construction and repair are already skills in your wheelhouse, you may need to experiment here. How much of this work do you want to do? How much of this work is enjoyable? How much of this work leads to a greater profit?

No matter which path you take, you need to do your research. If you do work yourself, you need to make sure you do it *right*, or you will pay more down the line getting someone to fix your mistakes. Don't rush; be patient with yourself as you go. Remember, you are a rookie! Finally, it's important to be honest with yourself about what you're truly capable of (and what you can realistically learn how to do).

The same advice applies if you choose to outsource the work: Be smart about it! Shop around for competing quotes to make sure you don't overpay. A common rule of thumb is to go with the middle-price quote. The cheap guy is cheap for a reason, and the expensive guy is overkill and will break your budget. Make sure you have developed a solid scope of work so you aren't surprised by any costs and can hold your contractors accountable. (I'll provide you with an example of this in Chapter 8.) Even if someone else is doing the physical work, you need to be mentally in the game.

Basically, either way, if you are doing rehab, you can't wing it!

## Accounting and Bookkeeping

Bookkeeping and accounting for real estate investments isn't like running a typical family or business budget; it's more involved than that. We will go over a profit and loss statement and a balance sheet that show all the different accounts you need to track and record. There are IRS (Internal Revenue Service) rules and regulations to follow. Again, depending on the size of your portfolio, this can be a big job. But it's not impossible. Lots of people do it, particularly those who are coming from a finance, banking, or accounting background. Remember, you can lean on your previous professional experiences to help you make the most of this new endeavor.

This may be your first business and first time ever bookkeeping. I know that it can feel like a lot to take on. Fortunately, there are several investor-friendly bookkeeping software packages out there to help you. Stessa is a great user-friendly, real estate-specific option if you are unfamiliar with bookkeeping. It's also free! Some property management softwares like RentRedi also have built-in accounting features. Make sure you try a free demo before committing to any software. You'll want to make sure it's user-friendly and appealing to the eye so that you actually use it.

You can also search websites like Upwork, Fiverr, and Zirtual for a bookkeeper that is specific to real estate investing.

Here is a sample of a job description I used to find a bookkeeper:

**ABOUT OUR COMPANY:** We are real estate investors with multiple LLCs. Each LLC ranges from one to five properties. There is a property management company in place. We are looking for someone who can input transactions from the owner's report supplied by the property management company and any entries directly from the LLC bank account. Entries and reconciliations will need to be made by the 15th of the following month. All bookkeeping will be completed through Quickbooks and uploaded to Google Drive after each month's reconciliation. Applicants must have knowledge of adding a new property to Quickbooks by using the closing statement along with doing entries by class.

**SERVICES AND DELIVERABLES:**
- Process bank reconciliations for business checking, lines of credit, and credit card accounts.
- Upload documents and files to Google Drive in a timely manner along with emailing the CPA monthly with Quickbooks file.
- Prepare monthly profit and loss statements and balance sheets.
- Sign NDA for being discreet and reliable in the handling of confidential information.
- Have experience with real estate bookkeeping and rental income (preferred).
- Be able to log in to online banking and property management websites to pull statements.
- Have experience with Quickbooks (required).
- Able to use a payroll service and be responsible for submitting biweekly.
- Experience with sales tax (NY state sales tax preferred).

In your proposal, please provide a short description of your bookkeeping business and why we should consider you. Also tell us about another client and how your skills made an impact on that business.

The bottom line is this: Know as you go into this that you have options. Take some time to do a deep dive (or, at the very least, a shallow skim!) of your options before making your decision on how you'd like to handle this part of your real estate strategy. The time you invest now will not only save you money but also save you lots of headaches later on!

## Profit and Loss Statement

A profit and loss statement (P&L), often called an income statement, is a valuable financial statement for your business. Even if you have decided that you don't want to tackle this task on your own and plan to hire it out, I want you to be able to read the statement and understand it.

As you look this over, know this: Income credits your account, expenses debit your account, assets increase your equity, and liabilities decrease your equity.

## ROOKIE PROPERTY, LLC

| PROFIT AND LOSS STATEMENT | JAN–DEC '22 |
|---|---|
| **ORDINARY INCOME/EXPENSES** | |
| **INCOME** | |
| Rental Income Unit 1 | $12,000.00 |
| Rental Income Unit 2 | $12,000.00 |
| Pet Income | $240.00 |
| **TOTAL INCOME** | **$24,240.00** |
| **EXPENSES** | |
| Filing Fees | $25.00 |
| Office Supplies | $194.00 |
| Repairs and Maintenance | $1,511.12 |

| | |
|---|---|
| Other Supplies | $35.29 |
| Property Taxes | $3,235.79 |
| Utilities | $428.28 |
| Landscaping | $1,200.00 |
| Property Management Fees | $2,160.00 |
| Interest Expense | $7,332.10 |
| **TOTAL EXPENSE** | **$16,121.58** |
| **NET INCOME** | **$8,118.42** |

The top of the statement shows the different revenue streams, aka where your income is coming from. This is money coming *into* the business. For rental properties, this is primarily rental income but can also include other sources such as garage fees and pet fees. The P&L statement can be for the month, over a set period of time—such as year to date—or even for the full year.

Most bookkeeping software will generate this for you. Still, it is important to know how to read, comprehend, and create a P&L. You want to be able to understand the profitability of your business.

For example, if you are renting out an up-down duplex, you would put the first-floor rent and the second-floor rent into rental income. If each tenant paid $1,000 per month, then your total rental income for the year would be $24,000. If you charge $20 extra per month for a pet and one tenant has a pet, then the pet fee income would be $240 for the year. The profit and loss statement would total up all your income at the top. In this example, the total would be $24,240.

Below the income, you will see the expenses. The expenses show money that is *going out* of the business. Common expenses include repairs and maintenance, professional fees, utilities, seasonal maintenance, and property management fees. Breaking down your expenses into different accounts can give you a better picture of where your money is going in your business.

You will likely have these expenses set up on automatic withdrawals, or you will pay through an online payment system or even written checks. This makes it easy to lose track of your expenses. It is important to track who is being paid, what amount they are being paid, and what they are being paid for. The "what they are being paid for" is going to determine what expense column the dollar amount is added to. If you pay Joe's Landscaping $100 to mow the lawn of your duplex for the month of June, the $100 would be added to the total of the landscaping column. If you paid National Grid Electric Company $35.69 for electric in June, then that amount would be added to the utilities expense row. You can always break down your expense columns to be as broad or defined as you would like. For example, instead of a "utilities" expense, you could have three different rows: water expense, electric expense, and gas expense.

One last example: If you pay an attorney to close on a property or to process an eviction or draw up a lease agreement, that expense could be categorized under "professional fees."

The expenses are subtracted from the revenue to show the net income or profit. This does not mean how much cash flow you have from your property. The reason for this is that debt paydown is not included on the profit and loss statement. This means the money paid out of your business for your mortgage principal or any capital improvements is not shown on the profit and loss statement. So don't confuse the net income or profit with your cash flow. The mortgage principal is not considered an expense because you are repaying a loan.

## Balance Sheet

The next step is to look at a balance sheet. The value of a balance sheet is that by organizing information this way, you can:

- See at a glance what your business is worth to you as an owner.
- See at a glance how your company is performing (for example, if you are overleveraged).
- Have something formal to provide lenders or potential partners.
- Have something formal for your tax returns and your tax advisor/ accountant to best understand your investments in order to maximize savings and avoid audits.

Getting an overview of the financial health of your business is extremely important. One way to do this is by creating a balance sheet.

It is called a "balance sheet" because your assets, liabilities, and equity will (or should!) all equal out. For anyone who likes symmetry, then this is a thing of beauty! It's a simple way to make all the numbers make sense.

The balance sheet has three parts: assets, liabilities, and equity. The assets are tangible or intangible items of value. Examples include cash, stock investments, real estate, machinery and equipment, and goodwill. Goodwill is not about how many Goodwill stores you own, nor is it the value of how much you care for humankind! In a balance sheet, goodwill is an intangible asset, meaning it is not a physical thing you can hold or touch. For example, if you purchase a business that has a great brand presence, you may pay more for the business because it is well-known in the community. You aren't paying for a physical asset, but there is still value. Another relatively common example you may come across is accounts receivable. If a tenant owes you money, then it would show under the assets that you are owed XX amount of money from that tenant as a "receivable." This increases the value of your company by showing you have money that you are expecting to come in and that is already owed to you. As a real estate investor, you will be dealing primarily with tangible assets, but it is still important to have an understanding in case you ever come across it on a balance sheet as your business grows.

When creating your balance sheet, list out the bank account of your LLC and the cash balance (on the date the balance sheet is created) under "assets." If you use software, this will be created for you in real time. You can run a report at any date and it will automatically populate.

For any property you own, list the cost of the property when you purchased it. Similarly, if you rehab the property, you can add improvements to the property on the balance sheet. Ever heard an investor talk about capital expenditures when analyzing deals? You must account for future expenses by adding into your numbers a percentage of capital expenditures (CapEx). CapEx includes repairs and maintenance to a property that increase the value of the property outside of general maintenance and upkeep. Examples could be new flooring throughout the property, gutting and remodeling the bathroom, installing new kitchen cabinets, or putting on a new roof. On the example balance sheet below, you will see "Property: 180 Sunset; $219,900" and then a line underneath it labeled "Improvements: 180 Sunset; $30,000." This would show that the total asset value of the 180 Sunset property is $249,900 on the balance sheet. This value is drawn from the actual cost of the asset, not the market value or appraised value.

CapEx improvements are not expensed and must be depreciated. If you are conducting repairs or maintenance, those costs are shown on the P&L statement as an expense from that year, but any capital improvements must be depreciated over a set number of years.

Next, we move on to the liabilities section. This is where you would show any debt or obligations you need to pay someone else. A common item that real estate investors have listed in the liabilities section is mortgages for their properties. The asset section would show the purchase cost of the property, while the liabilities section would show how much you owe on the house. This mortgage balance would be updated just like your cash balance. Each payment you make on your mortgage reduces the principal due on your mortgage, necessitating an update on this report as of the date you use for the balance sheet.

If you received any bills from vendors, contractors, or other parties you haven't paid yet, then those would be listed as payables. This is money you owe and that will be coming out of the business, so it needs to be factored as a liability. Another common liability that investors will see is tenant security deposits. These security deposits are owed back to the tenants upon their departure. Yes, a tenant may damage your apartment and so you may keep some deposits, but until their move-out date inspection, you are to treat their security deposit as it is owed to them.

Once you have all your assets totaled up and all your liabilities totaled up, you will need to pull the net income or loss from the profit and loss statement. When you incorporate your net income, the total assets minus net income minus total liabilities will equal your equity in the company. Hopefully, the statement will balance. The total liabilities and equity should equal the assets.

If you're more of a formula person than a narrative one, this might help!

**Assets = Liabilities + Owner's equity**

You can also use these sample images of a balance sheet to help you understand this crucial concept.

| BALANCE SHEET | DEC 31, '22 |
|---|---|
| **ASSETS** | |
| **CURRENT ASSETS** | |
| Checking Account | $8,620.75 |
| Accounts Receivable | $1,800.00 |
| **TOTAL CURRENT ASSETS** | $10,420.75 |
| **FIXED ASSETS** | |
| Property: 180 Sunset | $219,900.00 |
| Improvements: 180 Sunset | $30,000.00 |
| **TOTAL FIXED ASSETS** | $249,900.00 |
| **TOTAL ASSETS** | **$260,320.75** |
| **LIABILITIES & EQUITY** | |
| **LIABILITIES** | |
| Current Liabilities | |
| Tenant Security Deposits Held | $1,800 |
| Total Current Liabilities | $1,800 |
| Long-Term Liabilities | |
| Mortgage Payable | $198,120.27 |
| Total Long-Term Liabilities | $198,120.27 |
| **TOTAL LIABILITIES** | **$199,920.27** |
| **NET INCOME/(LOSS)** | **$8,118.42** |
| **TOTAL EQUITY** | $52,645.28 |
| **TOTAL LIABILITIES & EQUITY** | $260,320.75 |

# What now?

Whew, that was a lot. But thinking about your real estate journey as a business is a necessary step that you will be very grateful further down the line for having done. Let's do a quick recap by answering these questions. Afterward, jot down notes about the next steps you need to take for these action items.

| QUESTION | NEXT STEP | ADDITIONAL NOTES (?) |
|---|---|---|
| Do you want to create an LLC or get umbrella coverage? | | |
| Are you going to do your own property management or outsource it? | | |
| Are you going to do your own property rehab or outsource it? | | |
| Are you going to do your own accounting and bookkeeping or outsource it? | | |

As an entrepreneur, you need to stay organized and run a legal business. Having it all together and accessible will make your life easier as you grow and scale. Outsourcing a task doesn't make you lazy or incompetent. Do you think millionaires and billionaires have time to learn every task or role before they hire someone for a position in their company? Sometimes knowing what you don't know and hiring a person to fill that role is even smarter than taking the time to learn how to do it yourself. A lot of what you need to know will be learned as you go, but it is perfectly okay to not learn every single process. There are many things that will be done more effectively and efficiently (with better quality) if done by someone else rather than you. Finally, keep in mind that your life can change dramatically in an instant or over time. You want to set yourself up to have options and the ability to be passive, or at least to work from your phone from the beach!

# HOMEWORK

**1.** Decide if you'd like to start an LLC or do things differently. Schedule a meeting with your insurance agent to discuss the options available to you if you want umbrella insurance. Discuss your LLC implications with your tax accountant and attorney.

**2.** Make decisions about outsourcing (property management, rehab, and accounting/bookkeeping). If choosing to outsource, begin compiling a list of potential people you'd like to work with or start networking to receive recommendations from other investors.

# Chapter 4

# PARTNERSHIPS

## Vocabulary You'll Need to Know

**ASSETS:** Anything of value or a resource of value that can be converted into cash.

**FICO:** FICO (Fair Isaac Corporation) was a pioneer in developing a method for calculating credit scores based on information collected by credit reporting agencies.

**MULTIPLE LISTING SERVICE (MLS):** A database established by cooperating real estate brokers to provide data (photos, descriptions, and purchase price) about properties for sale. Some of the information (but not all) is then pulled to populate websites such as Realtor.com and Zillow, where anyone can search properties that are listed for sale with a licensed agent.

**JOINT VENTURE AGREEMENT:** Allows two parties to have separate legal companies that work together on a specific project.

**LEVERAGE:** To use (something) to maximum advantage.

**LIABILITIES:** A debt or financial obligation that a person is responsible for.

**PARTNERSHIP:** Union of two or more people on a real estate deal. Using LLCs and joint ventures to partner.

# What You Have to Offer

There are four items, or pieces of the puzzle, I think you need in order to get started in real estate investing: money, time, experience, and security.

Do you have all of those and are ready to dive in? If your answer is no, don't worry. Your real estate dreams aren't doomed.

When I started out, I was missing money and I had plenty of fear. I can't even tell you what my specific fear was . . . It was vague, but it was holding me back. I think part of it was that I didn't want to be sued. I didn't want the roof to blow off and be responsible for injuries, damages, and replacement costs. I didn't want to ruin my family's financial future. What if I lost everything?

At the time, I figured my best solution was to partner with someone who had money and resources (aka, a network that would help us if something awful were to happen) giving me a sense of security. Again, I had no idea what that awful thing would be, but it scared me all the same.

I didn't have any money either. At least, not enough money to buy a whole house! I had watched the investor I was working for buy property in cash. I thought that was the only way to do it. What I didn't realize as a rookie is that the cash could have come from many different places and been sourced using a wide variety of methods.

The point I'm trying to make is that you don't have to do this thing alone. Later on, in Chapter 8, we are going to talk about building a team of individuals to help you with the tasks of property management and maintenance, financial transactions, and legalities. If you were running a baseball team, these people would be the players—the ones who get things done. When we're talking about finding a partner, it's something different. With a partner, you are looking for a co-owner. A person who makes decisions for the team, writes the checks, and sits in the box seats to watch it all happen. Sitting in those box seats may seem like a cushy job, but at the end of the day, it's the owners who are ultimately responsible for the results. When I was first starting out, I wanted someone to sit with, someone to bounce ideas off, someone to help me pave the way. I figured if I partnered up with someone I could go farther, faster.

It's easy, especially early in the game, to think about what you don't have and operate from a deficit mindset. However, instead of focusing on what you (perhaps desperately!) need from a partner, flip the narrative and focus on what opportunity you're able to offer them. This way, when you meet the right person and the time is right (yes, this whole chapter will sound a little like a dating guide), you'll be able to present yourself as valuable, necessary, and desirable for a real estate partnership.

Here are five things to offer a new real estate partner.

## 1. Interest on Their Money

If your partner is investing money into the deal, you can offer them equity on the property as well as interest on their money. This gives them two revenue streams from the partnership. The interest can be paid out in a variety of ways including as interest only, in a lump sum, or through monthly principal and interest payments.

For example, in my first deal, I took on a partner who put up the funds to purchase a duplex with cash. We each received 50 percent of the cash flow, but he also received a monthly principal and interest payment. We set up an amortization schedule for his investment to be repaid over fifteen years at 5.5 percent interest. (There was also the option to refinance with a bank and to pay him off at any time.)

At the time, I honestly didn't even know you could go to a bank and get a loan for an investment property. I couldn't even tell you what my loan options were or what the interest rate would have been had I gone to a bank. I wasn't making a ton of W-2 income and didn't know if I would have been approved for a loan. What I did know, though, was that the process was simple and easy when I worked with my partner instead of a bank. He also earned a better interest rate than what his money was getting just sitting in a savings account. Where he was getting less than 1 percent interest on his money in his savings, he was able to jump that up to 5.5 percent through working with me. The deal was a win-win for both of us!

## 2. Real Estate Tax Benefits

Tax savings are a big benefit of real estate investing! Depreciation, capital gains tax, pass-through deductions for losses, deferred capital gains, and tax write-offs for real estate investors are benefits that not all people know about. It is important to point these out to your potential partner. I don't want to go too far into the weeds here, so to find out more information, I highly recommend reading *The Book on Tax Strategies for the Savvy Real Estate Investor* by Amanda Han and Matthew MacFarland and connecting with an investor-friendly tax advisor.

There are a few things I think are worth mentioning.

## DEPRECIATION

When you purchase a property, the IRS recognizes that property as an asset that must be depreciated for a certain period of time. The IRS believes that an asset has a useful life, and when you purchase a property, its "lifespan" can be expensed over a period of time instead of all at once in the year you purchased it. Most commonly, this amount of time is 27.5 years for residential real estate.

For example, if you purchase a property for $100,000, you cannot deduct $100,000 on your tax return as an expense in the year you purchased it. Instead, you must divide that $100,000 by 27.5, which equals $3,636. That is how much you can deduct each year until the twenty-eighth year, when the depreciation has zeroed out. Adding this depreciation amount to your expenses on your tax return each year reduces your taxable income and therefore reduces your tax liability without having to spend money like you would for other expenses, such as utilities.

## CAPITAL GAINS

Capital gains express the profit you would receive when you sell an asset. The basic formula is the sale price minus the asset basis. The asset basis is described as the original cost of the property plus the amount spent on any improvements.

Take this number and then subtract any depreciation that has been taken over the years of owning the asset. Capital gains are taxed differently than the income you generate from your business or even your W-2 income. It is usually at a lower tax rate, especially if you hold the asset for longer than one year. If you do hold it for longer than a year, then it is considered a long-term capital gain. The lower your tax rate, the more money you get to keep in your pocket, which is a win for you!

## 1031 EXCHANGE

A 1031 exchange could be described as a tax loophole—a legal one, of course. This situation provides the ability for an investor to never pay capital gains tax on the sale of a property. This rule (Section 1031 of the Internal Revenue Code) states that you can sell an investment property and use the capital gains on the sale to purchase another property without paying taxes on the capital gains. It is almost as if you are rolling over your profit from one property to another.

It sounds great, right? And it is, but there are certain rules and requirements you must follow to complete a 1031 exchange and not pay taxes on the gain, including following a strict timeline in which you must identify the new property you are going to acquire and close on the property. If you don't meet the timeline, the 1031 exchange falls through and doesn't qualify. You must also keep the ownership interest the same in the new property you are acquiring. Even though you aren't paying taxes now on the property, that doesn't mean they are forgiven. The taxes are deferred and will be due once you sell that new property unless you do another 1031 exchange and continue to defer. You must also use a third party to facilitate the transaction of the exchange. There are companies that specialize in this for you. The last time I assisted in a 1031 exchange, the fee was $1,500.

It must also be a like-kind investment (meaning the properties are both used for business purposes). One thing to note is that your gain doesn't have to cover the full purchase price of the new investment. You can use the capital gain cash as the down payment on the new property and get a mortgage for the remainder. This is a great way to grow and scale without paying taxes.

## 3. Monthly Payments and Payouts

You can help your partner increase their return substantially through this partnership investment by offering monthly payments (for the interest or for duties done on your co-owned properties). These types of payments need to be in place from the start of working together, so communicate this option early on and see if this is one your partner is interested in. It can be an enticing proposition if you make it clear that your partner would be receiving a monthly cash flow payment for a rental. Who doesn't love mailbox money? (Well, nowadays, direct deposit money!)

You can also structure your partnership so it provides an opportunity for your partner to earn extra money by putting together a fee schedule of tasks and their values. If a partner completes a task, they are paid out of the company account (your partnership account). For example, just like you would pay a vendor like Joe's Landscaping to cut the grass, you would pay your partner for cutting the grass. This would be paid out over and above any property cash flow. Here are some more examples: If a partner does the bookkeeping for the property, they could be paid $50 a month, or if a partner completes a maintenance request, they could be paid $20 an hour. This works great if you want to avoid duties becoming uneven or are struggling to find an equity percentage value that equates to the work each partner is doing. Instead, just have equal equity and then pay out what duties each of you complete; then outsource the rest!

## 4. Knowledge

If you are reading this book, you have probably already immersed your-self in podcasts, books, blog posts, and forum discussions on real estate investing. Knowledge is an amazing asset to a partner. There are a lot of people who want to invest in real estate but don't have the time (or don't want to put in the effort) to do the research. Sometimes people who have done tons of research get stuck in analysis paralysis and need a partner to take them to the next step. You can be that person for your partner!

Reading, listening to, and absorbing information is great, but you can also get hands-on experience too. Find a part-time job that will pay you to be a leasing agent, fulfill maintenance requests, or be a real estate agent assistant. There are many side hustles you can do in this industry that will give you access to a network of people, documents, and tools that you can leverage into knowledge. Don't forget about offering your services as an intern to someone. I like the idea of you getting paid for experience, but there are a lot of things you can do right from home to benefit an investor. Partners may come knocking at *your* door once you've acquired a few successful partnerships and can share that knowledge.

## 5. Time

Time is something you can offer someone who has a lot on their plate. There are a lot of people who want to invest in real estate but don't have the time to take a deal from start to finish. That's where you could come in. If your partner is incredibly busy but can bring other necessary pieces of the puzzle to the table, make it a passive investment for them. Sweat equity is real, and for busy people, time is a currency they can't get more of . . . unless they partner with you!

These are five of the main things you can offer a new real estate part-ner, but keep in mind that there are many more. Everyone has different assets when it comes to real estate investing. Reflect on these five aspects and then brainstorm an additional list of talents and resources you have to offer. This way, when an opportunity arises to speak with a potential partner, you won't be caught like a deer in headlights. You'll have confident answers already crafted, further proving that you are a great person to partner with.

# The Partner Presentation

When seeking a partner, you will want to gather a few pieces of information and data to share with them. This will greatly increase your trustworthiness in their eyes. Your goal is to be able to support and prove everything you are pitching to them; a collection of the right documents can help get the job done. I like to call this the "partner presentation." (Psst, this works great for seeking money lenders too! More on that in Chapter 5.)

For the partner presentation, you can put together a physical binder or pile everything into an online folder in a service such as Google Drive. For the purposes of this book, I am going to call this collection of documents a binder, because the first time I did this, I printed everything and put it into a physical binder that I handed to a potential partner over coffee.

The goal of the binder is to prove that what you are offering is a good investment. If you were analyzing a potential investment in a company, you would look at the company's financials, history, key employees, and future plans and projections. Through this binder, you are essentially laying out the facts in a clear, simple, professional way that will allow a potential partner to see that you are the real deal and worth partnering with.

The binder for your partner presentation will put a heavy emphasis on financials. The point of providing your financial information is not to show how much money you have, but rather how you manage the money you do have. If you do have money to show, that's great, but the focus should be on providing proof that you can responsibly pay your bills, live below your means, and understand the basics of a strong financial foundation.

In this binder, you can add in the following documents.

- Personal tax return for the past two to three years
- Personal financial statement
- Credit score report
- Bank statements and credit references
- Examples of deals you have analyzed
- Investment or real estate track record (if you have it)
- An outline of your investment goals and plan for your business
- Any additional documentation that demonstrates your value as an investment partner

You have an opportunity to go into business with someone, so remember that when you are delivering this presentation. I'm not talking about setting up a PowerPoint or Prezi and then making someone sit down and watch you deliver a forty-five-minute slideshow. But this is still about putting your best foot forward as a potential business partner. Your presentation can be an informal conversation at a coffee shop where you have this information handy; or you could simply email it to them after an initial discussion of partnering. The way you present the information and how you deliver it will depend on the person you are approaching. How do you think they would most likely appreciate it? Is this person busy and would rather receive everything in an email to peruse in their time, or do they value face-to-face interactions? Do some research and think about the partner you are approaching; your presentation will be about you, but its delivery should be tailored to them.

Before we break down these documents, especially the personal financial statement, let me tell you a little story. Once upon a time, I was talking to a group of people about sharing this personal information with potential partners. One person's immediate reaction was to ask, "How do you trust that person not to steal your identity? You just handed over access to your personal information, including your social security number!" I honestly was caught off guard by this question (even though it was a great question and completely valid). Here's how I answered:

"I believe that if you are concerned about a person stealing your identity, then you should not be partnering with them. Plain and simple. If you partner with someone who you are concerned will compromise your identity or financial information, then they are not the right person to partner with."

You can also redact social security numbers and account numbers on these documents, especially if you are giving them a copy to retain. If you become business partners with someone, you will at some point need to know their social security number to submit a document or form. I can't even tell you the number of times that I have needed to fill out my partner's personal information, including social security number, birthdate, full name, and even their spouse's information on occasion. As with so many things in business, exert caution, but understand that personal information will eventually factor into this arrangement. That is why trust is paramount.

## Personal Financial Statement

One item in your binder you may not have heard of before is a personal financial statement, sometimes shortened to PFS. This is a list of your assets and liabilities. When you have ownership of an item that provides value to you, it is considered an asset. Common items that are considered assets include cash, retirement accounts, jewelry, vehicles, property, and other investments. Take a moment and write down the assets you own along with an approximate value (or the exact value if you know it). The value is what you could sell it for today or turn into cash today. For cash, that would be the cash value, while property would be listed at the appraised value or market value, vehicles would be listed for the resale value, and retirement and investment accounts would be listed as the face value of what you would receive if you cashed out today. If your asset has debt against it, such as a loan on a car or a mortgage on a property, then you will add that amount later as a liability. For now, just list the value of each asset.

A liability represents money owed, just as with the balance sheet we went over last chapter. You could have credit card debt or a personal loan in which you owe someone money, for example. Create a list of how much debt you have, and then list the approximate balance for each debt owed, including your mortgage, any car loans, credit card debt, or even medical bills owed. These liabilities do not need to include your monthly expenses or bills you are currently paying, unless they have a particularly high dollar amount. For example, if you just had your landscaping done at your house and will have an abnormal expense that month, I would not add it into your liabilities unless you don't plan to pay the bill in full and are going to be making payments. This could go for furniture or any other purchases you have financed. To put it plainly, debt with recurring payments needs to be added to your list of liabilities.

The next step is to take the assets and subtract the liabilities. This will give you your net worth. This shows you what you'd be "worth" if you paid off all your debt and cashed out your assets.

What's your number? Is it positive or negative? Is it more or less than what you expected? Don't fret if the amount is negative. Real estate investing is going to help improve your situation!

Once you have completed your personal financial statement, type it up and make it look professional so it's not just a bunch of scribbles on a random envelope, and then add it to your binder. (I've provided you a template you can start with at **www.biggerpockets.com/rookiebonus**.)

Next up is your credit score. If you've rented an apartment or taken out a loan, you are likely familiar with the concept. For those who don't keep on top of their credit score, a simple way to get an estimate is to head to www.annualcreditreport.com, a website that tells you your FICO score. You can get a free report through this site from each of the three major credit bureaus once a year. Most credit card companies will also offer free FICO score updates. Just sign up through your credit card online portal. You should also be able to pull a history of your debt payments, which hopefully shows you pay things on time. Most banks, as well as financial management companies, have an app where you can even get updates on changes to your score, balances, and any time your credit is run. Do not go and run your credit through a credit agency just to see what your credit score is. Going about it this way could decrease your credit score.

If you have positively partnered with someone else in the past, you can use them as a reference as well. Previous or current lenders can supply a simple letter stating your payment history, letting your potential partner know that you made payments on time and fulfilled your obligation. You can even ask for them to briefly describe how easy you were to work with, such as that you provided all the information they requested in a timely manner. This would be particularly valuable if you are seeking a private money lender or money equity partner.

After your own financials, the next addition in the binder should be any deals you have completed and how those turned out. I always use the BiggerPockets calculator reports (**www.biggerpockets.com/calculators**) to showcase my deals. These reports are easy to understand, are visually attractive, and show a lot of information about both the deal and how it turned out. If you haven't done a deal yet, then you can use the reports to analyze a couple of deals that fit your criteria to show the investor what you'd be going after as well as your ability to complete this task.

## Strengths and Weaknesses

When approaching potential partners, it is also important to have a clear list of your personal strengths and weaknesses. You will want to compare this list to your partner's because you'll have the best success if you can compensate for each other's weaknesses. Similarly, leveraging each other's assets and abilities will be advantageous to building a successful business. Remember, using leverage doesn't always mean financing! You can leverage your time, network, assets, money, and more. One partner might be an introvert and have trouble networking, while the other could be an extrovert and excel at meeting new people and attending in-person events.

Let me show you one way a partnership benefited me when each partner contributed something different.

For the first couple of years that I purchased rental properties, I hired contractors to do any and all rehabs and repairs. However, when I purchased a quadplex, I wanted to learn to do the rehab myself. I asked my friend Joe to be my partner on this deal. He led the charge on the rehab and I worked alongside him, learning each and every step of the way. For this particular quadplex property, we did most of the work ourselves and only hired out contractors for electric and HVAC work. Even though Joe didn't invest any money in the property, he got 40 percent equity in the property for doing the labor and teaching me how he did it along the way. He earned equity, I learned a ton, and the rehab got done. Again, we both won.

If you want to learn something, provide an incentive for that person to teach you. Sometimes, giving them something other than money (in this case, equity in a property) can work out better for everyone involved.

## Partnership Structures

Okay, it's time to get into the nitty-gritty of how to get this partnership done right. While there are a variety of ways to structure a partnership, there is no right or wrong one. As I've been saying—and will continue to say—there's only the right way for *you*.

On the most basic level, there are four different things you can "bring to the table" of a partnership: equity, sweat equity, debt, and capital.

- **Equity:** your stake or share of ownership in a company
- **Sweat equity:** performing physical labor or services in exchange for a share of the company or ownership of the property
- **Debt:** having the mortgage in your name, meaning you assume the risk by actually holding the mortgage
- **Capital:** providing the cash needed to purchase a property or start up a company

If you look at this list right now, which of these four are you able to provide? Which would you be looking for a partner to supply? Knowing this information will be helpful for you as you look for potential partners. We often choose to spend our time with people most like us, but in this case, looking for a person who *has what you don't* and who *needs what you have* is going to work out much better than finding your investment doppelgänger.

As you consider the best partnership structure for you, you may be asking yourself:

- Is the structure fair?
- What would someone else want out of the deal to partner with me?
- How do I make sure it's a good investment for both of us?

These are good questions. It's important to know that a partnership structure is negotiable. You and your potential partner can discuss the structure and tailor it so it suits you both. When you do want to offer someone a partnership deal, have some kind of offer ready. This will give you both a starting point.

Think of it like an asking price on a home—even though the seller is asking $150,000 on the MLS, that doesn't mean that is actually what someone will pay for the property. The purchase price could wind up being either more or less than the asking price. The seller may accept an offer for $125,000 because the buyer is offering to take the property as is with no repairs. Or they may accept $160,000 because the buyer wants all contents of the property to be removed before closing (in this scenario, it's a hoarder house, and the seller knows it will only cost $4,000 to get the property cleaned out, netting him $6,000 out of the $10,000 after paying the junk removal company). In this scenario, there were different elements to the deal than just the purchase price. Keep this in mind when structuring your partnership—the equity split or the return your partner may get on the deal is not the only factor at play.

As you read, know that the terms partner's stake, partner's equity, and partner's shares are used congruently throughout the book, but they all mean the same thing.

An easy starting point is to look at what each partner is bringing to the table. Here are some elements to consider:

- Money put into the deal (capital)
- Who found the deal

- Where is the financing coming from and who is the personal guarantor
  - Let's break this one down a little more. If you have an uncle who is going to lend you money at 3 percent interest to fund the deal, that is a huge value that your partner might not have access to. Similarly, if you are using a line of credit that you have on your personal residence, that is of value in the partnership. This also means that you are the personal guarantor, so you are personally liable if you can't pay back that loan.
- Who is doing the rehab or managing the project
  - Is it going to be a short-term rental and one partner is going to set up the furniture and handle the communication with the guests?
- The exit strategy and who will oversee that?
- How long this partnership will take place
  - Will you hold the property for five years then sell unless both parties agree to keep the property?
- The values and resources each partner is bringing to the table
- What is important to each partner
  - Cash flow? Appreciation? A short- or long-term investment? Passivity?

**Let's do an example:**

Colt found a property for $100,000 (those of you living in expensive markets, are you cringing at my $100K examples yet?). However, Colt only has $30,000 saved. He ran the numbers and analyzed comparable properties that have sold in the area, so he knows that after rehab, a property in that area can sell for $200,000. Colt estimates the rehab on the property will cost $30,000 for materials and labor. The holding costs (insurance, property taxes, and utilities during the rehab process) would cost about $650 a month, and rehab would take four months, plus an additional three months to sell and close on the property. (Total holding costs of $4,550.) There will also be some closing costs (survey, title work, and/or attorney fees) estimated at $2,500. The total money needed, assuming the property is bought with cash, is $137,050.

Colt has been researching and analyzing deals for several months and feels confident in his analysis. He knows he can manage the rehab, hire contractors, and get the property finished, but he needs money. Fortunately, Colt's friend Maverick is a Realtor and has some money he wants to invest but no time to invest himself. Here is how Colt decided to structure the offer:

- **Colt's capital contribution:** $30,000
- **Maverick's capital contribution:** $107,050
- **Colt's responsibilities:** Get deal under contract at $100,000; manage rehab within budget of $30,000
- **Maverick's responsibilities:** Handle the design and book-keeping; list the property for sale without taking a commission

If you look at the capital contribution, Colt is putting in 22 percent of the money and Maverick is putting in 78 percent. The harder part is evaluating how much work each person is putting into the deal to earn that sweat equity. Being Colt's first investment, he may be willing to take a smaller equity piece just to get experience and get started in real estate. Or Colt may decide he wants to maximize every investment he makes, so the deal is only worth doing if he doubles his investment. That's him making a profit of $30,000.

The estimated sale price is $200,000, so subtracting $137,050 gives an estimated profit of $62,950. Since $30,000 is 48 percent of that final sum, Colt would need to have 48 percent ownership in the deal to double his investment (100 percent cash-on-cash return). Is this fair? Who decides it is fair?

In the end, both partners decide what is fair. If Maverick is making 1.5 percent interest on his $107,050 sitting in a bank account, then this may be a fair deal to him. He loves design, and bookkeeping is easy for him, but he would never want to manage contractors. Maverick sees it as an opportunity and agrees to have 52 percent equity, coming out with an estimated $32,734 in profit (a 31 percent cash-on-cash return). That's way better than what his money would make sitting in his bank account for seven months, and likely outpaces what he would gain on average in the stock market during that period. That's one way it could pan out.

Alternatively, Maverick could come back to Colt and say that he doesn't agree. Maverick's counteroffer might be that they split the equity based on capital contribution. Then they pay out fees to each partner who fulfills certain responsibilities. For example, their partnership agreement can state the following:

- **Bookkeeping:** $50 per month
- **Project management:** $20 per hour
- **Finding agent to list property:** 2 percent commission
- **Rehab labor:** $30 per hour

I like this method, because if a partner suddenly can't fulfill their duty, then you can outsource the task and not worry about the equity piece now being unfair.

When you are choosing to be in a partnership you can't worry or be tedious about who is doing what. One of the benefits of having a partner is that you can lean on each other. Make sure you are prepared to help each other out and that you look for a partner who will reciprocate!

If you are partnering with multiple different people and you are managing them or doing a lot of the tasks so your partners can remain passive, you can also create your own management or development company. A management company would oversee the daily operations of a short- or long-term rental. The development company would oversee the rehab process. Either company could charge fees for these services, and it would be disclosed to your partners up front what those fees are.

If you want to dig deeper, rookie, here's a BiggerPockets podcast episode on structuring a partnership: **www.biggerpockets.com/blog/rookie-174.**

## Partnership Bonuses

In addition to having another person to work alongside you and celebrate your victories, partnerships have additional benefits—included among them are life insurance policies, shotgun clauses, and buy/sell agreements.

First up? Life insurance policies. I highly recommend anyone entering a partnership getting a life insurance policy for each partner. Let's use Sara and Tyler as a business partner example. Sara and Tyler are real estate investors, operating under a shared LLC. Sara is married to Tony. Tyler is married to Zosia. Pretend Tyler passes away. Sara doesn't want to be partners with Zosia, Tyler's wife, so she takes the money from the life insurance policy on Tyler and uses the proceeds to buy out Zosia. Sara is happy. (You know, other than the death of her dear friend and business partner!) Zosia is happy because she has a big amount of cash that Tyler worked hard to earn while being a partner in this LLC, and Sara and Zosia don't have to be partners. Also, Sara gets to be 100 percent owner of the LLC without having to deal with, "Oh my gosh, how am I going to get $100,000 to buy Tyler's wife out of this partnership?" That money came from the life insurance proceeds. I know it can feel morbid or uncomfortable to think about business this way, but, just as in your personal life, in business you can better protect yourself and your loved ones by planning for any eventuality.

Next up, shotgun clauses. A shotgun clause forces someone to sell their stake in the company because of a reason specified in the partnership agreement (more on drafting that agreement in a minute), such as if one partner steals money from the company or commits a felony (even if it's unrelated to the company). Including these exit strategies in your partnership agreement will dramatically reduce your liability if a partner drops the ball or isn't who you thought they were. It might feel silly or untrustworthy, but a good partner won't be offended. They will know this is standard business practice and if they have nothing to hide (poor character included), they won't disagree with including these types of clauses.

Finally, there are buy/sell agreements. A buy/sell agreement states what happens if one person in the partnership wants to sell their shares. This can give the other partner the right of first refusal to purchase the shares in the company from the selling partner before they go and sell their stake. Would you want to risk being partners with just any random person? I know I wouldn't! Usually, within the buy/sell agreement, there is a predetermined formula created by your accountant or attorney that will determine the purchase price of the other partner's equity in the company.

Want more, rookie?
Here's another great episode on partnership!
**www.biggerpockets.com/blog/
rookie-podcast-73.**

# Partnership Fears

Just as it can be exciting and comforting to share the stress, workload, and joy of investing, it can also be overwhelming. If you are feeling a bit nervous about entering a partnership, don't worry. You aren't alone. And you're smart to really think this through before entering an agreement with someone.

Having a strong partnership agreement can overcome most fears of getting into business with a bad partner. First, think about what that fear is. What are you afraid of? This isn't a rhetorical question. I really want you to answer it. Once you identify it, create a scenario in your partnership agreement of how you will handle that fear if it comes calling. For example, if your fear is that your partner will steal money, then have a shotgun clause stating that they are forced to sell their shares of the company to you if that happens. Plan out ways to ensure checks and balances to prevent that from even happening in the first place. One example would be two check signers for each check or approval from both members over a certain amount.

Using different partnership structures such as an LLC or joint venture can also limit liability. It is important to consider what will work best for you and your partner. (Review Chapter 3 if you need a refresher on this!)

In order for a partnership to be successful, communication is key. Communication is a big part of any relationship, whether it is a parent and child, spouses, or business partners. You will need to *listen to understand*. What does your partner have to say? Are you really thinking about their words and intentions, or are you just thinking about how you will respond? Listening is an underutilized skill and form of respect, but it absolutely needs to be present if you want to build a successful (and enjoyable!) partnership. To help you create a partnership that values both parties, you need to write out an agreement clearly stating all of the aspects we have covered in this chapter. It is important to put systems and boundaries in place that protect not only both partners but also your ongoing relationship.

Once you find a person you'd like to work with, draft a partnership agreement. The partnership agreement should lay out all the answers, or at least outline different scenarios, so that if there is a disagreement between you and your partner you can look to the partnership agreement for the predetermined outcome or the next steps to take. To help you,

I've included a sample operating agreement at **www .biggerpockets.com/rookiebonus**. Revise and change it to your specific needs as necessary, and then have your attorney look it over to make sure the agreement is applicable to and in line with your state's laws.

## What Do You Think?

The term partnership is sometimes applied to romantic relationships, and yes, I am basically suggesting that you date your investment partner—getting to know each other, taking your relationship seriously, and treating each other with respect is key. Take it one deal at a time if you have to. At the very least, make sure you and your partner are on the same page. Have quarterly meetings where you sit down uninterrupted and review the goals you each have and where your business is headed. If, right off the bat, you don't want the same things long-term, then your partnership probably won't work out. You both could want to make money, but one person might want to make money and then sell everything in five years, while the other wants to build a massive portfolio and hand it down to their kids one day. It's better to know that up front!

Set meetings with your partners and their significant others to make sure you are all in alignment and agreeing as to where the company is headed and its growth. Identify different scenarios that could happen, along with exit strategies.

Before diving into a partnership, make sure you get to know the person you'll be working with. Sometimes, that means going out for coffee or lunch; other times, it might mean wading into deeper waters with something like a personality assessment such as DISC[6] or Enneagram.[7]

Finding a partner is one of the best things I did as a rookie investor. Through my partnerships, I was able to grow and scale my rental portfolio quicker than if I was on my own. As you journey forward into partnerships of your own, remember two things.

1. This process is repeatable! You can have more than one partnership, and each can be structured differently.

---

**6**  www.discprofile.com/what-is-disc

**7**  www.biggerpockets.com/blog/rookie-172

**2.** Be sure you go through the process with each partner. Vet them and don't cut corners. A bad partnership is bad for business. Make sure you are making a commitment to and with a solid partner.

I know I've touched on my own partnerships throughout this chapter, but as we close it out, I want to share a few more examples. As I've said many times already in this book, you get to create and pick what works best for you. But, by seeing my partnerships spelled out on paper, you can hopefully begin to think about people, structures, and agreement clauses that could work for you.

## Partner 1: Evan

Evan and I are each a 50 percent owner of our properties. Evan is a completely passive partner, bringing only capital to the table. He puts money into the deals we purchase, and I do the legwork, such as finding the deals, acquiring the deals, and managing the assets. As we have grown and scaled, I have contributed money into our investments, but at first Evan was the only one putting in capital. This is a great example of how partnerships can grow, change, and expand as time moves on.

## Partner 2: Joe

With Joe, I have one entity where we split everything 50/50. We each put in 50 percent of the money (if necessary, but we usually buy with little or no money down). We share 50 percent of the responsibilities and also evenly split the profit. Joe and I have a second LLC, of which I am 60 percent owner and Joe has 40 percent. We structure this second partnership this way because I do more work up front acquiring the deals and I also put more money in. This is a good example of how we adapted and pivoted our LLC based upon what each was capable of at the time.

## Partner 3: Daryl

Daryl and I are 50/50 partners. I handle the money aspects, focusing on funding and acquisition. Usually, we use lines of credits, private money lenders, and hard money. Daryl does most of the work on deal sourcing and project managing the rehabs. We split any cash flow and profits evenly.

I came into each of these partnerships at different times in my real estate journey and portfolio growth. For each one, I had different things I could offer to the partnership as well as different things I was looking for in a partner.

What do you think? Is adding a partner something you'd like to do? To get started on the process, create a list of why you think you need (or might want) a partner, as well as a second list of what you can offer someone else in a partnership. Then tell everyone and anyone what you are trying to do with real estate. This might feel a little scary, but you can do it! Ask people if they know anyone who would be interested in partnering on a deal. If someone says yes, ask them to reach out and make an introduction on your behalf. This not only creates a built-in recommendation for you, it also takes the pressure off cold-calling and asking your potential partner directly.

# HOMEWORK

You know what time it is! Time to put all this good knowledge into action with a little homework! Here's what I want you to do before moving on to Chapter 5: Financing.

- Look back at the list of five things you can offer a partner, even as a Real Estate Rookie. Make a list of your best qualities. Draft a pretend pitch, selling yourself as an amazing investment partner. What opportunity and strengths can you offer?

- Create a sample partnership structure that you could offer someone. As you draft this, keep in mind what is important to you. (Control? Equity? Cash flow? Experience?)

- Begin creating your partner presentation binder.
  - As a reminder, this includes: deal analysis, experience or track record, personal tax return for the past two to three years, personal financial statement, credit score report, bank statements and credit references, and any other useful documentation that demonstrates your partnership value.

# Chapter 5

# FINANCING

## Vocabulary You'll Need to Know

**401(K):** A retirement account provided by an employer to an employee that is managed by a third party (selected by the employer). Employees contribute pretax money to their 401(k) directly from their paycheck. The money is invested into the stock market and the employee receives a return on their investment, which is reinvested into the 401(k) account. Some employers may even contribute to an employee's 401(k) as part of a benefits package. There are no taxes paid until the person withdraws funds.

**CAPITAL EXPENDITURE:** An improvement, repair, or equipment purchase that will add value over time. Examples could include a new roof, tractor, or HVAC system. These are items the IRS considers to have a life span of over a year and shouldn't be expensed all at once, since the asset will provide you value over several years or more. Smart investors save for these big-ticket items well in advance. The IRS requires you to depreciate these assets—investors write off a portion of the cost of the asset each year until the life value of the asset has ended. For example, according to the IRS, a new roof should be depreciated over 27.5 years.

**COLLATERAL:** something pledged as security for repayment of a loan, to be forfeited in the event of a default.

**DEBT-TO-INCOME RATIO (DTI):** This formula compares the amount of your monthly loan payments to the amount of income you make. A bank will want to look at your DTI to make sure you can afford an additional mortgage payment; a lower DTI is a sign to them that you are not over-leveraged. This will include all types of loan payments, not just mortgages—for example, auto loans, lines of credit, or any personal loans.

**IRA:** A retirement account that provides tax advantages. Each year, the IRS sets a certain dollar amount that you can contribute. The money is invested in the stock market based on stocks that either you choose or a financial advisor chooses for you. The money contributed can be deducted each year on your tax return. At retirement age, you will pay income tax on your withdrawals.

**SELF-DIRECTED IRA:** Similar to an IRA, but instead of investing it into the stock market you can choose your investment strategy. For example, you can use the money in the retirement account to invest in real estate through a syndication or even as a private money lender. There are restrictions; for example, you cannot be an active investor in the deal that you are using your IRA to invest in.

**OPM (OTHER PEOPLE'S MONEY):** Borrowed capital (such as by using a private lender) to increase the potential returns as well as the risks of an investment.

**PMI (PRIVATE MORTGAGE INSURANCE):** A type of mortgage insurance often required when you have a conventional loan and make a down payment of less than 20 percent of the home's purchase price, to be paid until 20 percent equity is reached. PMI protects the lender—not the buyer—in case you stop making payments.

**SELLER FINANCING:** When the seller of a property decides to be the lender on the property being purchased, rather than having the buyer finance through a bank. In this situation, a buyer would negotiate the terms of the loan (such as interest rate, length of loan, and monthly payment) with the seller.

# Financing Real Estate Investments

One thing that holds many new investors back is money. If you're raising your hand right now saying, "Yeah, Ashley, that's me!" don't worry. You're not alone. Know that it is still definitely possible to make your real estate dreams a reality. You just need to think creatively and examine your situation from all angles.

Before I go on, I want to put a little disclaimer out here on the page: *Do not over leverage yourself!* It is imperative that you keep cash reserves and equity in your property. For a single property, I typically recommend you have six months of mortgage payments, property taxes, and insurance on hand (meaning having access to liquid money that you could pay the expenses on your property for six months if it was vacant with no tenant or sitting on the market unsold). Within six months, you should be able to get the unit rented, the repair made, or the property sold. If not, that's where it's important to have different exit strategies in place. If your strategy is to flip the property and it's not selling, are you able to turn it into a short-term rental? How about a long-term rental? When purchasing a property, you should know what kind of financing you will need in place for different exit strategies. If you can't sell your flip house and need to turn it into a long-term rental, are you able to get some long-term financing in place? Do you need your cash out of the flip to pay back yourself or someone else?

My goal in this book is to guide you in asking the right questions so that you're better equipped to start your real estate journey. It's one thing to read about financing strategies—it's another to strategically evaluate which option is best for you, to articulate *why*, and to have a backup or exit strategy in case of the unexpected. Keep this top of mind as you read through this chapter and do the end-of-chapter homework.

## Your Current Assets

To kick things off, I want you to think about your current assets. This could be your current home, retirement accounts, stock investments, or other cash reserves. Each of these assets can be leveraged for equity, which will in turn give you funds to move forward with your chosen real estate strategy. Let's take a look at your options.

### Current Property Equity

Do you have equity in any property you currently own? This could be your primary residence, a second home, or a current investment property. If the answer is yes, you have a couple of options.

One option is a cash-out refinance. The first step of the process is going to a bank and getting a new mortgage on your property. This is called a refinance. The bank will give you the money from the mortgage and you will use that money to pay back your short-term financing or the financing you had on the property before you increased the value of property. This will then allow you to take out a larger mortgage on the property and pay yourself back for any money you used out of pocket or from short-term financing to purchase the property or pay for rehab. Remember the BRRRR strategy? A cash-out refinance is a critical part of that strategy. (Hint: It's one of the Rs.)

The cash-out refinance strategy can jump-start your investing by using the "leftover money" from the refinance as a down payment on your next investment property. This is especially true if you have made major improvements to your property or the property values in your area have increased since you purchased. If interest rates have dropped since your original mortgage, this will also play out favorably for you because you'll be able to borrow more money at a lower rate. However much you originally paid for your property can now be used again to buy another property. If you purchased it with your own cash, you have that cash back now; if you used a private lender, then hopefully they want to lend the money to you again on another deal.

A HELOC, or home equity line of credit, is another great option for those who already own a home and want to tap into their equity to invest. Think of a HELOC like a credit card—you are opening a line of credit against the available equity in your house, and you can use as much or as little as you want of the available funds. Generally, you can borrow up to 85 percent of the value of your home, minus the amount that you still owe. A HELOC is different from a cash-out refinance, which is a complete origination of a new mortgage (meaning closing costs and a potentially higher interest rate, depending on the lending climate). Sometimes a bank will even waive the closing costs and appraisal fees for a HELOC, so make sure to ask! A HELOC is what you would get on your primary residence, but you can also get a LOC (line of credit) on an investment property. The only difference between the two is whether it is for your primary residence; they are pretty much the same product, except for the fact that the investment property LOC may have a higher interest than on your primary residence. You will have more success with options for an investment property LOC talking to a commercial lender than a residential lender.

I prefer this option over cash refinances because most banks don't charge closing costs on a line of credit. Another benefit is that you only have to pay interest when you are using the money. Plus, you can pull money out, pay it back, and pull it out again. It is a super-flexible and wallet-friendly way to have access to cash for investing. For long-term financing, I prefer mortgages, but if you are going to use the money over and over again to purchase properties or pay for rehabs and pay the money back within a short period of time, then a line of credit is the way to go. You are only paying interest when you are using the money, and most times it is interest-only payments.

Be smart with how you use and repay this money, as you are borrowing using your house as collateral.

## Stock Investment Accounts

Another way to get a line of credit is to use your stock investment accounts. If you have a (non-retirement) brokerage investment account you can sometimes put a line of credit against that investment account. The interest rate is usually very low since the collateral is your investment account, which is pretty liquid. By following this model, your investments could be making you 6 percent a year while your line of credit is only charging you 3 percent a year—with hopefully your real estate investments making much more than that! This way, you can continue to keep your stock investments and use the line of credit to invest in real estate. There are some requirements, such as that you must have a certain minimum amount of money in your brokerage account and the amount available to you on the line of credit may fluctuate depending on what the current balance is in your brokerage account. The benefit of this option is that you can continue to invest in the stock market, invest in real estate, and pay a low interest rate on the money you borrow to buy real estate. In my opinion, this option is more valuable than using your retirement accounts because you can stay diversified and continue to invest in the stock market while leveraging that investment.

## Retirement Assets

I am a big fan of holding index funds for the long term and not pulling them out, but if you have a retirement account, like a 401(k), you can also borrow from that. If you decide you want to take a loan against your 401(k), then you are actually pulling your money out of the stocks it is invested in. If you do this, you now have a loan payable to your 401(k). The benefit is that you are paying interest back to yourself via your 401(k) account. The company you work for will set up payments back to your 401(k) through your paycheck. Every time you are paid, a predetermined portion of your check will go toward paying back your 401(k) loan.

The downside to this strategy is that, of course, you are no longer invested in the stock market. If you can make yourself a greater return on your real estate investment than your 401(k) is making, then maybe pulling money out feels like a no-brainer. Be warned, however, there are some limitations. For example, you need to have a certain amount of money in your brokerage account in order to get a line of credit against it.

If you have an IRA (or plan to open one), I'd recommend looking into a self-directed IRA. This investment opportunity works by using the money you put into an IRA to invest in real estate instead of in the stock market. All cash flow, income, and expenses must run through the IRA and the same rules apply for pulling out the cash as for a traditional IRA.

A person might do this because they are not happy with the return they are getting in the stock market. Or perhaps they feel the fees they are paying to a financial advisor or institution to manage their investments are too high. Maybe they want more control of what they are investing in. Remember you are working to create an investment (or portfolio of investments!) that works and feels good to you. Doing what everyone else does, just because "that's what everyone else does" isn't always a smart investment plan.

You can't be an active investor in your self-directed IRA, but you can choose the operator. If you have any type of brokerage account or retirement account, I challenge you to take a look at your statement. The fees of how much the fund you are invested in is charging you will be listed. I personally love index funds because of their low fees.

I like being diversified and having money in real estate and the stock market, and the fact that I can use one portion of my financial portfolio to fund another is not only exciting, it can also be super profitable.

## Banks and Loans

Not all loans are created equal. Let's take a look at a few of your options so that when you have an appointment with a banker, you can go into it confidently and armed with knowledge. You should shop for the best rates and terms. Ask what the lenders have available based on your situation and what you want to invest in.

## FHA Loan

These loans are approved and insured by the Federal Housing Administration (FHA), aka, the U.S. government. FHA loans require only 3 percent down and are generally paid back over a thirty-year period. These loans have comparable interest rates to standard, conventional loans (lower than private money). Because they are backed by the U.S. government, lenders are willing to give these out, although some sellers may be hesitant to accept an offer from an FHA-backed mortgage because there are more stringent requirements for the property condition. Because FHA loans are intended to support and incentivize primary home buyers, they have more lenient credit score requirements (typically 500–580) and allow low down payments. As with most mortgages with a down payment less than 20 percent, you will have to pay private mortgage insurance (PMI). A common misconception is that FHA loans are only for first-time homebuyers. This is not the case, although you can usually only have one FHA loan at a time. If you want to use an FHA loan to purchase a second property, you must first refinance out of the first FHA Loan (this can be done by refinancing into a conventional loan).

### Requirements:
- 3.5 percent down
- 500–580 minimum credit score, generally
- $420,680–$970,800 loan limit, depending on location (as of 2022)
- Standard market interest rates, some of the lowest options; fixed options are common, although variable is also an option.
- An inspection on the property that is separate from the inspector you may hire during your due diligence period.

## Conventional Loan

These types of loans are not necessarily backed by the federal government, but the vast majority of lenders offer this type of mortgage. (Hence the term conventional.) Loans that meet certain requirements (called conforming mortgages, a type of conventional loan) can be bought by Fannie Mae and Freddie Mac, however, which are federally backed mortgage companies. This means that after your lender provides you a mortgage, they may go on to sell it to another lender (or Fannie Mae/Freddie Mac), which makes no difference to you as a borrower but does make this loan type more appealing to lenders. Because of this, conventional loans are among the most popular.

As with FHA loans, you will have to provide your lender with proof of income, statements of cash reserves with which you will purchase the property, employment verification, proof of your debt-to-income ratio (DTI), and your credit score. Conventional and FHA loans are generally not great options for individuals with very low credit, high DTI ratios, or little to no proof of income (the standard is two years of proof). Thus, buyers with less favorable qualifications will prefer FHA loans. As with other mortgages, less than 20 percent down payments will result in needing to pay PMI.

**Requirements:**
- Down payment as low as 3 percent in some cases, although standard is generally 5 percent or more, 15 percent for multifamily, and 10 percent for second homes. This is if the property will be your primary residence (if you are house hacking). The down payment will generally be at least 20 percent if it is an investment property.
- Minimum 620 credit score
- $647,200 loan limit, up to $970,800 in certain HCOL (high cost of living) areas
- Standard market interest rates, some of the lowest options; fixed options common, although variable is also an option.

## 203(k)

The Section 203(k) loan is a type of loan that allows homeowners to finance renovations along with the price of their home. Through a 203(k), you can roll your renovation costs into your mortgage and pay it off in your monthly mortgage payments. You can't use a 203(k) loan for homes that are so in need of repair that they aren't considered habitable, but this is a great option for homeowners and investors looking to buy a property that needs a little bit of tender love and care. There are more steps to take with this type of financing compared to a traditional FHA mortgage or conventional loan. You will have to create a rehab proposal (HUD, the Department of Housing and Urban Development, has a checklist for this) and get an appraisal to estimate the post-rehab value of the property. At this point, you can hire a 203(k) consultant if you want to, but it is not necessary—finding a loan officer who is knowledgeable in 203(k) loans and able to guide you through the process would work well too. If you take this route, however, you will need to be confident in creating your own budget, after-repair value estimate, and timeline, because the loan officer will not be able to help with that.

## Leverage in Action
How does this play out in real life? Let's take a look at one of my deals.

Once upon a time, I purchased a duplex with a partner for the bargain price of $35,900. To do this, I met with a loan officer from a small local bank with only six branches. I already had a relationship with this bank through my job as a property manager, which helped me walk into the meeting both confident and calm.

I handed the loan officer a BiggerPockets calculator report and he unexpectedly told me he would give me an unsecured short-term ninety-day interest-only loan for the purchase price. This would allow me to purchase the property with a cash offer! Our offer was accepted for $35,900 (asking price was $42,000). After closing, I invested $800 in the property in the form of a new fridge for the lower unit.

Previously, I had found that most banks I spoke with wanted me to wait six months to a year before refinancing based on appraisal value. But because I was familiar with this particular bank, they allowed me to start the refinance process the day after closing. They were also willing to offer me a mortgage based on the new appraisal right away.

Three weeks after closing, the house appraised for $55,000! I refinanced for 75 percent of appraisal. After paying off the ninety-day loan and reimbursing ourselves for appliances and interest, my partner and I walked away with $1,250 each. We decided to keep the money in our LLC for reserves.

I rented out both units three days after closing and have rental income of $1,200 a month, which comes out to around $200 a month in cash flow after PMI, fixed expenses, and saving for variable expenses. We pay extra principal on the twenty-year mortgage and save 15 percent of rental income for repairs and capital expenditure. This is not my best cash flow property, but it's definitely my best cash-on-cash return! Even though we didn't put in any of our own money on this deal, we still had reserves and cash available. There are great advantages to buying property with no cash, but it doesn't mean you should continue to operate without cash. There is always the chance of unexpected repairs very soon after closing.

So much of this was possible because of the relationship I had built with the bank. As a rookie, this kind of strong-relationship situation might not be available to you right away, but keep it in mind for the future. Remember that everyone you work with, be it buyer, banker, or Realtor, might cross your path again. Do your best to be honest, professional, and reliable from the start. People will remember this about you and be more likely to do deals with you down the road.

## Other Financing Options

The beauty of real estate financing is that we've barely scratched the surface by talking about your assets and mortgage options. Let's dive into a few more of the common tactics to fund deals.

### Private Lender

Another option is asking to borrow the money to purchase a property from someone you know. I hear a lot of investors tell me that their parents or aunts and uncles loaned them money. Some people asked for money when they were first starting out and others asked once they gained traction and wanted to level up.

The first time I heard the term OPM funding (other people's money) was while sitting next to my business partner's father at a pool in Arizona. We sat in that backyard and talked all things real estate and investing. By the time my business partner came out to join us, I joked, "I no longer need you! I have found the source of wisdom you had." My mind was already spinning as to how to use OPM going forward and to reduce the amount of money I was putting into deals.

Using OPM funding isn't only a winning situation on your part; it can be an opportunity for your lender as well. And don't worry! This isn't like *Shark Tank*. Getting money from someone else doesn't mean they have to be an equity partner in your deal. If you set up a note payable payment plan, the person who lent you the money can be paid monthly principal installments, plus interest. You get the money you need now, and they are earning interest on their investment. It's a win-win!

Start by making a list of the people you know who you think might be interested in loaning you money. Brandon Turner once told me to not directly ask someone but to ask if they know anyone who would be interested. It takes away the direct confrontation. Be confident in your approach and put together a small presentation. It doesn't have to be fancy, but you want to communicate that you have thought this through and you know what you are doing. You want to ensure your family member or friend that lending you the money is a smart investment. Your "presentation" could be as simple as a printout of a BiggerPockets calculator report for the deal you have analyzed and want to purchase. It will also be important to prove that you are financially stable and reliable. In your presentation to your future lender, provide your personal financial statement, tax returns, bank account statements, and credit report. Just like we talked about in the partnership chapter, once you gather experience and have done successful deals, there will be lenders who don't ask for anything—they are too eager to invest their money with you!

It is important to remember, for both you and your lender, that it's not about how much money you have—it is about how you *manage* the money you do have. Be confident! Make the pitch! See what happens.

There are also real estate–focused private lenders who run small businesses lending money to investors. These types of private lenders are a great middle ground between institutional lender and real-life acquaintance.

## Hard-Money Lender

A hard-money lender is not a bank; it's an institution that gives out loans specifically to people looking to purchase property. Hard-money lenders act like a bank, using the house as collateral for the money they give you. A hard-money loan can be acquired much faster than a traditional loan with a bank, though it is usually at a much higher interest rate and will come with points (payments you need to make right away). A hard-money loan must also be paid back quickly, usually within three to eighteen months.

Hearing all of this you might be asking yourself, "Why would I go this route? It sounds risky and expensive!" And you might be right; however, I will say that if the deal numbers crunch out in your favor (even with a higher interest rate), it's better than no deal at all. You'll just need to consider all the variables in order to make your decision.

To be totally honest, as a rookie, this option might not even be on the table for you. It is hard to get a hard-money loan without a solid and proven track record, something that you as a rookie likely do not have. If you'd still like to pursue a hard-money loan, ask other investors in the area for lender recommendations and also ask if they'd write a referral letter on your behalf. Who knows? Maybe a successful investor's word will be enough to get you in the hard-money door!

The last thing I'll say about hard-money lenders is that you need to be sure they are fully committed. There is nothing worse than sitting at the closing table, only to have your funding back out. Just as a hard-money lender will be vetting you, make sure you do the same to them and only choose to work with people who are dependable and have a proven record of following through.

## Cash/Savings

If you have saved up cash (including money in a reserves account) then deploying those funds can be a great way to get started in real estate. If your money is sitting in a bank account or under your mattress, then your cash could be losing money against inflation. If it's only making 1 percent in a money market savings account and inflation is at 3 percent for the year, you are missing out! Using this money toward a real estate investment could be a good financial move for you. Cash buyers also have an advantage in competitive markets because they can close in days (compared to weeks with financing other ways).

Keep in mind—don't spend it all! Rather than maximizing every financial opportunity with the money you have, having some cash on hand reduces a lot of risk. It is always good to have cash reserves in place for those unknowns or things that come up that you aren't expecting.

## Creative Financing

The options are endless for creative financing. I am going to give you a couple of examples to get the juices flowing and to start thinking outside of the box. The first thing to note is all the financing options I discussed above can be combined. Example 1 will demonstrate that.

**Example 1:** Purchasing an apartment complex for $750,000. A commercial bank will loan 75 percent of the purchase price ($562,500), leaving a down payment of $187,500 needed. The deal has lots of cash flow, and the purchaser asks the seller to do seller financing on the property for the down payment amount only. The buyer now has a commercial mortgage for 75 percent of the purchase and seller financing for 25 percent of the purchase. The buyer has zero of their own money in the deal! The cash flow can cover the bank loan, seller-financed loan, all expenses, and put some cash in the buyer's pocket. The buyer only needs to come up with closing costs and cash reserves.

**Example 2:** Subject-to deals. The master of this is Pace Morby (you can find him on YouTube, BiggerPockets, and Instagram, as well as on his A&E show *Triple-Digit Flip*). This is where you purchase a property from someone with the following happening:

- The property is deeded into your name as the new owner.
- The current mortgage on the property stays in the seller's name and you start making payments directly to the bank on their behalf.
- Depending on the deal, you could be paying the seller some cash or you could just be taking over their mortgage payments and they walk away from the property

There are more details than it being that simple, so check out Pace Morby's content for all of them. I did this once before to purchase a farm. So far it has worked well! The seller actually rents the farmhouse from us and we get to use the farmland. We had to pay some back taxes on the property, but the mortgage payments are so low compared to if we got our own mortgage as investors. The current mortgage has a low interest rate fixed over thirty years because the old owner had it as their primary residence. We wouldn't have been able to get terms that great without sub-to financing.

This is only the tip of the iceberg with creative financing. For example, you can take out a conventional mortgage for a property but use private money for the down payment and hard money for the renovation costs. That's three types of financing and no money of your own on the table! Do your research, talk to lenders and partners, and get creative. Just be sure to crunch the numbers conservatively and not overleverage yourself or wade into unfamiliar waters when taking on obligations to lenders.

## Seller Financing

Have you ever heard of seller financing? This strategy is one of my favorites! It doesn't hurt to ask if the seller of the property you plan to buy would consider holding the mortgage for a period of time. If they agree, you'll make monthly payments to the seller instead of paying them with a lump sum of cash at purchase or with proceeds from a mortgage. This arrangement would give you time to put in some sweat equity to increase the value of the property. Often, you will operate under this payment plan agreement for a couple of years and then refinance, paying the seller back with the refinance money. But this isn't always the case. You can also set things up so that you keep seller financing on the property for twenty or even forty years. With seller financing, you aren't held by the claws of the bank. Instead, you can make your own terms—terms that work for both you and the seller. I would recommend getting an attorney to assist in drawing up a contract to make sure the agreement is binding and everyone involved in the process is protected.

Using seller financing is a huge advantage if you can get better terms than a bank can offer you. Another bonus is that you don't have to pay closing costs or submit a trove of bank statements, along with all the other information a bank requests. This makes the process much more convenient and smooth all the way around.

See? I told you that you had options! A lot of them! Just like picking out your investment strategy in Chapter 2, take some time to think about which of these financing options would work best for you. Check out the homework listed below and then, on your calendar or to-do list, write down at least one step you are going to take and a deadline for completion. This book is subtitled "90 Days to Your First Deal," after all, and in order to make that happen, you need to make some moves!

# HOMEWORK

Time to put this knowledge into action. Here is your homework for this chapter.

- Research which type of funding you want to use and rank your top three choices.

- Check in on your business binder and fill in any new information.

- Check in on your goals—are you making progress?

- Reach out to lenders to get approved or take steps to put your funding in motion. Set it up!

# Chapter 6
# MARKET ANALYSIS

## Vocabulary You'll Need to Know

**PRICE TO RENT RATIO:** A ratio of home price compared to rent price, determined by dividing the median price of a property in a market by the median rent that is charged in that same market.

**VACANCY RATE:** The percentage of time that a property for rent is vacant over the course of a year.

**BUYER LIST:** A list of people who want to purchase property. Wholesalers typically send the people on the list information about the deals they have under contract to see if any of them would like to purchase the deal.

**DRIVING FOR DOLLARS:** Driving, walking, or biking around neighborhoods looking for properties that fit your buying criteria, and then mailing, cold-calling, or door knocking to contact the owner about whether they are interested in selling.

**OUT-OF-STATE INVESTING:** Purchasing a property in a state that is not where you live. For example, if you purchase a property in Florida but live in New York, that is investing out of state. The laws, regulations, and key people you need on your team may be different than if you are investing in the market you live in.

## So Many Markets, So Many Possibilities

How many real estate markets are there across the United States? I honestly have no idea! What I can tell you is that there are too many to analyze as a rookie investor. It would be an extreme waste of time and put you into analysis paralysis. The good news is, not only should you not analyze all the markets—you don't have to. I recommend that you, as a rookie, focus on analyzing three to five markets (city, zip code, or neighborhood) at first, and then narrow it down to one where you will purchase your first deal.

You might be saying to yourself, "I don't need this chapter! I already know where I'm going to invest!" But I'd caution you to slow down and let me help you think this through. If the reason you have picked your market is because that's where you live, that's the wrong answer. It may be a great place for you to live or be convenient for you, but that does not mean it's the best market to invest in.

When I first started out, I invested in the town where I grew up. In fact, I still live close to there today, so I understand your desire to stick close to home. I had been working in that town as a property manager for two years when I first entered the real estate arena. The town was a convenience for me. The rental rates, house prices, vacancy rate, job industry, and town amenities were all familiar to me. I also had the experience of managing other units in town. I felt like I knew everything I needed to know! And perhaps I did . . . for that town. But I never even took the opportunity to analyze another market. To be completely honest, I didn't even know what a "real estate market" was!

Fortunately for me, it all turned out okay. Investing in that market has worked out for me. It was great being close to my properties, since I was actively managing them. Focusing on one market and one strategy in which I could become an expert helped me gain experience and confidence. But just because I lucked out, that doesn't mean everyone will. I know better now. And if I knew then what I know now, I would have done it differently. That "differently" is market analysis and what I want to share with you in this chapter. Through the next few pages, I'll help you look for qualities that make a market worth investing in.

I did eventually spread out to other surrounding towns. My real estate agent was actually the one who introduced me to the South Buffalo market. I was nervous investing in the city, a new area to me. I never went there! I didn't know the streets and how they could differ drastically by just turning a corner. But, based on my agent's recommendation to consider it, I looked into a neighborhood and ended up buying two duplexes. They are two of my best properties. If I hadn't been brave enough to venture into a place that was new to me, I'd never have found them.

The point I want to get across is, don't just invest in a market because you live or lived there. You can listen to the recommendations of others, but the bottom line is you need to do your own research. As we go through the items to review for market analysis, you will realize that the internet is extremely beneficial in finding factual data and statistics. When analyzing a market, you will pull more information off the internet than you will find from physically standing in the neighborhood.

Finally, I want to take a minute and say that in this incredibly important market analysis step, we are *not looking for individual pieces of property*. We are looking for a desirable area in which to focus our real estate efforts. Do not be distracted by a single home, apartment complex, or foreclosed property. In this step, we are thinking *big picture*. What county, town, or neighborhood will produce plentiful property purchasing and sales? (And continue to do so over and over again?) This is what we are looking for right now. Finding individual pieces of property will come later.

## Market Analysis Factors

There are a lot of factors that can go into analyzing a market, but the three basics we're going to cover first are jobs, population, and cost.

### Job Growth

Whether you are trying to find a market in which to wholesale, flip houses, or rent out houses, there is always an end transaction. No matter the real estate strategy you choose, you will always need someone to buy or rent the property. What do people need to purchase or rent a house? They need money! And most of the time, that money comes from a job.

A good market will have more than one stable job industry. If one industry or employer closes or moves from the area, another should still be there to support the town. Some common examples include a medical facility or hospital, manufacturing plants, tech companies, gas and oil headquarters, a college or university, and tourism.

Have you ever driven through a small town or even a city that once had a large manufacturing plant that had been shut down? It's devastating!

In the absence of the jobs the large business provides, the town withers into desolation. Even in a city where there is a lot going on, the loss of a major job production industry can cause a migration of people as they look to find jobs elsewhere. Closings like these can also result in a huge decline of people migrating to that city. Cities often offer huge tax advantages to large companies for opening facilities or headquarters because of the job growth it can cause. With a strong job market, you will have income-earning individuals. People with income can buy and rent property. Therefore, selecting a market where the job growth is stable (if not strong!) is a necessity.

You can use the Bureau of Labor Statistics website to help you find information about the job growth of the area you are interested in.[8]

## Population Growth

Along with job growth and steady job industries, there should be population growth. Looking at migration patterns can show you what areas of the state and country people are moving to.

This might be obvious, but it's worth stating plainly: Your renter or buyer pool gets smaller if the population is declining in an area. This can happen for many reasons, including a lack of jobs, poor climate, or even because of state laws. When reviewing the population of a city, you want to make sure there isn't a slow decline in population, and especially not a rapid decline. If you do come across a market where this is happening, find out why. Are you able to understand a certain event or change in that market that started the decline? If so, do you think the situation will continue to persist and negatively affect the population? Or do you project it will bounce back? For example, some major urban areas saw temporary population dips during the COVID-19 pandemic as the world was in flux and remote work environments changed the employment landscape.

If you see a dip in population growth, it might be wise to wait it out and watch for a bit before making a commitment to the area. If you can find a market with population growth, however, that would likely be a better choice for your investment. My hope is that you'll use the information in this chapter to help you choose a profitable and stable market to invest in. For this particular aspect of market analysis, that means choosing a market with population growth instead of one with population decline.

---

[8] www.bls.gov/eag/home.htm

To calculate the population growth rate, just find the difference (subtract) between the initial population (e.g., one year ago) and the population today, then divide by the initial population, and multiply by 100. You can use websites like www.census.gov to find this information. This will give you the rate of population growth as a percentage so you can see how much larger the population is relative to what it was before, making it easy to compare different markets.

You can also use the Crane Index to help you determine population growth; the Crane Index measures the number of operating crane towers in a given market, providing a simple measure of the rate of new construction.[9] If there is a lot of construction in your chosen market, that's a good sign! Usually, significant development in an area means there is population growth and likely also a demand for housing (and even retail).

Whether you are looking at job or population growth, tax payments, or estimated rent amounts, it is very important to verify your data. If someone tells you something, even a real estate agent, make sure their data is accurate. Sometimes people dole out information that they didn't even verify themselves and unintentionally give you the wrong information. Protect yourself and your future investments by double-checking what you hear and learn so that you can make informed decisions.

## Housing Costs

Cost is another key factor in market analysis. In fact, it might be the first factor you think of when considering a property. But there's a good reason I'm listing it third. You could find a piece of property within your budget, but if it's in an area with a declining population that lacks job opportunities, it is going to be very difficult to rent or sell. In that scenario, it isn't going to be worth your time, energy, and resources. Yes, the dollar signs are important, but don't let them be your only guiding factor. Promise me you understand this and will remember it as you analyze markets . . . then you can keep reading!

The cost of a house can vary from market to market. For example, a house in New York City with three bedrooms, two bathrooms, and 1,500 square feet is going to be vastly more expensive than the same property type in Buffalo, New York. Part of your market analysis should be looking at average home prices. First, you want to make sure the houses are

---

**9** www.rlb.com/americas/insight/rlb-crane-index-north-america-q1-2022

within your budget. If you have $10,000 for a down payment, then you probably won't be buying a house in San Francisco (or at least your options will be very limited!). Secondly, you want to set yourself up for success by investing in a property with a return on investment that makes sense for the time and energy it is going to require of you. Knowing average prices for a market can help you make a choice that best fits your situation.

The average cost of a home can be found using real estate listing websites. On them, you can search current properties for sale as well as the prices for those that have recently been sold. From there, you can collect data on properties and separate them by square footage, number of beds/baths, etc. This collection of information will give you an idea of what the average home value is and if it's in your budget.

Next, even if you are using OPM to finance the purchase of a property and none of your own money, it is imperative to still have reserves in place. You want your reserves to cover at least three to six months of expenses. For example, if your mortgage payment with insurance and property taxes is $3,000, then you need *at least* $9,000 in reserves. I like to recommend six months of expenses or more to be cautious, but you can skim by with three months, especially if you are purchasing a high-cash flowing property where you can quickly build up the reserves or use cash flow to cover those unpredictable expenses.

Using the average home value of a market can help you narrow down your choices by getting rid of the markets where homes are out of your reach (for now!). Remember, there are no limitations in real estate, but going too big too fast can be risky. For your first property, I want you to feel comfortable and confident. I don't want you to put yourself in a bad situation. The whole goal of this endeavor is to create a life you love! Going into bad debt that increases stress and anxiety is not what you had in mind when you dreamed of your new reality, is it? I didn't think so. For now, play it safe; later on, when you have outgrown my advice, you can go buck wild building your real estate portfolio.

Another one of the costs to consider when looking into markets is property tax rates. You can find this information by looking at resources provided by each county. For example, I invest in the Erie County area. The county's website helps me identify at what percentage property taxes are calculated, as well as how and when those payments should be made.

If you are interested in doing short-term or long-term rentals, there are different rules and regulations in different cities and states. You don't want to spend a lot of time analyzing a city, thinking that it's perfect for short-term rentals, and then close on a house and find out the city doesn't allow rentals that are under thirty days. (Meaning someone must stay at the property for thirty days or more if they are renting it.) Similarly, if you are doing long-term rentals, you may be more intrigued to invest in a state that has landlord-friendly laws. I recommend checking out www .avail.co/education/laws for insight into regional landlord-tenant laws.

## Market Analysis

It can be super appealing to jump in the car and drive around to "just see what's out there." I get it, I really do. I'm not saying you can't do this, but in my experience, it isn't the wisest plan of action. Instead, I'd recommend doing a market analysis. Find these sixteen pieces of information first. Then, if everything checks out and looks good, you can go for a drive.

This might not feel super fun or sexy, but I promise you, it will prevent you from falling in love with a property you can't afford or making an impulse purchase you'll regret for years.

These are the sixteen items you should consider when completing a market analysis.

1. Job industries in place
2. Population growth rate
3. Average home value
4. Average rent in the area
5. Price-to-rent ratio
6. Tax assessment percent
7. Anything unique about the utilities (e.g., only has propane, no city water)
8. Seasonal maintenance required (e.g., snow plowing)
9. Specialty insurance required (e.g., flood insurance)
10. Average income, age, and education level of renters
11. Percent of homeowners versus percent of renters
12. Crime statistics
13. School district rating
14. Average age of properties (i.e., Will you need to save for a lot of CapEx?)
15. Average vacancy rate
16. Exit strategies (e.g., Can you flip it if you can't rent it?)

To help you keep track of what you find, you can use this Market Analysis Worksheet (downloadable at **www.biggerpockets.com/rookiebonus**).

# Market Analysis

Date: _____

| ITEMS TO REVIEW | MARKETS | | | | | | |
| --- | --- | --- | --- | --- | --- | --- | --- |
| | 1 | 2 | 3 | 4 | 5 | 6 | 7 |
| Job industry #1 | | | | | | | |
| Job industry #2 | | | | | | | |
| Job industry #3 | | | | | | | |
| Population growth rate | | | | | | | |
| Average home value | | | | | | | |
| Average rent | | | | | | | |
| Price-to-rent ratio | | | | | | | |
| Tax Assessment percent | | | | | | | |
| Utilities (anything unique) | | | | | | | |
| Seasonal maintenance | | | | | | | |
| Specialty insurance | | | | | | | |
| Average income of renters | | | | | | | |
| Average age of renters | | | | | | | |
| Average education level | | | | | | | |
| Percent of homeowners vs. percent of renters | | | | | | | |
| Crime statistics | | | | | | | |
| School district rating | | | | | | | |

| Average age of properties | |
| --- | --- |
| Average vacancy rate | |
| Multiple exit strategies? (long-term rental? short-term rental? flip?) | |
| **CRITERIA REQUIREMENTS** | **NOTES** |

These sixteen pieces of information cover a lot of ground. Some aspects are more important than others, and depending on what you plan to do with the property (sell, flip, rent, etc.), some criteria will rank higher than others.

For example, if I were looking for a unit that I could use as a medium-term rental to traveling nurses, criteria such as job industries, average rent in the area, and education of renters would be most important for me. However, if I were looking for a fix-and-flip property, the average home value and crime statistics might be more important. As you make your list, be sure that those three factors we talked about at the beginning of the chapter are on it (jobs, population, and cost). Without those pieces of information, you may wander into a bad deal, and I don't want that for you!

After you've analyzed a few markets (again, I'd recommend at least three, but not more than five), pick out the best one or two to go visit. Once you physically arrive in certain areas, you'll be able to visibly verify what your research has hinted at—you'll likely learn additional information too. Sometimes you will see that one end of a street is flourishing while the other end is full of crime. Being physically in an area will help you get a great visual of what neighborhoods are A, B, C, or D class that will help confirm your analysis of the market.

Note that by "classes" of neighborhoods, I am referring to the way neighborhoods are categorized from a real estate perspective. The breakdown generally looks like this:

- **A class:** High-end neighborhood, generally with luxury upgrades, good schools, and low crime. A-class residents tend to be high-income earners.
- **B class:** Economically middle-class neighborhoods where properties are in good shape but could potentially still be improved. Schools in this area are good and crime is low.
- **C class**: Residents in C-class areas are middle-to-low income and property values/rents tend to be lower, often due to higher crime and worse schools than A- or B-class neighborhoods. More homes may have deferred maintenance or need major upgrades.
- **D class**: These areas are low income and high crime, with low school district ratings. A large percentage of homes in these neighborhoods might be run down or need major, large-scale revitalization.

There is no set rule for these classes, and investors' preferences range in terms of what class markets they are willing to invest in. The further down the spectrum you invest, the more room for improvement (especially for value-add investors who will breathe new life into a property). You can take several neighborhoods in your market and rate them based on these guidelines. D-class neighborhoods may produce high cash flow due to the cheap price of the properties, but remember that nothing is free—they are more likely to come with break-ins and damage to the property due to high crime, and risk nonpaying tenants due to the economic disadvantages of the area. With A-class neighborhoods, on the other hand, you risk lower cash flow or a higher financial barrier to entry, as well as low vacancy during a downturn where renters can no longer afford luxury apartments in nice neighborhoods. There are pros and cons for each. Many new investors take the Goldilocks approach and aim for the middle.

If you flip-flop these steps and drive first, you are likely to waste a lot of time. What looks good in person might end up having a whole lot of analytical flaws. Remember, your goal is to find and secure this first deal quickly and efficiently so you can grow and move on to bigger things. You don't have time to drive around neighborhoods that look nice but turn out to be a bust on paper! Do your research first and only go where you know the deals are worth your gas money and time.

If you are analyzing out-of-state, use Google Maps' street view feature to virtually walk the streets to check out the neighborhood. Make sure to take note of the date of the street view—when it was captured—because a lot can change if the view is from over five years ago. It is also great to have a boots-on-the-ground team to physically tour the area while video calling you or sending you videos and pictures. Or, of course, you can always buy a plane ticket and visit it yourself!

## Sourcing Deals in Your Desired Market

I'm going to assume, because you are a very smart rookie, that you've successfully found a market. Congratulations! But it's not time to pop the champagne yet. You're getting closer, but you have a few more steps to go. After you've decided on your market, you need to find specific properties, and in this section, I'm going to tell you about several ways you can get the job done. Browsing MLS listings, working with a wholesaler, using direct mail, cold calling/texting, searching online marketplaces, getting word-of-mouth referrals, and driving for dollars are all options available to you. Let's look at each of them one by one.

### Browsing MLS Listings

The most obvious deal source is to get a property off the MLS (multiple listing service). Contact a real estate agent in your area and let them know the type of property and criteria (e.g., price rage, neighborhood, number of bedrooms) you are looking to purchase. The Realtor will put this information into an automated email program that will notify you every time a property with your criteria goes on the market. This is the easiest way to have deals sent to you (so much easier than scrolling Zillow and Realtor.com every day).

There is a prevailing stigma out there among some investors about using the MLS. Some people say that it doesn't produce results, but I absolutely disagree. I have multiple properties that I purchased through this deal source, so I'm proof that it works.

### Working with a Wholesaler

A wholesaler is a person who finds a property, puts it under contract for an assigned price, and then sells it on to its final buyer, keeping the difference in price without having to own any property. These properties can be both on- or off-market.

The best way to find a wholesaler is to get on a buyer list. To do this, head to Google and do a simple search. For example, type in "sell my house fast in Buffalo" or "sell my house for cash in Denver." You will get a list of wholesalers in your area you can check out. Once you find one you like, fill out the form on their website and they'll contact you.

Another way you can find a wholesaler is to talk to other investors in your market and ask them who they work with. Wholesalers get a bad rap sometimes, but if you can get a trusted wholesaler (like someone a colleague has already vetted) to put you on their list, that's great! As you build a relationship with a wholesaler, they will get to know the kinds of properties you are interested in and will cherry pick the best options for you.

If you are ever contacted by someone asking if you're interested in selling your primary residence, it is likely a wholesaler! You can tell them, "No, my house isn't for sale" (or maybe it is, for the right price), "but I'd like to get on your buyer's list."

## Cold Calling and Texting

Use the list you have created—via PropStream or another similar software, or via driving for dollars—and reach out to the owners by phone. You can send out individual messages/make individual calls or do a "blast" by sending out multiple messages at the same time.

Be cautious around cold calling or texting. There are rules and regulations about this kind of activity, and sometimes it can be viewed as spam. Look up the rules in your area to make sure you are compliant and your communication will not be seen as harassment. Also, be sure that you are not using your personal phone number when making these texts and calls.

If you are feeling super brave, you can also just knock on doors and begin a conversation with a potential seller. There is a lot to be said about personal interaction and its effectiveness compared to cold calling, especially if you are skilled at relationship building.

## Using Direct Mail

There are a couple of different ways you can put this strategy to work. One option is to hire a service to send you mailers of available properties based on your criteria. Another option is to handwrite postcards to properties you have come across that look vacant (particularly if you know you could sell it as a flip).

While it might sound old school, direct mail is actually a pretty popular strategy among investors. First, use an app like PropStream to enter your criteria. Once you pull a list of matching properties, use a direct mail company to create a mailer for you. Ballpoint Marketing is a company I have used and would recommend. Once they are delivered to your house, add in your message. There are tons of free scripts out there on the internet if you aren't sure what to write, but my main advice is to keep it simple. Don't overthink it! For example:

Hi _____,

I am interested in purchasing your property. If you'd like to talk about it, call me at _____.

Sincerely,

Ashley Kehr

If they are interested at all, they'll call you. If not, they won't. But more than likely, a long and rambling letter wouldn't have convinced those people to call you either. So, like I said, keep it simple.

Another bonus of direct mail is that it's an inexpensive and cost-effective method, which is great for many rookies. Phone calls are sometimes poorly received, but mail doesn't feel as invasive.

## Searching Online Marketplaces

You can also search for properties in online locations like Craigslist and Facebook Marketplace. Oftentimes, these properties are for sale by owner. Frequently, these listings lack a professional marketing campaign and services, resulting in a lower level of competition. The end game is the potential of a better (and bigger!) profit for you.

## Getting Word-of-Mouth Referrals

My favorite way to find properties is letting everyone and anyone know what I am looking to purchase. This is an especially good strategy if you have friends who do work on houses or do lots of driving! Get the people in your life involved and working with you. Chances are they frequently come across vacant or distressed properties. For example, one of my friends works as a landscaper. He gets a lot of contracts with the local gas utility service to repair people's lawns after gas companies dig them up during line repairs. He is constantly sending me addresses for properties that look vacant or distressed. By letting your people know you are in the market, you'll increase your knowledge of the properties that are available. Plus, you'll save time and money aimlessly driving the streets to find new properties. To sweeten the deal and increase their motivation to call you first, offer them a referral fee if you end up closing on a property they recommend!

When it comes to word-of-mouth referrals, staying connected with other investors and maintaining a good network can be huge in accomplishing this task. If you have positive relationships with investors, they might send *you* deals that they are passing on (or partner with you!). Never underestimate the power of connection.

## Driving for Dollars

Did you know a major source for investors comes from doing something you may do every single day? This is especially true for the deals that are not listed on the MLS or have big for sale signs in their yard. Driving for dollars, though it sounds like it, is not about driving around looking for money on the ground. Instead, it is basically just keeping your eyes peeled for distressed and abandoned properties as you are riding around in a car. This method works great when you are looking for properties that you can rehab because they are usually easy to spot from the street. Driving for dollars isn't a great deal source if you are out-of-state investing (unless of course you are already in the area for a visit), but if you live in proximity to your desired market you might want to consider this as a way to find properties. I'm a big believer in this method of deal sourcing for rookie investors, and it's a process that has a few steps, so let's dig into them.

You likely pass property that is for sale every day as you drive to work, the store, or school. If not, take a Sunday drive! To make driving for dollars effective (rather than a waste of time), set up a seamless process you can put on repeat each time you get behind the wheel.

When you are actually out driving (or, even better yet, riding) in the car, you will want to be able to record the addresses of the properties. One of my favorite ways to do this is to use an app. You can use your mapping app to drop a pin at the location of a property of interest and then review the properties when you get home. If you are more of a "pull over and analyze right then and there" kind of person, I'd recommend using an app like DealCheck or PropStream, which will automatically pull information on the property from the MLS and even county websites. Through Deal-Check, you might also be able to see recent sales history, any photos from when it was last for sale, property tax estimate, and a few other things.

While distressed or vacant properties can sometimes be easy to spot, that's not always the case. Let's go over some key indicators you should look for when driving around.

- Think about *when* you are going driving. A good day to pick is trash day. Which houses don't have trash out? This likely means no one is living there and they are vacant, which could make them ripe for selling.
- Look for unkept yards, tall grass, and overgrown landscaping. These are good indicators that the property could be vacant or that the person living there is incapable of upkeep on the property financially and/or physically.
- Look for deferred maintenance. The paint is chipping, or the gutters are falling off. These signs don't necessarily guarantee the house is vacant but that the property owners may have a hardship and aren't able to take care of it, which may also mean they'd be interested in selling it.
- Look for any papers taped in the windows. This could be a notice from code enforcement stating violations that need to be taken care of. The notice could also be for a maintenance company that is caring for the property while it is owned by a bank, meaning it has been foreclosed on and the bank hasn't sold it yet.
- Look for mail piled up or newspapers and telephone books littered around the yard. These are clues that could mean that a person moved out of the property and, since no one has retrieved the mail, it is vacant.
- Lastly if you are looking for multifamily property, look for separate utility meters on the house. (Hint: Investors with children: This is a great thing to train your kids to look for when they are riding with you! Have them look for gas and electric meters and shout it out if there is more than one.)

Properties that are distressed, such as ones with a bad roof or plywood in windows, show that the property has some potential for value-add, especially if it is in a good neighborhood. A situation like this could also be the result of a homeowner who can't afford to fix up their property. There are lots of reasons why people are motivated to sell or why they haven't listed on the MLS. A common one I hear is people don't think anyone would buy it. I once had an investor tell me about a woman who didn't want to sell. After trying to negotiate with her, they asked her the simple question, "Why don't you want to sell?" Her answer? She didn't know how to move. So they hired movers and helped her find an apartment. It turned out to be a win-win situation. Driving for dollars helps you find the people who may be in a situation where they need help like that.

Remember that the goal is not to take advantage of someone in a difficult situation but rather to assist them out of their difficult situation while making a profit. There is no reason it can't be a win-win for both of you. You may be someone's only option before their house is foreclosed on or taken for back taxes and they get nothing. You could be providing some relief for the seller. If your intent is to misguide or to fool old ladies into selling their homes to you while they are left worse off than they were before, then your reputation as an investor will get ruined quickly. No one will want to sell you their house or work with you.

Okay, so you have a list of addresses of property leads! Good work! Now what do you do with them? The next step is to create a process. The goal is to figure out why the property is in disrepair, who owns it, and whether they might be interested in selling.

For example, if you are looking for properties with high equity, you'll want to look to see if a property has been owned for quite some time or if it was bought with cash. This will impact the purchase price. If the person owes a large mortgage balance, then there isn't much wiggle room on the purchase price. A great option here would be doing a sub-to deal (where you take over their mortgage payments). If they don't have a mortgage on the property, it is more likely that they can be flexible on purchase price or even offer seller financing. Knowing this information up front will help you decide whether a property is worth further consideration or if the margins are too small and you should move on.

Let's go through a list of resources you can use to find information on a property that could be valuable to you.

1. You could go to your local assessor's office, but you can also find a lot of information on the county website. Personally, I'd start there first. Most counties have a Geographic Information System (GIS) mapping system. This technology will map out parcels of land to show approximate lot lines, current and previous owners, property taxes, and the owner's mailing address.

2. You can also do a search for the tax bills. Tax bills will have the owner's name and mailing address. The town, county, village, and school taxes (if applicable or of interest to you) can usually be found online with a simple search.

3. You can also use apps like LandGlide or OnX Hunt to locate some of this information. OnX Hunt is actually an app my dad showed me that he uses for hunting. Turns out, its GPS capabilities also double as a great real estate tool!

4. Another great software is PropStream. It's a paid app specifically built for real estate investors that allows you to get a lot of information on a property with just a few taps of your screen.

Here are my top tips for talking to off-market sellers. A couple of these tips are from an investor friend, Nathan Robbins, another great person to follow online and learn from! I mention this not only to give him some of the credit but also to remind you that you don't need to recreate the wheel. There is so much free knowledge out there.

- Manage your expectations. Know that you don't have to close or convince someone they need to sell to you during your first conversation. Your first objective is simply to get them to answer one question: "Are you open to an offer?"

- The number one reason you'll get hung up on or told no right away is a person's natural guard and protective defenses. No one likes a cold call. To combat this, try using the following phrase within the first five to seven seconds of your interaction: "The reason for the call is . . ." You'll be amazed at how this up-front declaration of your purpose and intention eases the mind of the person you are talking to. No more guessing on their part . . . They know why you are there and can now focus on responding rather than figuring out who this stranger is and if they are in any danger.

- Know your why. It is easy to get discouraged and not to make the call, especially if you've had a few no (or "Get off my lawn!") comments recently. If your *why* is strong enough, you can overcome your fear of making the call. Remember that if you are kind and genuine, the vast majority of people will be kind back.

If they ask for your offer, don't panic. Instead, have a mini celebration in your mind, and then let them know you don't have enough information to make a fair offer at this exact moment. Ask if they can show you the property. This will help tailor a fair offer that works for both of you.

Once you have located a mailing address and an owner's name, it is now time to contact the owner. My preferred method is direct mail, but you also have the option of door knocking or cold calling. Again, the direct-mail strategy involves writing a letter or postcard to the owner of the property stating your interest in purchasing it.

There is no right or wrong way to write this. It's really going to depend on the seller if they are receptive to your letter or not. I have received letters that are typed out and some that are handwritten. One even included a picture of the couple who wanted to purchase the property. You can write or print your own letters or use a printing company

When sending your letter, don't forget to include your contact information so they can respond to you. You can set up a Google Voice number for free and have it connected to your cell phone so you don't have to hand out your personal information. Download the Google Voice app, create a phone number, and receive calls and texts directly to your cell phone. You can put this number on all your mailings. When you send your first letter, don't let it be your last. Even if you don't hear anything from the owners the first or second time you reach out, follow up at least every six months with another letter.

You can track your leads using Microsoft Excel or a customer relationship management tool (CRM). A CRM is technology you can use to manage all your relationships and interactions with customers and potential customers. Personally, I'd recommend using Monday.com or Asana to build out your own CRM. These programs and similar ones are free or low cost to use to track your relationships along with tracking many other aspects of your business.

In some cases, your letters might be mailed back to you. The postal service may have marked it "return to sender," meaning that person is no longer at the address you found. Don't worry! You still have a couple of options. You can return to the property and leave a note on the door or garage. Another thing I have done is talk to the neighbors. If they are willing to talk to you, they can provide a lot of information on the owners and the property condition. You might also hear the neighborhood gossip, which can be helpful in its own way!

Finally, before you start mapping out routes and skipping your kid's baseball games to drive for dollars, let's also talk about outsourcing this task. This is a task that you can easily hand off to your friends and family. It's as simple as this: "Hey, Mom, if you are driving around and see a house that looks like it needs work and is run down, can you please send me the address? If I buy it, I'll give you $500." You can also tell people who are on the road a lot in your market area to keep an eye out for you in exchange for a referral fee. Just be cautious that government employees can't accept a referral fee (e.g., paying a postal worker $50 a lead on addresses that have mail piling up showing a sign it might be vacant). One of my business partners has a landscaping contract with a large natural gas company in our area and he is constantly sending me houses he sees that look vacant, distressed, or have red tags on the meters alerting that the gas has been shut off. Chances are pretty good that if I follow his leads, I'm going to find a few pieces of property to buy!

## Let's Recap!

Okay, so we've covered how to find your market and then properties in that market. I have a little bad news. Once you have chosen your market it doesn't mean you are done researching forever. Markets can change and real estate investing strategies can pivot. This type of searching is not a one-and-done kind of thing. It's ongoing. I highly recommend doing a yearly reevaluation of your market to see if it's still the best market to help you reach your goals.

Have you ever gone on a drive with your parents through their old hometown? They often comment on how much things have changed. Maybe you are even noticing that yourself as you revisit areas you used to spend time in. Just because a market fits your strategy now, that doesn't mean it will always fit. Reevaluating your market at least every year will give you the chance to be proactive instead of reactive if there are changes coming that will force you to pivot.

For example, if you are investing in medium-term rentals that house traveling nurses and the local medical center shuts down or moves to a different campus, then you no longer have the same customer base. At this point, you would need to look at your exit strategies on the properties you already own and decide where to start purchasing next to keep your current business model. Or consider: Do you need to pivot your property to a long-term rental? Should you sell the property? Do you need to find a new market? Keeping tabs on your market is key if you want to continue to have success.

Another great reason to occasionally review your market is that laws and regulations can change, resulting in dramatically different results and outcomes for your real estate business. This could be for both short-term rentals and long-term rentals. If your state changes the tenant-landlord laws in a way that is not in your favor, you may want to change markets. For example, a city may decide to suddenly enforce strict and costly short-term rental regulations, which could decrease your profit and may make you want to find another market. There are many reasons to stay up to date on your market, as well as to keep an eye out for other markets in case the day comes when you need to change it up.

One last point to consider for the future. I know I told you to focus on one strategy for now, but investing in several different markets can also diversify your portfolio. Imagine if you have all your rentals in one town and there is a flood or a hurricane. Yes, you can have insurance to cover most natural disasters, but that doesn't mean you will receive a check the day after the disaster hits or even by the time your mortgage payment is due. Maybe a huge industry shuts down and limits the tenant pool. If you have other properties in other markets, they could support the market that isn't doing well during that time period. Doing business in multiple markets will prevent a single change from impacting your entire investment portfolio. Focus on one market for now, but keep it in the back of your mind that you can always diversify to other markets.

## HOMEWORK

- Complete a market analysis using the worksheet at **www.bigger pockets.com/rookiebonus**.

- Narrow down your list of potential markets to one you will focus on.

- Identify your preferred way of finding deals. If it is driving for dollars, make a list of "drivers" you can ask to send you deals.

# Chapter 7
# DEAL ANALYSIS

## Vocabulary You'll Need to Know

**CAPITAL EXPENDITURES:** Improvements to a property that increase the value and construction of the property. These are items that will extend the life of the property and will therefore be depreciated for tax purposes and not a repairs and maintenance expense.

**CAP RATE:** The ratio of how much income you receive from a property compared to how much you purchased the property for (or compared to the current value). This is often used for commercial property valuations.
**FORMULA:** Cap Rate = Net Operating Income ÷ Market Value of Property

**CASH FLOW:** The amount of income left in your business after all the bills have been paid. This amount is often expressed as a monthly dollar amount.
**FORMULA:** Cash Flow = Total Income − Total Expenses

**CASH-ON-CASH RETURN:** The ratio between how much cash you put into the deal versus how much cash flow you are getting out of the deal
**FORMULA:** Cash-on-Cash Return = Net Operating Income ÷ Total Cash Investment × 100

**COMPS:** Comparable properties that have like-kind features to the property you are analyzing to determine what your property is valued at.

> **ROI (RETURN ON INVESTMENT):** What you will receive back from your investment compared to how much the investment cost up front.
>
> **FORMULA:** Return on Investment = Annual Returns ÷ Cost of Investment × 100
>
> **VACANCY:** When a unit is not occupied by a tenant and there is no income currently being generated.

## What Are Your Criteria?

You know how you sometimes go to the grocery store for three specific items, come home with five, but forget the one thing you really needed? It's an annoying mistake for sure, but an inexpensive one. Make that same mistake in the real estate world, though, and it could end up costing you ... a lot.

There are many things to consider when analyzing a deal. It is important to think about your price range and the cash flow a property will produce. There is both cap rate and financing to consider—and more! Having a checklist will help you make sure you cover all your bases while analyzing a deal to determine if it is a good deal. You'll want to create a "buy box" that lists out what type of property you want with certain performance criteria. This will help narrow down your search.

Ask yourself what makes a good deal for you. Be aware that your response might not be the same as every other rookie investor's. That's not only okay, that's great! The beauty of working with real estate is the variety of ways you can find success in it.

Finally, one last reminder before we dig into this chapter's content: The point of investing is to make money. You picked up this book because you want to make some money, right? Deal analysis is an important step in making that happen!

Without further ado, here are the criteria I recommend you consider when analyzing a deal.

### Market

You should already have a pretty good handle on this based on the previous chapter, but let's do a quick recap. It is important to choose a piece of property within an area that has good job and population growth and meets all the other market must-haves on your list. If you need more of a review, turn back to Chapter 6 to refresh your memory. Make sure you have niched down into a neighborhood and it isn't a super broad area.

## Price Range

Once you know how you are going to fund the deal, you will need to create a budget. If you have a private lender or bank that will lend you 80 percent of the deal, that means your max budget will be based on what you have saved for the 20 percent down payment, cash reserves, and closing costs. If you are using cash or money from a line of credit, then your budget may be based off that amount. Knowing your budget can help you narrow down your search results and focus on finding deals that will work for you, rather than having a widespread range of options to consider.

## Cash Flow

Cash flow is the money coming into the business minus the cash coming out of the business. This is not your net income or net profit. This just shows the cash in your pocket at the end of the day.

### *Cash Flow = Income – Total Expenses*

Let's break this down in an example:

| | |
|---|---|
| January rental income from Unit 1 | $500 |
| January rental income from Unit 2 | $600 |
| January snow plowing | $125 |
| January mortgage payment, including insurance and property taxes | $432 |
| Principal | $80 |
| Interest | $190 |
| Insurance | $62 |
| Property taxes | $100 |
| January repairs | $45 |

Now we take the total income for the month ($1,100) and we subtract the expenses. The expenses are the snowplowing and repairs ($170), as well as the insurance, property taxes, and interest ($352). Note that this does *not* include the principal payment.

$1,100 − $170 − $352 = $578

$578 would be your profit for January but not your cash flow. The last item to subtract from your income would be the principal payment; in this scenario, that is $80.

$1,100 − $170 − $352 − $80 = $498.

$498 would be your cash flow for the month of January.

> Why hold off on subtracting the principal payment until the second step? That's because on a P&L, you are calculating profit. Principal payment is loan repayment and therefore is not an expense for the business, so it is not used to calculate net income or loss. Net income and cash flow have different calculations, and your principal payment is cash coming out of the business to pay down a loan, which is why it's used to calculate cash flow.

In just a little bit, I will show you how to account for reserves such as vacancy, repairs, maintenance, and capital expenditures. For this scenario, though, we are showing that this month you pocketed $498 in cash.

While it can be easy to see this number and let it mentally determine your level of success, I want to remind you that you should never rely on one metric. Instead, use a variety of measurements and indicators to help you know when you have truly found a good investment.

## ROI

Return on investment (ROI) is a performance metric used to evaluate the efficiency of an investment. ROI tries to directly measure the profitability (amount of return) on a specific investment, in relation to the investment's cost (both initial cost and ongoing costs/expenses).

Let's take a look at an example.

$$ROI = Net\ Income \div Cost\ of\ Investment \times 100$$

If a property generated $50,000 in revenue and had $20,000 in expenses, then the net income would be $30,000. Let's say you purchased a property for $220,000 and put in an additional $60,000 in rehab.

Your total cost of investment would be $300,000.

$$\$30,000 \div \$300,000 \times 100 = 10\% \text{ ROI}$$

Make sense?

In my opinion, the most important use of ROI is to compare multiple investments against one another and then pick the strongest one—again, not only relying on this metric.

## Cash-on-Cash Return

Cash-on-cash return, sometimes abbreviated as CoC, is the amount of money you made in profit via cash flow during the year divided by how much money you put into the deal. This number is usually communicated in the form of a percentage. It's another good way to assess whether a deal is worth your time, money, and energy.

$$\textit{Cash-on-Cash Return} = \textit{Net Operating Income} \div \textit{Total Cash Investment} \times 100$$

For example: If you invested $1,000 and made back $100 in one year from that investment, that is a 10 percent return. Different investors have different targets. Many say 8–12 percent return when doing a cash-on-cash investment is good, but those in more expensive markets targeting appreciation might go as low as 5 percent. To know what is considered "good" in your market, ask around or analyze a lot of deals to see what the average is.

Let's look at it another way. You might be making $200 in cash flow on a property, but if your initial investment was $1 million, the cash-on-cash return shows that even though the deal meets the cash flow criteria, it isn't giving you a whole heck of a lot.

My advice to you is to never rely on one formula to analyze a deal. There is no single formula that you can use on its own to tell you if you've found a great deal. Look at a deal and take into consideration several formulas and factors. This will give you a much better indication of your future success.

## Cap Rate

Cap rate is the ratio of how much operating income you receive from a property compared to how much you purchased the property for (or compared to the current value). Cap rate measures what the return currently is or should be. Return on investment (ROI) states what your return could be over time. Cap rate is often used for commercial property valuations. There is much debate on whether cap rate is a useful metric, since it is so specific in what it measures. Just like many other formulas, it does not take many other factors into consideration, such as the condition of the asset, the time the investor needs to add value to the deal, and if there is any value to be added to increase income and in turn increase the cap rate. Cap rate is measured when you purchase the property (the current income and the purchase price), and it can be measured again after you increase the income on the property, which will in turn increase your cap rate.

$$\textit{Cap Rate} = \frac{\textit{Net Operating Income}}{} \div \frac{\textit{Market Value of Property}}{} \times 100$$

Let me show you cap rate in action.

When you see a commercial property for sale, you will often see it being sold at something like an 8 percent cap rate. This can actually be misleading, because sometimes they will tell you what the net income will be after you make X amount of money in improvements—meanwhile, the current cap rate is actually a lot lower because the property is underperforming.

For example, if a commercial property has $50,000 a year in rental income and its expenses are $30,000, then the net income is $20,000 for the year. If you purchase the property for $210,000, then your cap rate is 9.5 percent ($20,000 ÷ $210,000 × 100 = 9.5)

If you are able to increase the rental income by another $5,000, however, your cap rate increases to 12 percent!

If the rents are below market and all you have to do is raise your rent prices without putting money in, then that's great! But if you have to put more money into the deal to increase your profit, then you really aren't getting that cap rate; you had to put additional money in, plus the purchase price. If the money put into the deal does increase the market value of the property, then you would use a new market value instead of purchase price to show the new cap rate based on the value you have put into the property with increasing the profit.

## Financing Criteria

Another thing to consider is how you are paying for the property. This may factor into the kind of deals you can purchase. If you are using an FHA loan, you will not be able to purchase a property that is dilapidated and lacking adequate plumbing. Remember, an FHA loan requires you to use the property as your primary residence. There is also an inspection on the property to make sure it is habitable and up to code. A major fixer-upper will not qualify, putting you back at square one trying to find money to purchase the property or looking for a different property that qualifies.

Knowing how you will pay for a property will significantly help you build out your criteria and limit the number of deals you are analyzing (which means you'll be able to pick the deals you offer on faster). Along with knowing your financing options, you need to know your budget. If you are preapproved by a lender for a certain amount, then you know you can purchase a property for that amount plus the cash you have for a down payment, reserves, and closing costs. Again, I highly recommend having enough cash reserves for three to six months of expenses. The reserves should at least cover your insurance, property taxes, and mortgage payment for each of those months. If you use your reserves at any point, you should replenish the pot with cash flow from your property until it is at full capacity. Then you can start taking cash flow again.

## Equity

Does it matter to you how much ownership you have in a property? This will come into play when you are deciding to partner. (Think back to Chapter 4!) Can you purchase a property without a partner and retain 100 percent of the equity? Or are you willing to give up more equity to someone who can contribute to purchasing a more expensive property? Along with percentages, you may also care how much leverage you have on the property. I don't recommend having a property that is worth $100,000 and taking a $100,000 mortgage against it. You want to retain some equity in the property so you are not overleveraged.

## Turnkey vs. Rehab

Is your property a turnkey or does it need some rehab? The answer will play a role in your involvement and amount of work you must put into the deal. Take that into consideration when you are analyzing an investment.

If the property is turnkey, you can expect a lower return because there is less work you have to do.

> Keep in mind that work does not have to be the actual swinging of a hammer. It might mean making calls to contractors and organizing the work that needs to be done. This may not seem like "work" now, but I can tell you that the mental gymnastics of managing a renovation project is real. Don't dismiss the time and energy this will take, no matter which way the labor gets done!

If you are purchasing a property that needs rehab, you are going to need to know the rehab cost. Whether you are flipping or renting out the property, there will be a cost associated with the work that needs to be completed. It's easy to think, "I can purchase a property for $80,000 and then sell it for $100,000," and then say, "Woo-hoo! We made $20,000!" If you needed to repair the property and that cost $20,000, then your profit is actually zero. It is super important to know your rehab costs and budget so that you can accurately determine what your profit is going to be.

To start understanding how to estimate rehabs, I want you to open up a blank spreadsheet. You are going to build a spreadsheet for materials and labor. You can create one spreadsheet containing both materials and labor or a spreadsheet for each—whichever is easier for you to track and process.

Let's start with the materials. If you have some knowledge of rehabbing a property, you can probably start creating a list of materials you would need on your own. If you don't know what materials go into a project, then this is where YouTube comes into play. Remember, you're not actually going out to buy this stuff right now; this exercise is to get an estimate. If you miss something, it's okay—it most likely won't be a large cost if you are including everything else, particularly the main components needed to do the rehab. If you are replacing a half bath, for example, here are some items you would need.

- Toilet
- Wax ring
- Three water lines
- Vanity
- Countertop
- Sink
- Faucet
- Seventy-five square feet of tile

- Grout
- Mortar
- Spacers
- Wood trim
- Thirty-two-inch door
- Door hardware
- Two pull knobs

Now you can take these items and search for them on your local hardware store website. Copy a link to the product and paste it into your spreadsheet. Add a column to show the cost per unit, a column to show the quantity you need, and then a column for the total cost of that material. This will be very time-consuming, and you can get as detailed as you want. I recommend starting out with all the details, but after a while, when you've estimated several rehabs, you'll be able to ballpark the cost without having to enter in every line item.

The advantage to this is that once you add these materials into your spreadsheet for each rehab you estimate, you can use it as a template for future rehab projects. Simply plug the quantity you need in and get your estimate. Of course, this sheet will need to be updated every once in a while to see if costs have changed or if you need to use different materials (for example, wood can drastically fluctuate in price).

Estimating labor costs will be the same format. Most labor items can be figured based on the square footage. Call around to local contractors and ask for their pricing. A lot of times, your local hardware store will advertise how much they charge for flooring to be installed at a price per square foot. Flooring, tiling, painting, roofing, installing trim work, and a few other trades may be able to get you a decent estimate; but there will, of course, be variables that change this cost. Cathedral ceilings for painting, pitches for roofs, or the number of windows for trim work are all factors that will affect an overall price. For installing cabinets, vanities, light fixtures, and other items, a general contractor or handyman may be able to give you an estimate per unit. Enter these numbers into your spreadsheet.

After you have built out a list of costs for material and labor, you can use this to estimate your rehab. You will want to add in some kind of contingency buffer since your cost will not be exactly what you estimate. There will be changes to your plan, costs will change, or you may forget to add something in. A buffer of 10 percent added into your budget can be a good starting point.

Besides building out your own rehab template, you can also find a contractor who can give you an estimate before you even offer on a property. The problem with this is that you might not get the property, and a contractor isn't going to want to chase you around town to showings. To combat this potential problem, offer to pay the contractor for their time if they agree to give you an estimate on a property before you purchase it. This way, you have the information you need and you've still kept a good relationship intact.

Also, if you have a family member or friend who has construction experience, you can reach out to them for help or assistance in building out the estimate. (Psst. I'd offer to pay them too! Even if they turn down the money, the gesture will still go a long way.)

If you have no idea where to even start on the materials you need for a project or the work that needs to be completed, my advice is to just go one room at a time. Use your own house to identify materials. (I'm not recommending you take apart your toilet, but if you do, make sure you shut off the water first!) A simple YouTube video can show you the elements to many renovation walk-throughs, and I recommend learning through the power of videos on the internet rather than actually taking apart your house.

You can also use the house renovation checklist and master material list worksheets at **www.biggerpockets.com/rookiebonus** to help plan your rehab!

## Analyzing a Deal

Before we dive into all there is to know on deal analysis, I want you to find the tool you are going to use to crunch the numbers. Are you a pen-and-paper kind of person? Or would you rather use a calculator that computes some of the formulas for you? I recommend the latter, but either way will work! Just please know that you don't need to go and buy some fancy deal analysis software.

### Calculators

Here are a few recommendations of where to look for deal analysis calculators to get you started because, let's all say it together now, *there is no point in recreating the wheel.*

# BiggerPockets Calculator Reports

These are calculators that allow you to input the income and expenses for a property and then generate a report that shows the results of your deal. This includes the results of formulas such as your cash-on-cash return and your purchase cap rate.

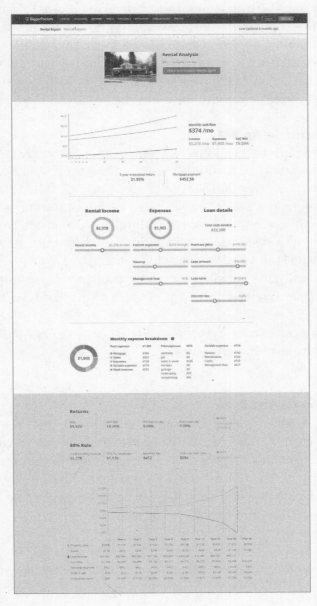

## Creating a spreadsheet
*(or using someone else's from the investor community)*
When taking this route, I recommend looking at as many deal analysis calculators as possible and then combining the best features to create your own tool that works for you. Your creation will likely always be a work in progress, but the beauty of it is that you can tailor it to your specific needs and preferences. There are investors who offer their calculators for free if you simply give them your email address. They do this to get you onto their email list. You can always unsubscribe later on, but there also might be some valuable information in those newsletter emails, so wait for a few deliveries before automatically dismissing the content.

## Downloadable Apps!
A couple of options that make it easy to analyze on the go are DealCrunch, Top Deal, Backflip, and DealCheck. You can find these tools in your app store. Even if you don't use them for every deal, it's helpful to learn what their inputs are and what they calculate, because they may give you an idea of something else you should be adding to your analysis. For example, two things I never see people add in are their accounting fees or LLC setup fees. And I think they should! Plus, getting used to using a variety of methods to analyze deals will get you more familiar with reading different reports and more confident with the types of results you want to look for.

 No matter which calculator you use—or if you create your own—you'll want to find out if the numbers make sense.

## Scenarios to Analyze
When analyzing a deal, I recommend running through three different scenarios. Using the BP calculator or the analysis calculator of your choice, run the numbers three different times: once for the property as it currently stands, once for the worst-case scenario, and, finally, one more time for what you expect the numbers to be for the property.

Let me explain a bit further.

### AS IS
The first time you run the numbers through the calculator, put them in for the property as it currently stands. What is the rental income right

now (aka, what were the previous owners charging)? What are the current fixed and variable expenses? These are expenses you know will happen every month and ones that could vary every month.

## WORST-CASE SCENARIO

The second time you run the report, you are going to play into all your fears. What is the worst-case scenario? What if you don't generate the rental income you hoped? What if the property taxes go up? What if there is more maintenance than you had originally intended? Enter all the doom-and-gloom financial worries into this report.

When I run this report, I am always increasing the expenses and decreasing the rental income. I am projecting that I will get the bare minimum for rent or that my units will have a lot of vacancy. This could be because of a remodel taking longer or because there ends up being something wrong with the unit that doesn't make it desirable. Or maybe the rent is priced too high at leasing. It could be a variety of things. When I run this worst-case scenario report, I want to know what the lowest rent is that I could get for this property and if I would at least break even.

For example, if I run comparables on surrounding units for rent and I see that properties with similar finishes, similar approximate square footage, similar amenities (such as a garage), and the same bed/bath count are renting on average for $1,000, then I am going to look at the lowest comparable. If that one is $900, then I am going to be super conservative and use $850 as my worst-case scenario.

If you run the worst-case scenario numbers and it still turns out to cash flow, then you know you are safe.

## EXPECTED

Finally, be realistic. Run the report a third time, entering your most realistic estimates. What do you expect your rental income, expenses, taxes, and rehab costs to be? Do a little research. Check neighboring properties and make educated guesses off what you find.

In our last example, for the worst-case scenario, we found that similar units rented for $1,000 on average. That will be the rent income projection I use for my expected scenario. I will actually list the property for $1,100 because I want my units to be better than average, but if I do end up renting the units for that increased amount, the additional $100 will just be bonus money.

Remember, though, it's always better to be conservative and not over-reach. Stick to what the comps show you, even if you are seeing rental prices in the area increase. If you can get more, that's great! But first make sure the deal works with what the market is at right now.

Don't forget that lowball offers are acceptable! The only number I like to manipulate when analyzing a deal is the purchase price. That is one number that is negotiable. Don't manipulate the rental income by increasing it just to make the deal work. Don't stretch it. The same goes for expenses: Don't lowball expenses to make the deal work. Just because you really want it to be a good deal, that doesn't mean it will work out that way.

## Income: How to Price It and How to Get It!

To help you know if you are on the right track in setting your price and rent amount, you can pull comps, aka prices of comparable properties nearby.

As you do this, you need to be asking, How much income are you going to generate for your property? What (about the property) is going to generate income?

Let's look at the different streams of income your property could generate. Realizing the different revenue streams is my favorite part of looking at a property! There are just so many ways to generate income from an investment property. For example:

- **House flip:** the sale of the house
- **Short-term rental:** daily rental income, cleaning fee income, or even a pool heating fee
- **Long-term rental:** monthly rental income, garage fee income, or pet fee income
- **Campgrounds** (less conventional but a favorite asset class of mine because of the many revenue stream possibilities): nightly campsite fees, ice sales, firewood sales, dump fees, activity fees, glamping site fees, seasonal RV rental fees, and more

Once you have identified what ways you will generate income on the property, then you must find out what you can charge for each income stream. If you are selling your property as a flip house, you will need to identify the ARV (after-repair value). This will be based on what other similar properties in the area have sold for. This number will be your income on the sale of the property. Note: This is not your profit. This is just the sale of the property. You'll need to add up and deduct your expenses to figure out your actual profit.

If the property is a rental, you will need to figure out the monthly rent of other similar units in the area. Whether you are trying to find the ARV or the rent of the unit, there are similarities in how to find these numbers to add to your analysis. To begin, let's look at some different places where you can find the sale price of homes, or prices for rental units.

Pull comps from these sources.
- BiggerPockets Rent Estimator
- Facebook Marketplace listings
- Apartments.com
- Zillow rents
- Calling local property management companies
- Asking local landlords and/or real estate agents

Several of the sites listed post units for rent, but, unfortunately, they will only show you the rent amount the current owner is asking for, rather than the amount their current or previous tenants actually paid. But the BiggerPockets Rent Estimator will show you that info!

Using the websites that only show the currently listed price, you can start to track them. Take time once a week and look to see what is available in the market you are looking to invest in or in the area of a property you're interested in. Organize or sort the listings starting with the newest. Each week, take some time to enter similar units into a spreadsheet. If you don't see a unit listed anymore that was there last week, know that it was most likely rented. You can use the rental price it was listed for as a comp. You'll want to make sure that you are only using listings that have the same bed/bath count and similar square footage. If there are pictures, gauge the quality of the unit and also the finishes. Is it completely remodeled? Is it older and outdated? Does it have laminate countertops and carpet, or granite countertops and hardwood floors? Give the listing a rating: poor, good, or great. The same will go for house sales. You will want to use the same criteria to match properties that are similar.

In some states, it is not public knowledge what properties sold for. Texas is one of them. It is considered a nondisclosure state. If a property is sold between two private parties and was not listed on the MLS, the price is not public information.

Another important reason to have a reliable agent on your team is so they can assist in pulling comps. If you are going to ask frequently and you aren't continuously buying and selling (where they are getting business from you), I would recommend offering some kind of compensation to the agent. Building those relationships is key. You don't want an agent to feel used; you want them to want to work with you!

There are also paid software programs like PropStream that will show you sold prices on properties (along with a ton of other data). You can view who owns it, their mailing address, if they took a mortgage out on the property, what the mortgage amount was, the property tax amount, and other additional information. All for free! The software simply compiles it in one place. In Buffalo, New York, the city has a database called OARS (www.buffalo.oarsystem.com), which provides lots of data on different parcels. Take a look at it and play around with searching for different properties. They even have a button to view comparables. It may take some googling or even a phone call to the assessor's office to ask if your market has a similar database, but it's definitely worth the time and effort.

When it comes to rent, there is the 1 percent rule, which states that the monthly rent should be at least 1 percent of the purchase price; while it can be harder to find deals these days that meet the 1 percent rule. I couple this with the 50 percent rule, which states that your fixed expenses should be half of the monthly rent.

For example, if you purchase a unit for $100,000, you should charge $1,000 per month for rent and expect that you will pay $500 per month in expenses on that unit.

Be aware that the 1 percent rule is a common guideline—emphasis on guideline—to quickly review if a deal is a good deal. But please, by no means solely rely on this formula.

In the example above, this rule states the property is a good deal if you buy for $100,000 and you can rent it out for $1,000 a month. However, this back-of-the-napkin math does not take into account so many other factors that go into analyzing a deal. This rule also varies depending on your market. In high-cost markets, it is hard to hit the 1 percent rule, but despite that, you may still have good cash flow because your expenses such as property taxes are lower or the property is turnkey so you have no work to put into the deal.

I once bought a duplex that ended up having monthly rent at 4 percent of the purchase price. The reason I was not super excited about this was because the property needed constant repairs and became a headache. It wasn't in a great area. The property taxes on this $17,500 property were $2,500 a year!

I feel the same about the 50 percent rule. That same property that I purchased for $17,500 did not meet the 50 percent rule, mostly because the property taxes in New York State, where the property is located, are so high.

When you use these two rules, understand what is common in your market. Head over to the BP forums or to a Facebook group of local investors in that market and ask them what they are currently meeting for the 1 percent rule and 50 percent rule in your market. You can also pull some data on purchase prices, rent prices, and expenses—but asking will get you the answer a lot faster. One thing I love about real estate investors is that the large majority is willing to share so much information!

My point here is there are plenty of ways to figure out how to price your property and how much to charge for rent. As a rookie, it might feel like a lot to take in and process, but the longer you are in the industry, the more you will know and the more comfortable you will feel. For now, take in as much information as you can stand to hold in your head and then make your best educated decision.

## Fixed Expenses

Fixed expenses are things that need to be paid for repeatedly, throughout the entire year. They are typically the same amount every month (or year or quarter), making it pretty easy to get an accurate estimate of what they will be. Some are large and obvious, like the mortgage, while others are more easily overlooked or forgotten. Combined, these expenses add up and absolutely need to be taken into consideration when you are trying to figure out if you can afford a property.

The best way to find out expenses is to ask for a profit and loss statement or tax return from the current owner to show what they reported as income and expenses. Of course, you don't want to rely solely on the information that they give you, but it can at least give you a starting point. If the owner wants to sell the property, many will also give you a breakdown. If they are unwilling to give you information, there are other ways you can find it on your own. Let me walk you through the primary fixed expenses you can expect.

**ONE ADDITIONAL NOTE:** This is an excellent time to brainstorm if there are ways to cut expenses that are unnecessary or being overpaid.

## Mortgage

This is the big one, and the obvious factor you probably think of first. But don't forget to add in your insurance and property taxes. Oftentimes, these are escrowed and paid each month at the same time as your mortgage. There are many mortgage calculators out there online for free, so find your favorite and have a look at the price breakdown based on your real (or estimated) interest rate, loan amount (the property price minus your down payment), insurance, and taxes.

Also have a look at an amortization schedule, either in general or for this property, to get a sense of the breakdown. This will show you what percentage of payments are equity and what are interest. You'll notice that the first few years are always skewed toward interest, and later in the life cycle of the loan, you will be paying more heavily into equity. This is the bank's way of reducing risk and ensuring they get more money up front. It's also why so many people recommend you not sell a property within a couple of years of getting it, unless you have forced appreciation—you will have gained much less equity early on, compared to what you've paid in interest and closing costs.

If you escrow your property insurance and taxes, the bank or lending company you use will pay those from the escrow account on your behalf each month, so they are rolled into the payment.

## Utilities

These should also be pretty easy to figure out. You can either call each utility company and ask for the previous year's average payment or you can talk to the seller and get the numbers from them. Even though things like electricity may vary from month to month (based on seasonal and geographic factors), you should be able to get an average expense. If your tenants are responsible for paying the utility bills (electricity, water, etc.), then this is a fixed expense you can cross off your list of things to count and manage.

Make note that the utility company will usually only give you an average of the billing for the year and can't give you the exact amount for each month. Make sure you request it for the full year; if you only gather six months of information, it won't be an accurate average, particularly if you're in a market with distinct seasons (e.g., a gas-heated house in a cold climate will have much higher bills in the winter than the summer).

If the property has separate meters for each unit, then it is quite common for the tenants to pay their own utilities. To do this, each tenant will contact the utility company and put the utilities in their name. If they move out, you as the landlord will switch the utilities into your name. You must then cover the costs until a new tenant moves in. If you are looking at property, ask the agent or owner to view the leases, which would state what utilities are included in rent and what the tenant is responsible for.

There is one market I invest in where the village requires the owner of the property to have the water bill in their name. You can still have the tenant pay the water bill, but if they don't pay, it's on you. Oftentimes a landlord will bill their tenant for the water usage or just include it in the rent. If you are going to include any utilities in the rent and not have the tenants pay it separately, make sure you are accounting for that when you decide on the rent price. For example, if comps show you can rent your unit for $800 but you will be including utilities because they are not separately metered between each unit, then you need to increase the rent you are charging to cover the cost of the utilities. (Unless the comps also state that utilities are included.) If you get the average cost of the utilities, add that amount to the rent. Let's say the water, gas, and electricity average out to be $125 a month for that property. You could then change the monthly rent from $800 to $925 or even $950 to give a little buffer. I prefer properties that are separately metered. There is nothing more painful than driving by a property with electricity included in their rent and seeing an AC unit in every single window on full blast when no one is home!

## Insurance

Insurance is one more major expense that you need to be aware of.

Several years ago, I became a licensed insurance agent to help another investor open his own insurance agency. I love starting new businesses and I learned a lot, so that was the upside. The downside was that I also learned that *I really dislike insurance!* I heavily rely on licensed agents who are practicing and active in their field. Like with an accountant or CPA, you want to interact with an insurance agent who is up to date on current regulations and policies. The insurance industry is ever-changing, just like tax and law.

When it comes to property insurance, there is a lot going on. It can be difficult to estimate your insurance costs because there are so many variables. Some common details that will affect the price of the insurance quote are:

- Type of roof
- Age of roof
- Age of HVAC
- Type of electric panel. Breakers or fuses?
- Does it have a pool or trampoline?
- Any dogs? Breed(s)?

These are just some of the aspects that can affect your insurance rate. And despite the difficulty of the process, I do have a couple recommendations on how you can get an estimate.

First off, talk to other investors in the area and see what they are paying for similar properties. If you talk to someone who is using the property as their primary home, know that their insurance is different since it will have different coverage. It is not apples to apples. For example, a primary residence insurance policy will have coverage for the personal contents of the home. On a rental property, you don't have contents in the home, so your tenants will, or should, get their own rental insurance.

The second way is to talk to an agent. I recommend going to an insurance broker who can get you quotes from multiple insurance companies instead of just one company. If you go to a State Farm agent, they can only quote you for State Farm. If you go to an insurance broker, though, they can shop around and get you quotes from multiple companies, which you can then compare and select the best fit. If you already have an agent or broker for your homeowner's insurance or auto insurance, start with them since you already have a relationship.

There are also websites where you can enter property information and get a quick quote back. Policygenius is an example of one site where you can do this.

In the inspection period—known as the due diligence period—make sure to get an actual quote on the price of your insurance with all the correct information before you move forward with the deal.

If you are flipping the house during the rehab, you will have the holding cost of insurance. You may be required to get some type of builder's risk insurance since there is a renovation going on. The insurance pricing will also vary based on whether you are doing the work yourself or using contractors.

 Builder's risk insurance is a special type of property insurance that indemnifies against damage to buildings while they are under construction.

### Additional Fixed Expenses

Finally, geography can play a role in fixed expenses in the form of fees paid for things like landscaping and snow removal. This is just another reason why knowing your market (and knowing all aspects of what it's like to live there) is beneficial. Other fixed expenses may include HOA fees and garbage removal. One area of expense that people often forget to factor in is professional fees. If you are hiring an accountant, attorney, or other professional, remember to add in their fees to your fixed expenses.

## Variable Expenses

While variable expenses will change month to month and are more difficult to estimate, they are definitely still important to factor in when analyzing a deal. Because these expenses vary, it is common practice to list and set aside a percentage of the property's rent for the expense rather than a dollar amount (e.g., assuming 10 percent of the income will go to maintenance).

### Repairs and Maintenance

A huge part of this expense will depend on the age and state of the property when you buy it. Purchasing an older property or one in disrepair might be cheaper on the front end, but if you are having to constantly put money back into it, it might not turn out to be the deal you thought it was. Ever seen the old-school Tom Hanks movie *Money Pit*? If not, do yourself a favor and stream it for a great cautionary tale.

If you are doing the BRRRR strategy and rehabbing your property, you hopefully won't have to deal with repairs for a while. Of course, issues may still come up, but if you are doing a rehab that requires updating a lot of the mechanics and cosmetic pieces of the property, it should be done right and will hopefully last a long time before things start breaking.

That being said, it is almost impossible to estimate exactly how much you will be spending on repairs and maintenance. It's hard to say what will break, so it's even harder to estimate what the monthly costs will be. Repairs and maintenance can range from a hot water tank needing a new valve to a closet door falling off its track to every self-managing investor's worst nightmare: a 3:00 a.m. phone call reporting that the toilet is overflowing. These are all things you can't account for at an exact cost when running your numbers, so use a percentage of the monthly income to accommodate future repairs. Keep this money squirrelled away in an account for future use. You don't want to be dipping into your own pocket every time something breaks—especially for more costly repairs.

To gauge the percentage, first take into consideration the condition and age of the property. If you have a property that received only a cosmetic update and has older mechanics and bones, then you'll probably need to expect more repairs and maintenance. If you are completely rehabbing the property, then you can expect a lower percentage. If a property is older and hasn't been completely updated, I prefer to use 10 percent of the monthly rental income as my number. If the property is in great shape, I use 5 percent. If the property is somewhere in between, 8 percent is a safe bet.

Don't be a cheapskate! If you already know that something needs repair or is going to break in the near future, you should fix it during the rehab period or before you get tenants in there.

Along with utilities, you may also have something in the lease agreement that states who is responsible for paying for certain repair and maintenance costs. It is very common for landlords to be responsible for all repairs and maintenance (unless, of course, the tenant causes the need for the repair). For example, a toilet or drain clog could have been an issue from the tenant and the expense for repair could be placed on them. This could be stated in your lease agreement, noting that the drains are clear upon renting. If the drain clogs it could be from the tenant's hair, grease, or . . . other things.

When I managed a forty-unit apartment complex, one of the buildings had eight units. One night, four of the tenants called to report that their toilets weren't working. We sent out a plumber, who ended up scoping one of the drains with a camera. There was a crushed beer can in the pipe! One of the tenants had somehow flushed it. At the time, there was no way to find out who had done it, since half of the building's toilets backed up from it. In this case, the property owner covered the bill, but if we had been able to figure out who caused the problem, we could have passed the buck on down the line to that particular beer-can-flushing tenant.

## Capital Expenditures (CapEx)

Capital expenditures are payments for large repairs that must be done. These payments can be depreciated and should also, despite being in the variable category, be somewhat fixed once you know the size and scope of the things that need to be repaired and/or rehabbed. Some potential CapEx may include replacing a roof, siding, or hot water heater. Anything that will repair or improve the structural or mechanical presence of the property is considered a capital expenditure.

## Property Management Fees

Typically, a property manager is paid a percentage of the rental income. Therefore, you are only paying based on the amount of rent money coming in. If your property is experiencing a period of vacancy, then your property manager isn't collecting a fee. Paying a percentage rather than a fixed salary incentivizes your employee. The more units that are full, the more work they will likely have to do, but also the more they will get paid! Keeping tenants happy and continuing to rent from you works out in everyone's favor. A nationwide average for property management fees is 10 percent, and this percentage is a good rule of thumb; however, still call around and ask managers what they charge. You might want to mark up that percentage a little over what they say just to account for the additional fees that can be charged.

## Vacancy

Thinking that your property will be rented out all the time from the day you buy it is an easy trap to fall into. But, quite honestly, that's rarely the case. It's hard to predict, but it is wise to consider how much time your units could potentially sit empty (not earning any rent). It is always better to overestimate when it comes to vacancy.

When you are analyzing the deal, you are estimating the average of every month. If you have one or two months when your property is vacant, that could be a good chunk of your yearly cash flow disappearing right out the window! To mitigate this, you want to estimate when the property will be vacant in order to be financially prepared. Not only will money not be coming in during a vacancy but you will also have other "holding costs" until a new tenant moves in. Even though the unit is vacant, you will most likely keep the utilities on for showings and any repairs that need to be done during a turnover. Don't forget that you will also have all your fixed expenses during this time too, such as mortgage payments, insurance, and property taxes. Just because there is no "customer" doesn't mean your overhead stops.

## Verify Your Expenses

Before we leave this section of the chapter, I want to be sure to tell you to verify your expenses.

There will be all sorts of people and places offering up numbers when it comes to the expenses on your property. They could come from the MLS listing, from the seller, from the Realtor, or from a property management company. I say this in the kindest way possible—don't trust anyone! I'm not saying everyone is trying to hide information and mislead you. But people are sometimes misinformed or simply do not have all the information (even if they seem confident in their answer).

For example, on an MLS listing, you may see the property taxes listed. This information could have just been given to the agent from the seller. The seller could be someone who inherited the property and wants to unload it without even knowing that there are three separate property taxes a year on the house. They only know about two and so that's what they sent the agent. The person isn't trying to be shady ... They just only know what they know. There are so many scenarios that are the result of a simple mistake, and that's why you need to be thorough in your research—so you can really and truly know what you are getting yourself into. For this example, call the assessor's office or pull data from the county website.

Another good example is insurance. If you are looking at a property and the seller tells you what the insurance costs for the year, ask to see their policy. They could be underinsured. I looked at a property once where the insurance seemed way too cheap. The property had a wood-burning stove, which the insurance policy didn't state. When I looked into it further, I discovered that there was no coverage if the property burned from the wood-burning stove. That's why it was cheaper than what I thought it should be (and also cheaper than what I was quoted).

As you get better at analyzing your deals, you will be able to ballpark some numbers for that market. If you know the average water bill for that town is $50 per month per unit, you can ballpark to run your initial analysis. During the inspection period or your due diligence, you should still verify those numbers. In the meantime, call the utility provider or ask the seller for copies of statements.

Again, I get it. This can be a lot to think about. It's nearly impossible to hold all this information in your head at one time and try to decide what to do. That's why I recommend writing everything down—three times. It's great to know how good things can be, but you also need to prepare for the worst. What is your worst-case scenario? If the worst happens and you can handle it, that's a pretty good sign that this deal is one you should make.

Don't get locked into analysis paralysis. There is never going to be a perfect deal, especially when you are just starting out. Your first deal may not be the best deal ever, but it is going to be the one that gets you started.

# Ideal Deal Criteria

Just as I had you list out must-have criteria when analyzing a market as a whole, I want you to do the same for individual deals as well. Here is an example.

- $100–$150 per unit with no money in deal, which increases as more capital is put into the deal
- Leverage no more than 80 percent of property
- Minimum 10 percent cash-on-cash return
- 12 percent cap rate
- Separate utilities if multifamily
- No HOA

These are examples of the different metrics you should set criteria for. You'll be able to begin identifying criteria that are important to you.

### Cash Flow

State your minimum cash flow requirement for a property. If you are going for appreciation, then maybe cash flow isn't as important to you. However, you should still have a minimum, even if it is a negative amount (that you are willing to lose). This benchmark measurement will help keep you on track.

## Funding

What kind of funding can be used to purchase the deal? If you need to use an FHA loan for your funding, you won't be able to purchase a dilapidated property that needs lots of work because FHA loans require an inspection to show that it is habitable and up to code. If a property requires more work or states cash offers only, then you know this property will not be in your criteria.

## Cash-on-Cash Return

The cash-on-cash return is just one of many formulas you can look at, but this plays a major role in how the deal is performing compared to other deals you are analyzing. If you have $20,000 cash to invest in a property, you are able to look and say, "Okay, if I put that in the stock market, I know I'll average an 8 percent return. I want to make at least 12 percent." Again, this measurement will help you determine if a deal meets your criteria for investment.

## Cap Rate

A cap rate is used more for commercial real estate investing than residential. There is the cap rate when you purchase the property and the cap rate after you add value. Are either of these important to you? There is a lot of controversy around whether this is an accurate measurement of a good deal, but I think it can be built into your criteria as long as it is not the sole metric you are relying on. If the deal does not meet the cap rate requirement at purchase, ask yourself if you are going to be able to add value to increase the income, therefore making the new cap rate meet your criteria.

## Market

What market are you buying in? If the property is in a different market from the one you've honed in on, then it doesn't fit your criteria. This will help you from going all over the place and force any of you shiny-object chasers to focus in the area that you have analyzed and chosen.

## Property Specifics

Are there specific features of the property that you require? Does it need to have a driveway because you know that gets a higher rental rate in your area? Do you only want multifamily properties that have separate electric meters so you don't have to pay the electric bill for the property (since there is no way to bill each tenant without having a meter to show how much each tenant used)? You can also identify features that you want to avoid. For example, if you've settled on short-term rental as your strategy, you might want to avoid any property in an HOA that is able to dictate how or if your property can be used as a short-term rental.

Keep in mind that your criteria can change as time goes on. Some people choose to check and reassess after a certain amount of time, while others do this after a certain number of properties. Everyone gets to be the captain of their own ship, but I recommend reassessing deal criteria if your goals change or there are market changes nudging you to pivot. If you're investing in short-term rentals and the market you are in puts restrictions on them, requiring that rentals be at least thirty days or more, you may need to change markets or strategies. Change isn't necessarily bad, but it often requires work.

# HOMEWORK

All right, it's homework time. Before moving on to Chapter 8 (Building a Team), I want you to complete the following tasks.

- Create your list of criteria.

- Find a good deal. It doesn't have to be perfect, but make it match your criteria. Send your criteria to your accountability partner or group. Ask for comments and recommendations. With their fresh eyes, others might see holes or possibilities you have inadvertently missed.

# Chapter 8

# BUILDING YOUR TEAM

J ust like most everything we have talked about in this book so far, building your team goes back to the vision you created in Chapter 1. What do you want your life to look like? How active or passive do you want to be?

Let your level of commitment guide you as you think about how many people to bring on, who those people are, and what you want them to be doing. Remember to also think about your strengths and weaknesses (or gaps in your personal knowledge) and to bring people on to your team that complement your skill set and compensate for what you lack.

## Do I Actually Need a Team?

There are things I don't like to do, things I am not good at, and things that take me a long time to complete. Personally, knowing what kinds of tasks fall into each of these categories for me has been helpful. For example, it cost $1,500 to obtain a liquor license for the store I own. It would have taken me a long time to learn how to get this license and follow through on the necessary steps, so I hired it out. That was money well spent and lots of time saved, allowing me to work on other things. My partner and I hired his current retail manager from one of his other businesses to help get the store open, since she has experience in retail and managing day-to-day operations. We already trusted her and knew she'd do a good job, so why not use her? This is just one example. There are many more I could give. One time, I even had my kids unload a pallet of flooring into a building in exchange for donuts, using my kids' sweet tooth to maximum advantage.

Personally, I believe everything is more fun with friends and that many hands make light work. I'm all in favor of adding team members to my investment strategy. But there's another common saying that comes to mind when I think about building a team: too many cooks in the kitchen. Sometimes, managing the efforts of a team can be more work than simply doing the task yourself. All these sentiments can be true at the same time. That's why it is important to take the time to think through who you want to bring on and what (specifically) you want them to do. There are many factors that will determine who you need on your team or if you even need a team at all. Remember, it takes time and energy to train people and teach leadership. You can't build an empire or scale efficiently and effectively all on your own. Building a team isn't always easy, but it's worth the effort. Let's look at some things to consider right now.

One factor that will likely force you to add a team member is choosing to invest in an out-of-state property. It is not impossible to run this kind of real estate business remotely and entirely by yourself, but it's certainly easier when you have a team to lean on. Sure, you can always fly out to your property before buying it or if there is an issue that comes up, but what happens when you are a twenty-hour drive away and a tenant no longer has a working AC unit on a hundred-degree day? Having boots on the ground that can be your eyes, ears, and hands on the property can be a huge help. For example, a handyman or licensed HVAC tech as a contact—or, better yet, a team member—to call could be a lifesaver.

As we go through and refer to team members, keep in mind that not everyone on your team has to be a hired employee. Your team members are people you work with, such as vendors in different trades of construction for repairs and remodels. They don't necessarily work directly for you—rather, you build a relationship with them so that when you do need them, they make themselves available while also caring about your property and performing good work for you.

Another factor is the type of real estate investing strategy you have chosen. Typically, when you purchase from a turnkey provider, they have all the team members in place that you need, whereas BRRRRs, fix-and-flips, and a few other strategies don't usually have a fully stocked team ready to go and served on a platter. A team-based approach works well for these kinds of investments because of the amount and variation of work that needs to be completed. For such strategies, you will have to find and create your own team.

As we go through different team members in this chapter, you should start to consider who you will immediately need in your tool belt. Will it be an agent and a property manager? Will it be a contractor? As you grow and scale, your team may even continue to build with an acquisitions manager, a marketer, or your own in-house leasing agent.

## Compensation

Your first thought may be, "How can I pay all these people? I can barely scrape enough money together to buy a property!" I get it. That's why it can be beneficial to use contractors or services rather than hire employees. That way you only pay for their services when you use them, rather than giving them a salary.

Remember again that having someone on your team doesn't mean you are hiring them to be an employee of your company. For example:

- An agent is paid by the seller when you purchase a property.
- A property manager is paid based on the tenants paying rent, so you aren't paying them unless rental income is coming in on the property.
- A contractor is only being paid if there is a repair or issue that needs to be fixed.

So what do you say? Ready to build your team? Let's take a look at some of the key players.

# Team Members

## Partner/Spouse

The first team member I want you to think about is perhaps one you'd overlook. I'm talking about your partner or spouse. Investing of any kind takes commitment, both in terms of time and resources. If you don't have support at home, this will be much, much harder (and a whole lot less fun!). Having a significant other who is on board doesn't mean that they have to be involved or do any of the work, although they can. It simply means that their energy isn't working against yours, nor is real estate investing a touchy subject between the two of you. You'd be surprised at how far a genuine interest in your efforts and kind words of encouragement can go. I can't say it enough: You are building a life you love. Do all you can to avoid adding negativity anywhere in your plan, including pessimistic vibes from someone living under the same roof.

## Real Estate Agent

It is hard to be an expert in all the things and harder still to *do* all the things, especially if you want to do them well. In my opinion, adding a real estate agent to your team is a no-brainer. It costs you nothing to have a highly trained professional find real estate deals that match your criteria. An agent can also update you from time to time about what's happening or shifting in your market, as well as draft offers that will pique the interest of sellers. What's not to like?

Even if you have decided that you want to take a very active role in this investment, having an agent on your team is still a good idea. Sure, you can do your own research and look for deals the way we discussed in Chapter 7, but it's great knowing that when life gets busy and you don't have time, someone else is still working and moving your business forward. You can even have an agent email MLS listings right to you through an automated service! Setting up notifications this way will get you info on potential properties faster than simply relying on a website like Zillow.

So how do you find one? One of my favorite places to search is the BiggerPockets investor-friendly agent directory. Think of your favorite matchmaking dating site. This is it, but better. Through it, you will be matched with an agent who will help make you money by finding a good deal, except you won't have to spend a bunch of money like you would on a date. Instead, you'll be taking a step toward *making* money!

I am often asked by rookies if they should become an agent. The answer is different for each person. There are pros and cons that mostly boil down to the amount of time you want to invest.

First, let's talk about what a real estate agent does. An agent acts as an intermediary between buyers and sellers in a real estate transaction. To achieve this goal, they do a multitude of tasks including, but not limited to, the ones on the list below.

- Evaluate their clients' financial abilities based on proof of funds and preapprovals, and then find properties within their price range and identified criteria

- Compile lists of potential real estate properties of interest with details regarding their location, square footage, and features
- Build and maintain relationships with a wide variety of individuals and businesses, including lenders, appraisers, home inspectors, escrow companies, contractors, attorneys, and more
- Prepare documents such as contracts, addendums, and purchase agreements
- Promote properties through open houses, the MLS (multiple listing services), networking, and advertisements
- Assist in negotiation

I currently don't have my real estate license and don't have plans on getting it. In my opinion, you don't need a real estate license to be a real estate investor. However, there are a few reasons why you might not choose to add a Realtor to your team. For example, if you did earn your real estate license and take over this portion of your investment strategy, you would be able to save on commission fees (or even earn commission yourself!). But again, think about how much time these duties would take and if the return (money not paid out in commissions to someone else) is worth the trade. It also depends on how many on-market deals you are looking at. If you are primarily buying off-market, you shouldn't spend much time finding the perfect agent if you will rarely use them.

To help you decide, make a list of pros and cons specific to you, your dream life, your personal goals, and your target market. Research what it would take to train and maintain an agent license in your market. If you are super stuck, remember that you can always ask your accountability person/group for their opinions. Sometimes it's easiest to take advice from someone you know in real life who has experience in your neck of the woods (rather than take the word of some author you've never met).

## Lender

Even if you are a cash buyer, it is beneficial to start building a relationship with a bank. I'd recommend starting with local, small banks. If you can, start with banks you already have a relationship with for your personal accounts, mortgage, or vehicle loan. Banking is very much a relationship business. Even if you aren't ready to purchase anything yet, set up a meeting with a lender at a bank to introduce yourself and share your intentions. Get a vibe of the person before you have to do business with them. If the meeting feels like a bust or a bad fit, that's good to know! It's especially good to know before you are tied to them for multiple months of screening, paying, and interacting. And if you hit it off, that's great to know too.

The lending standards are typically stricter for real estate investors than they are for buyers who are purchasing their primary residence, especially on the residential side of lending. Once you move to the commercial side of lending, then it may be more lenient, but you usually won't get as good of terms. Either way, it's important to have someone you trust who can help you end up with a financing option that makes the most sense for you. Again, start by working with a small, local bank. They are more likely to lend on a property in their neck of the woods; they may have even lent on it before. When purchasing a property, look who has the current mortgage on the property, and if it's a local bank, reach out to them!

If you don't have a local lender you'd like to work with or you simply want to shop around, I'd once again recommend looking to the Bigger-Pockets lender directories to help you find a reputable lender.[10]

## Contractor

For repairs, maintenance, and/or rehabs, you likely want to have a contractor on your team. This is especially true if you have chosen a strategy, like BRRRR or fix-and-flip, that inherently comes with a lot of construction. You may also want to have a contractor on your team for occasional (or emergency) property maintenance, as well as for inspections and project estimates before you even purchase a piece of property.

Finding and hiring a contractor can be difficult, but don't worry. I have some tips that will hopefully help make it a bit easier.

### FINDING:

- Look for and pay attention to yard signs. People don't let bad contractors put a sign in their yard. That little sheet of weatherproof plastic is as good as or better than a Yelp review. If it's someone's yard you know, then reach out to them and ask how it went.
- Ask for referrals from friends and family or other investors. Be warned, though—sometimes people don't want to share their good contractors because they are nervous they'll get too busy and

---

**10** www.biggerpockets.com/loans; www.biggerpockets.com/hml

become unavailable for their own projects. If that's the case, you have be understanding but worth the ask.

- Pull building permits in your market so you can see what contractors are listed. This way you know who is working on projects in your area.
- When touring houses, look for stickers of contractors on electric panels and HVAC units. If you end up buying the house, it can be an advantage to talk to the last contractor who either installed or worked on the system.
- When in doubt, you can use databases like HomeAdvisor, where you can enter your project information and get bids and calls from available contractors. Just be sure to vet them as well—there's nothing wrong in asking for references or examples of past work.

## HIRING:

- Have a contract that includes a scope of work detailing the jobs to be completed.
- Get a set price for labor and materials.
- Avoid hourly payments and go instead for project fees or milestone payments.
- Set a timeline or dates for work to be started and finished.
- Add in a buffer. If work is completed early, then entice the contractor with a bonus. For example, for each day they finish early you can pay them an extra $100. This could offset your holding costs, so if they finish early you will have to pay less interest on your loan before you sell it or refinance (depending on your chosen strategy). On the flip side, if they fail to finish on time, you can have it go the other way with $100 per day coming off their total due. Of course, you'll have to be flexible and understanding with material delays or delays that are out of the contractor's scope of work, but in theory, this practice can motivate your contractor to complete work on time or even ahead of schedule.

My friend Chris Lawrence, a flipper turned self-storage investor, gave me this tip: When he buys a property that needs work, he does a video walk-through, calling out everything that needs to be done and what should stay as is. He then gives the video to the contractor along with the scope of work. This way, the contractor could refer back to the video and Chris doesn't need to repeat himself multiple times. This also prevents project delays while the two communicate back and forth. Having a complete scope of work is important. In fact, the more detailed the better.

I've made a sample scope of work for you, which you can also find in my bonus materials at **www.bigger pockets.com/rookiebonus**.

---

## PROJECT SCOPE OF WORK
8892 Cushing Pl

*The work shall include, but not be limited to, all labor, materials, tools, equipment, incidentals, insurance, overhead, and profit to perform the work as outlined below:*

*Materials will be purchased with Development, LLC credit card.*

### DEMOLITION        $2,500
Scope Items
1. Complete gut; remove all drywall, appliances, cabinetry, insulation
2. Remove debris and garbage
3. Completely remove first-floor bathroom near stairs
4. Remove stairs to second (and third, if applicable) floor

### LANDSCAPING, DECKING, AND CURB APPEAL      $7,000
Scope Items
1. Remove deck on front of house and add new deck
2. Pour sidewalk to driveway

### EXTERIOR DOORS AND WINDOWS      $2,800
Scope Items
1. Door
    a. Remove and replace 3 exterior doors
2. Windows
    a. Remove and replace 6 Windows
3. Miscellaneous Items:
    a. Install caulking, flashing, trim boards around doors, windows to provide watertight installation as needed

### SIDING      $5,000
Scope items
1. Remove and install new vinyl siding

### INTERIOR      $15,000
Scope Items
1. Drywall/Framing/Insulation
    a. Insulation and drywall throughout first and second floor
    b. Reframe kitchen layout
    c. Reframe upstairs layout

2. Miscellaneous Items
    a. Skim coating walls as required where wall covering is removed
    b. Patching/wall prep of miscellaneous cracks in walls/ceilings
    c. Patching/wall prep of miscellaneous holes in walls/ceilings
    d. Install shoe molding and transition moldings as needed
        for laminate flooring install

## CABINETRY INSTALL         $7,000
Scope Items
1. Install kitchen cabinets per the layout shown
2. Install kitchen cabinets, base, upper and lower
3. Install filler panels, end panels, and trim pieces
4. Install cabinet door pulls
5. Bathrooms:
    a. Install new vanity cabinet each bathroom
6. Miscellaneous Items
    a. Provide all necessary shims and fasteners as required
    b. Butcher block countertop

## INTERIOR DOORS AND TRIM INSTALL         $3,000
Scope Items
1. Doors
    a. Install 3 interior doors that are 6-panel doors
    b. Install all new door latches and handles
2. Trim and Woodwork
    a. Install wooden stairs to 2 lofts
    b. Install trim along floor after LVP and tile installed

## FLOORING         $2,200
Scope Items
1. Carpet in loft area
2. LVP in living room and bedroom on first floor

## TILING         $3,500
Scope Items
1. Install tile flooring in kitchen, entry, and bathrooms
2. Install tile shower from basin up
3. Miscellaneous Items:
    a. Install cement backer board or cement board
        (contractors' preference) at all tile areas
    b. Install all grout

## INTERIOR PAINTING         $2,500
Scope Items
1. Paint drywall throughout; one paint color

## APPLIANCES         $2,500
Scope Items
Install and connect owner-furnished kitchen appliances

1. Range with exhaust fan hood
2. Fridge
3. Dishwasher
   a. All cords, hoses, and connections to be installed

## PLUMBING                                          $5,500
Scope Items
1. Kitchen
   a. Install water supply and new waste lines to sink
   *Note: Sink to be installed by countertop installation contractor*
   b. Install new kitchen faucet
2. Bathroom
   a. Install water supply and waste lines for new toilet, shower,
      vanity sink & faucet
   b. Install new plumbing fixtures for first full bath
      i. Toilet
      ii. Shower head kit
      iii. Vanity sink and faucet
   f. Install plumbing fixtures for half bath
      i. Toilet
      ii. Vanity sink and faucet

## HVAC                                               $6,000
Scope Items
1. Install furnace with central air

## ELECTRICAL                                         $7,000
Scope Items
1. Replace all existing outlets w/new white outlets
2. Run new electric throughout
3. Install new breaker box
4. Kitchen
   a. Install new GFI protected outlets along new kitchen
      cabinet layout as required by code
   b. Install new outlets for appliances as required
   c. Install new light fixture
5. Main-level bathroom and half bath
   a. Install new GFI protected outlet at vanity cabinets
   b. Install exhaust fan with light
6. Existing light fixtures
   a. Add new light fixtures throughout

## MISCELLANEOUS ITEMS                                $250
Scope Items
1. Install bath accessories (toilet paper bar, towel bar)
2. Install bathroom mirror

## TOTAL REHAB BUDGET:                        $71,750.00

## Property Manager

Being your own boss can be great, but sometimes we expect less of ourselves than we do of others, especially when we are paying for that other person's services. Granting yourself some grace as you grow is one thing. Allowing yourself to do a crappy job because no one else is checking in on you is another thing entirely. If you are choosing to take on the role of property manager (or any role in this journey) yourself, having a job description will help you stay accountable, get the job done right, and make the most of your investment.

A property manager handles all the daily tasks of managing both your properties and your tenants. If you own multiple properties, seemingly small issues can pile up big time. Do you want to be the one your tenants call when their screen door slams too loud and the garbage disposal leaks? A property manager can take care of those menial tasks and more, from showing the properties to signing leases to handling tenant disputes and unclogging toilets. Many people will insist they can do these things themselves, and they are right. They absolutely can. You absolutely can. The real questions are: Do you have time? And do you want to?

Let's say you do want to hire a property manager. It is important to know what questions you should ask before you hire them. Hiring a poor property manager can be worse than having none at all.

In my experience, no one will care for your property to the level that you care. Keep that in mind. Even with property management in place, there will still be oversight and work to be done. It is a common misconception that your investment becomes passive after you hire a property management company. You will still need to check your monthly owner's statement to make sure expenses are charged correctly, check that leasing is on top of getting vacant units rented, and check that your tenants are receiving maintenance and communication in a timely manner. At the end of the day, it is your investment. If you want it to go well, you need to make sure it is going well.

If you are on the hunt for a stellar property manager, check out the BiggerPockets property management directory[11] or referrals from other investors in your market.

---

[11] www.biggerpockets.com/real-estate-companies/property-management

## Accountant/CPA

If you are investing for wealth, you will want to use the tax advantages of real estate. In addition to keeping track of income and expenses and managing ongoing tasks like payroll, an accountant can do your taxes. Real estate investment taxes can get really complicated. Unless your day job is in accounting, I'd highly recommend passing this job off to a certified professional. If for no other reason, having an accountant or CPA do your taxes decreases your personal liability if you were to get audited. Accountants can also be a great source of good financial planning to lessen your tax liability. The bottom line? Often an accountant can save you more money than the fee you pay them.

To find an accountant, attend local meetups and ask who other investors are using. Accountants can perform their services virtually so asking investors across the U.S. can also work. I highly recommend finding an accountant who specializes in real estate investing and can not only prepare your tax return but also help you tax plan too. This is especially true if you plan on growing your portfolio.

## Attorney

An attorney can help you with many real estate investment tasks. They can draft and review legal documents as well as provide you with professional advice when dealing with tenant issues. A real estate attorney can also help you put legally binding agreements in place with contractors. If you can be guaranteed the contractor's work will be finished as specified, you can protect yourself from dealing with problems related to renovations down the road. These agreements can also legally and financially safeguard you from problems with the finished product.

Ask for drafts of docs so you can reuse them. A lease is a great example of this. You don't want to have to pay for your attorney to prepare this document every time you have a new tenant moving in. Not sure what kind of documents you'll need? A great starting point is BiggerPockets landlord forms.[12]

## Insurance Agent

And finally, last but not least, you might want to consider adding an insurance agent to your team. This could be the same agent who handles your

---

personal home and auto insurance, but it doesn't have to be. Be aware that if you are out-of-state investing, you may need to find someone new who is licensed in that state.

Again, building a relationship with someone you can work with long-term is always the best option. If you aren't happy with the agency you currently use for your personal insurance needs, ask around. Working with a broker who has access to different insurance companies is a big benefit.

You also want an insurance agent who has the availability to make quick changes for you. You never know when you will be at the closing table and your lender needs a last-minute change to your policy as a mortgagee. I know because this has happened to me! Ask what the usual turnaround time is for policy changes.

## Finding Team Members

One of the great things about the real estate world is that oftentimes, the people you are interacting with "know a guy." If you're having trouble finding a contractor, ask your property manager for recommendations. Chances are, this isn't their first job in the industry. Their past experiences have probably filled their contact list with all sorts of helpful people (and maybe a few you should avoid!). Alternatively, see if your real estate agent has a lender they love working with and would help you set up a meeting. The benefit and deficit of being a rookie is that most everyone will know more than you, including knowing the people to get the job done. That's okay! Even as an expert at anything, it's always okay to ask for recommendations. You want to work smarter not harder! Leveraging your relationships (and the relationships of your relationships) can be a huge stepping stone on your journey to success in this kind of investing.

Here are a few other ways of finding people to join your team.

- Join a few local Facebook groups and keep your eyes peeled for people asking for recommendations.
- Do a search online and call or email at least ten people/companies. Become familiar with the professionals in your geographic area and market.
- Attend virtual and in-person meetups to meet new people, network, and make connections.
- Keep a list of vendors or people to use even if you don't need their services right now. My business partner, Daryl, tracks all of his

vendor contacts in Monday.com, a project management platform but you could do this in a spreadsheet too. If a truck drives by that says, "ABC plumbing 716-941-6379" on the side of it, he will snap a picture and later add it to his vendor list for future use.

## What to Look For

Finally, I want to close out this chapter by listing out a few questions you should be able to answer before officially onboarding a person to your team. Some of the questions will need to be answered by you, and others by the person you are interviewing.

The first two questions to ask yourself are "What do I want?" and "What do I need?" Don't be fooled. The answers to these questions aren't always the same, especially if you don't have the funds right off the bat to pay a lot of people. Remember that most of the team members we've discussed (outside of the property manager) are paid based on the work they do, rather than via a salary. That should help!

Speaking of payment, you will want to make sure it is clear up front how your team member will be paid. Will they bill you like an attorney would? Will they be paid by the seller of a property if they are your agent? Will they have a set monthly fee like a bookkeeper? Know your contractor's rate for maintenance and for how payments or draws will be made if they are doing a large project for you; this can help you stay on budget.

A great follow-up question is one you ask yourself: "Is this person within my budget?" This is twofold. First of all, you want to make sure you can afford them. And secondly, does this person have experience within your target market and price range? For example, do they sell million-dollar homes and you want to look at $50,000 homes? Or do they put laminate countertops in all their rental renos, while you are looking to complete luxury remodels? Hiring a qualified person who is a bad fit for your needs will not get you to where you want to go. In fact, it will probably lead straight to conflict and disappointment. Have clear expectations for both parties.

Another question to ask is: Are they an investor?

This isn't always important, but knowing the answer will give you an idea of what you can lean on this person for. If an agent is an investor themselves, they may know more about the rental market than a typical agent. If you need help with a lot of your processes and aren't confident that you are getting a good deal, then having investor-friendly team members is beneficial. If you are confident in your deal and only need an agent to show you the property, then you won't need to lean on them as much. Ask yourself, what skills do you need to complement yours, and does this person fit the bill?

What is their availability?

Can they offer you anything unique?

Do they bring value you didn't know you even needed or was an option?

Finally, let them know your goals and your strategy, and ask if their motivations match yours. A person can be great at their job, but if they aren't aligned with a similar vision, there could be problems. Do your best to make sure that everyone is on the same page to ensure smooth sailing from the start. In fact, this might be a better place to start than end. If the answer to this question doesn't line up, it is likely that the rest of the answers won't matter.

## Finalize the Relationship

I think it is important to build a relationship with someone before you officially invite them to join your team. Get to know them and their skill set before you even have a deal. This could mean monthly dinners in which you chat about your investment hopes and dreams; it could mean getting preapproved for a loan; it could mean getting on an agent's email list; or it could mean doing a meet and greet with a property manager and touring one of their other properties. There are lots of ways you can get to know each other and your market before officially working together, so that when a deal comes along, you can feel confident both in the opportunity on the table as well as in the person you have by your side.

I want to make two final points before closing out this chapter. One distinct difference between a partner (which we discussed at length in Chapter 4) and a team member is that a partner has equity in the property or the company. If someone on your team does not have equity or ownership, then they are not a partner. However, a person who is your business partner could be an important team member. It is important to know that you can have someone on your team without giving them equity or ownership in the property. There are many ways of structuring your team; there is no "one size fits all" model.

And finally, accountability groups are usually formed with people who are doing similar strategies as you and who are also on your same level. The goal of accountability groups is to motivate one another to reach their goals, along with brainstorming and providing advice to one another. It is best to find members to be in your accountability group who aren't part of your current business. These people should be separate from your team members and partners in order to help you gain fresh ideas and get insights from third (uninvolved and unbiased) parties.

Partner, team member, and accountability group members are three important but distinctly different roles. Knowing the difference between them and keeping them separate (on paper and in your mind) will keep you from muddying the waters and increase your chances of creating a well-oiled and high-functioning investment machine.

# HOMEWORK

- Make a list of the team members you think you might need.

- Generate a list of possible team member leads and then start reaching out to them.

- Write out the questions you want to ask your potential team members in advance so you're prepared to have the necessary conversations.

- Organize team member information in the worksheet below (also provided at **www.biggerpockets.com/rookiebonus**).

| TEAM MEMBER | List ten potential team members to call/email. If you already have a role filled, ask if they are able to help with what you want to do. E.g.: Does your lender lend in out-of-state markets? | What do you need from them? | List your top questions to ask each. |
|---|---|---|---|
| PARTNER/ SPOUSE | | | |
| REALTOR | | | |
| LENDER | | | |

| CONTRACTOR(S) | |
|---|---|
| PROPERTY MANAGER | |
| ACCOUNTANT/ CPA | |
| ATTORNEY | |
| INSURANCE AGENT | |

# Chapter 9

# MAKING AN OFFER

## Vocabulary You'll Need to Know

**CONTINGENCIES:** Your offer only stands if certain (listed) criteria are met. These criteria are called contingencies. For example, your offer purchase price is only valid if the property passes an inspection or you sell your current house, if you need the funds from that sale to fund this purchase.

**EARNEST MONEY DEPOSIT:** Also called a good faith deposit. An amount of money a buyer agrees to submit before the closing. The money will be held in escrow by the attorney or title company until closing. At closing, the money will be credited toward the amount due for the purchase price. If the purchaser does not follow through on the contract and purchase the property, then the money will be retained by the seller.

You have a market and a team in place. You have your financing all set and you are confident in your market and deal analyses. Now it's time to make an offer! Or even better yet, multiple offers!

Before we dive into getting your offer accepted, we need to talk about how to make an offer in the first place. What is the process? Is there a certain, specific channel to go through? These are the questions that may be running through your mind. They are good ones! Even with a real estate agent guiding you through the process, you should still know the basics.

# Offer Basics

Let's begin with the basics. There are two different purchasing situations you might encounter out there in the real estate world: on-market and off-market. The type of situation you are working with will determine the way you craft and present your offer. Let's start with on-market first.

If you are purchasing the property on-market, this means it is listed on the MLS (multiple listing service). A property on the MLS will have a real estate agent representing the buyer, an agent whom you will submit your offer through. The agent will then present the offer to the seller's agent who will present it to the seller. In some cases, one agent will represent both the buyer and the seller; this is called a dual agent and is disclosed to both parties before entering into any agreement.

If you are purchasing a property that is off-market, meaning it doesn't have a real estate agent representing the seller, then you will most likely deal directly with the seller. So how do you do that? You start with a letter of intent.

A letter of intent states who you are, the property you'd like to purchase, how you'd like to finance the purchase, and any other terms you'd like to include. The purpose of this letter is just as it's named—declaring your intentions to the seller. This is informal and shouldn't be the only contract you draw up between the buyer and seller. It should just be an agreement to make clear what the terms are that both parties have agreed to.

If both parties agree to the items listed in the letter of intent, it can be passed along to an attorney to draw up a contract, and, after that, to the title company. Let's take a look at a sample letter of intent so you can see what I mean.

# LETTER OF INTENT FOR PURCHASE OF REAL PROPERTY

DATE

Owner Name
Address

Re: Letter of Intent
    Building Name
    Property Address

Dear Mr./Ms. Owner:

Subject to the execution of a definitive and mutually acceptable agreement of purchase and sale ("Purchase Agreement") within seven (7) days after execution of this Letter of Intent (the "Contract Negotiation Period"), the undersigned offers to purchase the subject property in accordance with the following terms and conditions:

Seller(s): Name and address

Buyer: Buyer Name, with contact information as follows: PO Box XXX, TOWN, STATE, ZIP. Buyer may assign his/her interest to any corporation, partnership, or limited liability company in which he/she is the controlling party or to any other third party without Seller approval.

Subject Property: The property, which is the subject of this offer ("Subject Property"), is identified as PROPERTY NAME, ADDRESS.

Purchase Price: $750,000

Terms of Purchase: $1,000 Cash Held in Escrow with Seller's Attorney until closing. $75,000 down payment to seller. $650,000 Land Contract. Amortized over 30 years at 4.5% interest. $25,000 balloon payment after year 1, $25,000 balloon payment after year 2, $25,000 balloon payment after year 3. Loan callable at year 8 with 6 months written notice.

Deposit Toward Purchase Price:

Initial Deposit: The sum of One Thousand Dollars ($1,000.00) as a refundable deposit toward and applicable to the Purchase Price ("the Initial Deposit").

Due Diligence Period: Buyer shall have fourteen (14) days after agreement is fully executed to perform due diligence for subject property. Deposit is payable within three (3) days after due diligence.

Buyer's Contingencies: Following the expiration of the Due Diligence Period, Buyer's obligation to close shall be subject to the following conditions:

The nonexistence of any development, building, construction, flood, or moratoria affecting the Subject Property.

Seller to provide Buyer possession to property free and clear of liens except for nondelinquent bonds and taxes.

Contingent on Seller and Buyer's attorney approval. Purchase Agreement (Contract) will be in accordance with Erie County Bar Association Standards.

Seller's Contingencies: Seller's obligation to close shall be subject to following conditions: No contingencies.

Closing: Closing to be on or around June 15, 2021

Expiration of Offer: This Letter of Intent shall constitute an open offer until April 15, 2021, at which time it shall be automatically terminated if not executed by Seller.

If the above outline of terms and conditions is acceptable, please indicate by signing below.

BUYER:

_____          Dated: _____


SELLER:

_____          Dated: _____

In some rare cases, you may have to submit an offer with the seller's attorney if they are handling the property transaction.

Before we get to submitting an offer, I want to talk a bit about creating an offer. My first piece of advice is that you should create and submit more than one. When you get to the negotiation table, you'll be able to discuss what the seller values most and make adjustments that best meet everyone's needs. However, when you first put together your offers, you are doing a bit of guesswork. Unless you already know exactly what the seller wants and what their motivation is.

For example, let's say you'd like to purchase a house listed at $150,000. Here are three ways you could make an offer.

1. **Bank financing:** You could offer $130,000 with 20 percent down and the bank's interest rate of 5 percent to be paid back over thirty years.
2. **Seller financing:** You could offer $140,000 with 10 percent down and an interest rate of 7 percent to be paid to the seller over twenty years.
   - See an example of a seller financing offer breakdown at **www.biggerpockets.com/rookie bonus** or at this QR code.
3. **Cash Offer:** $120,000, all up front, no financing required

As long as you are able to meet the demands of each offer and will benefit from each one, why not throw them all out there and let the seller pick what is most appealing to them? This strategy of submitting multiple offers can be especially powerful in a competitive market. Get creative!

Hopefully, based on my advice in Chapter 8 about building your team, you already have an agent. They can help you through the process of putting in an offer. Once you decide on a price and terms to offer, your agent will put together a contract; this is usually a standard contract that agents use to fill in the blank spaces.

The agent will fill in the following pieces of information.

1. **Seller's information:** This piece of information would include the name (or names) of the current owner(s) of the property, along with their address. The address could be the address of the property or it could be a separate address. For example, if the property is a second home or rental property, you may use their personal residence address. I prefer to look at the tax records and use the name and address the tax bills are sent to.
2. **Buyer's information:** This is where you will write in your name or your company name. You can use your personal name, or, if you have an LLC, you can put the LLC name. You will also write in your preferred mailing address. Some people choose to use a PO box and others their primary residence. I recommend that you

use whichever you receive your mail at and check most often. This information will go onto the deed at closing.

The name on the contract as the purchaser is the person or entity that will go on the deed. Sometimes I don't know right away what LLC will own the property, so I like to add "and/or assigns" after the name, which gives me option to change the name of the buyer. I have one company that I always put on a contract, and then after I get the offer accepted, I evaluate if I will take on a partner or not and what LLC I will end up putting the property in (as in, what LLC will own the property and be on the deed). This also gives me the option to wholesale the property if I'd like. I can assign the contract to someone else, and they can be the end buyer. Doing business this way just leaves my options open.

3. **Property information:** This is the address of the property along with an SBL number (section-block-lot number). The SBL number identifies the parcel and is used for property tax purposes too. You can also include what the property consists of including buildings, acreage, and any property features (e.g., 2.5 acres with one single-family home and a shed). If there are other items you want included (e.g., a lawn mower), this is where you could add in that you would like them included in the sale.

4. **Purchase price:** This number is the total price you are offering to pay for the property, excluding any fees but including both the amount you have financed and the cash you're bringing to the table. For example, you might offer $235,000 on a $250,000 house in the hopes of bringing the seller down in price. That $235,000 is the purchase price, and $250,000 is the list price.

5. **Earnest money deposit:** This is an amount of money you are willing to risk to give to the seller if you do not end up purchasing the property. There can be contingencies, such as inspections, that are done before your deposit is given. If you are very confident you are going to close on the property, you can offer to pay a higher deposit. This may reassure the seller that you can close, and they may be more willing to accept your offer. At the closing table, this money is credited toward the purchase price.

6. **Any contingencies:** If you are in a competitive seller's market, the seller may have options for offers and will more likely accept an offer that doesn't have any contingencies. Take my advice on this:

Don't waive contingencies you aren't comfortable with just to get your offer accepted. If you are very unfamiliar with the mechanics of a property and don't know what kind of rehab to expect, then don't waive your inspection. This is a good way to get in over your head in a hurry!

Instead, have a contingency in place that your offer is based on an inspection. If the inspection shows that there needs to be a lot of repairs, you can negotiate the price, ask for repairs to be done, or walk away from the deal with no money lost except for the cost of paying for the inspector. In most cases, you will not pay your deposit until after the inspection has been met anyway.

Recently, I had a self-storage property under contract. There was an auto repair shop renting one of the buildings on the property. I asked for an environmental study to be completed. I had this property under contract with seller financing for three years, after which I would need to refinance with a bank to pay the seller off. On a commercial property, a bank will usually require an environmental study to be done on the property. This is to make sure the land is not contaminated with chemicals. Banks don't want to lend on something that could have a huge remediation cost down the road. When the environmental study came back, the company recommended that a Phase II study be done. The first phase was around $800 and the second phase around $3,000. The second phase recommended a third phase for further investigating. The estimate for this was around $6,500! The seller denied my request to do a Phase III study—the reason being that if something was to come up in the study and I did not purchase the property, they would be responsible for remediating it.

Isn't there a saying that if you don't know about it, then it didn't happen? Or what happens in an inspection stays in an inspection? (I might be thinking of Vegas!) Regardless, since the seller would not let me proceed with the Phase III environmental study, I was entitled to my deposit back. I also did not give them a copy of the Phase II report—just the letter stating the result. I sold them the full report for half of what I paid for it. This was a benefit to them because they could supply it to another seller without wasting time having to do the environmental study all over again, and it was a benefit to me by reducing the amount I'd paid into a property I didn't get.

All this is to say that contingencies can protect you while you are in the due diligence process when purchasing a property. Don't be afraid to lose money because it can actually be an opportunity cost. It is better to lose hundreds now than thousands later on after you bought into a bad deal.

7. **Any additional terms of the purchase that aren't standard:** This part of the offer is up for creative license! You can add items and information for your benefit or to sweeten the deal for the seller. For example, you could offer to let the seller leave all contents of the property. If this property will be used as a short-term rental and is in turnkey condition, this may be an advantage to you in that it will help you quickly (and affordably) furnish the space. On the other hand, if the seller is the daughter of a deceased hoarder, allowing her to leave all the contents may be offering her a huge relief. You could work the cost of a garbage removal company into the numbers.

Once your agent has filled out the contract, you will initial and sign in various spots. While it might be tempting to simply slap your initials on the page and move on, it is imperative that you read through the contract, paying specific attention to where the agent filled in the blanks, made check marks, or added any further descriptions. Yes, it is their job to get it right, but this is your investment and *your money*. Taking the time to fully read through the contract will not only familiarize you with the process and vocabulary but it will also give you the opportunity to check that all the data was entered correctly.

The majority of agents send the document by email, and you are able to electronically sign.

## Multiple Offers from Different Potential Buyers

Oftentimes, when you are buying a property off-market, there aren't as many (or any!) competing offers. There are many scenarios for this good fortune, but it occurs most often when you connect with the buyer directly before they've advertised the sale of their house. If you are buying from a wholesaler, usually it is only the purchase price that matters because the wholesaler is only going to accept an offer that's a quick close and accepts the property as is. There isn't a ton of wiggle room to use contingencies or different negotiation techniques. Everything is pretty simple and straightforward. This can be a drastically different situation when compared to purchasing a property listed with an agent or direct from seller.

If you are purchasing in a hot market where offers are competitive and you want to have an edge, then what can you do? The first thing is to rely on your agent to get as much information as possible. Sometimes they can get hints or an idea of what you are going up against. They can also inform you of what is typical for offers at that time and in that geographic area.

One time I went to look at a property with my brother in a different market and learned about escalation clauses from the agent. Even though I had never heard of such a thing, they were apparently very common in that market and most offers had them.

For example, you would offer $200,000 but would pay $1,000 more than the highest offer with a max of $220,000. This means if someone else offered $212,000, your new offer would automatically be $213,000 and you'd be the highest offer now. If someone else offered $221,000, your escalation clause canceled out at $220,000 and they would stay the highest offer. The advantage of an escalation clause is that you are only paying a certain amount over someone else's offer. If you had gone ahead and just offered your max at $220,000 and the next highest offer had been $201,000 you would have offered $19,000 higher than if you did the escalation clause.

The following factors can also help make your offer more attractive.
- A large earnest money deposit
- Find out why they are selling and add something in the deal that is attractive to them. Some examples include: rent back until they find a new house (even after you close), leave behind garbage and junk that you will clean, take care of an eviction after closing, and not have the house vacant at closing.
- Cut their costs to sell the property. There are a variety of methods to make this happen, such as paying their closing costs and/or accepting a survey that was from years ago with an affidavit of no change to save the seller from paying for a new survey.
- Let them know that if your offer is not accepted and another offer falls through, they should come back to you.
- Offer to close quickly or in a time frame attractive to them. I have a friend who sold his house and the buyer wanted to wait four months to close because they didn't want to move in winter. This worked for him too because his new house wasn't ready yet.

I know this book is about getting your first (or next) deal. It may feel counterintuitive to walk away from a deal . . . but you must be willing to walk away if you can't meet what the seller wants or beat what someone else is willing to pay. If the numbers don't work, they don't work. I know that's disappointing. If you lose out on a deal (and during your real estate journey, you *will* at some point), it can feel demoralizing. It may not feel like it in the moment, but there will always be another. But I'm not going to leave you there all alone and deal-less. Let's move on to talk about the fine art of negotiation and get that deal in your pocket.

## Offer Negotiation

Now, just because you make an offer, that doesn't mean it will automatically get accepted. Especially in highly competitive markets.

The most important thing I can tell you about negotiation is this: LISTEN. Your primary goal is to figure out what is most important to the seller. You can't do that if you are only listening to respond. You need to ask questions and determine why they are selling (or, perhaps, why they *aren't* selling). You can use this information to help you achieve your goal of buying the property.

Let me tell you a story.

I was working on purchasing a piece of property through seller financing, and by listening to the seller, I learned that what was most important to him was a large down payment (so he could purchase a new home) and a monthly payment of $2,500. These two factors trumped everything on his criteria list, meaning he didn't really care about things like interest rates. I took this information and crafted an offer that gave him exactly what he wanted and gave myself a 3.5 percent interest rate—a rate much, much lower than I would have been able to get at a bank. We both won, due in part to my listening skills.

Each seller's story, reasons, experiences, and criteria will be different, but knowing some examples might help you identify the kinds of questions to ask and what you should keep your ears trained to listen for. Here are several potential reasons and/or obstacles a person might have when it comes to the sale of their property.

- They want to have a quick sale because they are moving out of state.
- They need a large down payment because they'd like to buy a piece of property themselves and need the money ASAP.

- They are looking to obtain monthly income.
- They inherited the property and don't have the time or resources to clean it up and make repairs, so they want to sell it right away, as is.
- They want the current tenants to be able to stay.
- They want someone who will continue to love, enjoy, and care for the property the way they did for so many years.

If you can listen for these gold-nugget pieces of information and then help the seller get what they want and need, your offers will be accepted more often.

Still, I want you to remember that this is not just about pleasing and accommodating the seller. You want to craft an offer that will get you what you want too. In order to do that, you need to decide what's at the top of *your* wish list. For me, at this point in my investing journey, it's cash flow. If a deal will generate good cash flow, even at a high interest rate, that's what I'm looking for. But that's just me and my situation. As a rookie, you might feel differently and be on the lookout for something else entirely. To help you identify what offer criteria is at the top of your list, here are some potential options.

- High cash flow
- Ideal interest rate
- Low down payment
- Opportunity for appreciation on the property
- Low monthly payment

Your plans for the property—and whether you plan to sell it immediately or hang onto it for a long time—will affect the criteria that are most important to you. Be sure to factor that decision in when deciding on your top offer priorities.

## Offer Presentation

If you have the opportunity to present the offer in person, absolutely do it! If you are using a real estate agent and the seller has their own, this may not be an option but worth the ask. If this is an off-market deal and you are working with the seller, this is a lot easier to make happen. This way you will be able to gauge the seller's reaction as well as allow them to voice their concerns. Rather than receive a phone call from your agent saying the seller passed on the deal, you can be present for negotiation. Again, *listen!* Take the feedback you are given at the table (both verbal and nonverbal) and adjust from there. Even if you are not ready to make a new offer on the spot, you can say, "Let me consult with my partner/spouse and think about this. I think there is room for improvement and that we can work this out. May I call you tomorrow with a new offer?"

It is very rare that people flat-out say no and do not counter an offer. If they do, ask questions and, yep, you guessed it, *listen.* For example, if they say the offer price was just too low, ask, "What is the lowest price you would accept?" and then go from there. Do all that you can to keep the lines of communication open and the negotiation going.

Another great tip for presenting an offer is to clearly outline the benefits of your offer. I like to do this by printing out an amortization schedule showing them a breakdown of the monthly payment—how much will go to the mortgage principal and how much will come to them in the form of an interest payment if you are presenting a seller financing offer to them. I take it one step further by pointing out how much they will earn in five years off the interest (on top of the purchase price) and again how much they will have earned at the end of the payment schedule.

This is so powerful! Selling a property can feel big, overwhelming, exciting, and emotional. Use this opportunity to show the seller the ways in which they (and their bank account) will benefit. You can also use this opportunity to point out tax advantages. I always ask the seller if they have talked to their accountant about the benefits of seller financing. This usually piques their interest in the topic.

# HOMEWORK

- Write up two offers for one deal!
  - How can you get creative?

  - How can you make both work for you?

# Chapter 10

# UNDER CONTRACT

## Vocabulary You'll Need to Know

**DUE DILIGENCE:** A period of time allotted by the seller for the buyer to gather information to make an informed decision on the costs associated with the purchase of the property, the condition of the property and verifying data about the property. That may include doing an inspection, verifying leases or expenses, and looking into permits or zoning.

**ESTOPPEL AGREEMENT:** Also called tenant estoppel letter. A binding document that clarifies the current status and terms of the lease agreement between a landlord and a tenant for a prospective purchaser of property. This information is supplied by the tenant and compared to what the lease agreement stated or the seller told you if there is no lease agreement in place.

**FULLY EXECUTED CONTRACT:** You are considered under contract on a property when the contract is signed by both the buyer and the seller.

## The Work Isn't Over

You've made it! You have your first property under contract. You and the seller have agreed on a purchase price and terms. Are you having a rush of emotions? Do you feel excited? A little nervous? Overwhelmed? All these feelings are normal. Take a moment to get that Instagram selfie in front of the sold sign to celebrate this milestone, and then come back to me, because the work is not done.

After the contract is signed, it's *not* time to sit back and relax. The first thing you should know is that a property is not guaranteed until you *close* on the property. There are a wide variety of things that can happen to make the contract fall apart, meaning you don't end up getting the property. I know this may not be a pleasant situation to think about, but I want you to be prepared.

Sometimes, when a sale doesn't go through, it is your decision. Sometimes it's the seller's, and other times uncontrollable circumstances prevent the deal from being D-O-N-E. Rather than focus on the reasons a contract can fall through, let's focus on what you have to do when the property is under contract to keep it moving forward.

One thing I regret not doing on my first couple of properties is creating a checklist of everything that needs to be done when a property is under contract. Even though every property is different, there are many tasks that you repeat for each property. Having a checklist will help you remember to do all the things, every time. That's why I made one for you! Feel free to customize this as suits your strategy. Again, the downloadable will be at **www.biggerpockets.com/rookiebonus**.

# PROPERTY ACQUISITION CHECKLIST

Project Name: [Name of Construction Project]
Date: [Start Date]
Location Address: [Complete Address of Construction Site]
Applicable Village: [Name of village property located in]
Property Owner: [Complete name of owner on deed]

The purpose of this checklist is to ensure that the processes of the rehab are appropriately covered. This contains the steps needed for the rehab process including the acquisition, contract, bidding, actual construction, and the final touches of the project.

| DESCRIPTION | NOTES | REFERENCE NUMBER OR DATE |
|---|---|---|
| ☐ Offer Accepted on Property | | |
| ☐ Attorney Approval | | |
| ☐ Deposit Check Sent (note: amount, date, any mail tracking) | | |
| ☐ Closing Scheduled | | |
| ☐ Closing Statement and Cashier Checks (Note: date and amount) | | |
| ☐ Insurance Policy | | |
| ☐ Gas into Property Owner Name | | |
| ☐ Electric into Property Owner's Name | | |
| • • • • | | |
| ☐ Electrical Inspection scheduled if Electric off for over 1 year | | |

- ☐ Water/Sewer into Property Owner's Name
  - •
  - •
  - •
  - •

- ☐ Schedule walk-thru with contractors; electric, plumbing, drywall before closing

- ☐ Create timeline of rehab

- ☐ Document items needed to be done and ask for bids

- ☐ Select bids and write up contracts with start date

- ☐ Process and submit legal permits

- ☐ Confirm insurance with contractors and file certificates
  - •
  - •
  - •
  - •

- ☐ Hire demo crew with tentative start, day after closing

- ☐ Order dumpster to be delivered on day after closing

- ☐ Secure unit with new locks on closing date

- ☐ Before pictures and video walk-thru of property on closing date (2 angles of every room; video of whole property starting with exterior then interior, first floor then second then continue to roll footage as exiting the unit)     Add Pics to Specific Property Folder; Name "Before Pics"

The most important task is to finalize the funds you are using to purchase this property. If you are using a lender, then the contract needs to be sent to the lender. You will also need to send the contract to your attorney or the title company you are using. This procedure will vary depending on your state. You can do some research online or even just ask a real estate agent for the process in the state you are purchasing the property in.

> Remember that the laws and processes you have to follow will be for the state you are purchasing the property in, not the state you live in or even that the seller lives in.

## The Key Players

If, as a rookie investor, you are feeling overwhelmed with this stage of the process, know you are not alone. Figuratively and literally. There will be several other people involved in the closing. Here are a few of the key players.

### Title Companies

These are the people who check the owner history, including verifying the current owner of the property and if anyone else has a claim to owning the property. You can purchase insurance through the title company that will cover you in case there is an error and someone else does claim the title later on. If the property is at high risk of being claimed by someone else and does not have a clear title, you may not be able to get title insurance. Lenders, including most private money lenders and investors in your deal, will want you to have title insurance before they hand over any money to you.

### Inspectors

Licensed professionals who go through the property noting repairs that are needed, including things that are not up to code or that are safety hazards. There are various types of inspections you can have done on your home, including a general inspection of the interior and exterior of the property, a radon test, a mold test, and even an environmental test on the soil of the property.

## Appraiser

An appraiser will evaluate your property based on the determined market value of the property. Think of an appraisal as more of an art than a science. There is no exact formula to know how an appraiser will value your property, and, as frustrating as it might be, different appraisers will come up with different amounts. If you are unhappy with how an appraiser values your property, you can request to have the appraisal disputed. All you have to do is bring in another appraiser (at your cost) or ask the current appraiser to review the information you have showing that the property is worth more than it was appraised for.

## Real Estate Attorneys

In certain states, such as New York, you are required to use an attorney to close on a property. They will be your intermediary between you and the title company. They will also file the deed and necessary paperwork with the county. In most circumstances, buyers and sellers each have their own attorney representing them. You can use the same attorney to represent both parties if you all agree to it.

## Contractors

Vendors hired to perform repairs and remodels on the property to upgrade and update the property to your specifications and desires. You can hire a general contractor who performs or supervises all the repairs or you can hire out several job-specific contractors who have different skill sets or are licensed in a particular skill, such as plumbing, electrical, HVAC, or landscaping work.

# Doing Your Due Diligence

If your contract states you will be doing an inspection during the due diligence period (the time allotted by the seller for you to perform your information gathering), now is the time to schedule it. You will need to contact a local inspector and get a quote by giving them details on the house, such as its size and number of units. Other things to do during this time are verify leases or expenses and look into permits or zoning.

When creating your contract, state an earnest money amount (you might have already stated this during the offer period). This dollar amount is the deposit you will give to the seller, which will be held in an escrow account. The earnest money is not due until after the due diligence period is complete. It is your responsibility to get the information you need before that period ends. Once the earnest money deposit is made, it is very rare that you will get that money back. If the property closes, the earnest money is put toward the purchase price.

Make sure that you find a reputable inspector. Your best bet is to ask real estate agents or other investors for a reference. If you are using a real estate agent, they will often have one or more inspectors to recommend. If you have friends or family who have purchased houses for their primary residence, reach out to them to ask who they used. Inspections are common for both investment properties and primary residences. You will also want to make sure they are available to come to the property within your inspection window. In my experience, inspectors have been able to come out to a property within a week's notice. If you don't think you will have all of your information within the inspection period, it is better to ask for an extension than to put in your earnest money deposit without knowing all of the facts or information.

An inspection report should be delivered to you in a timely manner. When choosing an inspector, ask how far out they are scheduled as well as how long the report will take after they visit the property. It is typical to receive the inspection report back within one to three days. You can usually expect to have it emailed to you; you can request a physical copy, but it may take longer to get to you. Some inspectors may even give you the report the same day. Depending on your time crunch, you should ask this question when choosing your inspector.

During the inspection, the inspector will walk through and examine the property, following a checklist. Afterward, they will create a detailed report on their findings. If they find any issues, they will be classified as low-level problems and high-level problems. You can ask the inspector to write out a list of what needs immediate action within the next year and within five years. This will give you an idea of what your costs will be for repairs and CapEx down the road. Keep in mind that these are guidelines. The report is just their recommendation and doesn't mean that you are required to follow an exact timeline. Nevertheless, it's incredibly helpful from a budgeting standpoint to know at this stage what repairs you can count on in the coming years (for example, a water heater nearing the end of its life span).

When you get the report, it will not tell you what the cost is to make a repair or who can fix it or how to fix it. This will be up to you to find out. There are several ways to address the findings and to handle them. The first thing to do is to get an estimate of the repairs needed. If you have no idea what the costs associated with the repairs are, that's where you will need to lean on experts. (Preferably members of that fantastic team you have already built!)

For my first investment property, I leaned on my real estate agent for everything. She was a family friend and I couldn't have done it without her. I had never even purchased a house on my own, let alone done an inspection. She reached out to her contacts to get estimates for me on the small repairs that needed to be done. Luckily, there weren't any necessary huge repairs. If you have a friend or family member who is a handyperson or in construction, don't be afraid to ask them or even to pay them to take some time to estimate the costs of what needs to be done. If there is a large repair outside the scope of your personal network's abilities, then it is worthwhile to get an actual quote from a contractor.

## Negotiating During the Inspection Period

Next, it's time to make a decision with the information you collected. You have several options.

1. Your first choice is to move forward with the contract and current purchase price. You will end the inspection period and send in your earnest money. Your agent, title company, or attorney will let you know where to send the funds (it is usually also stated in the contract). The money will be held in an escrow account where neither the buyer nor the seller have access to it. Depending on your state and who is involved with the transaction, it will be controlled by the seller's agent's brokerage, the seller's attorney, or the title company.

2. Your second option will be to completely back out of the deal. It is important to remember that you always have the option to *not* proceed with the contract.

3. Your third option is to ask the seller to make the repairs to the property.

4. Your fourth option is to decrease the purchase price to cover the cost of the repairs that you will make after purchasing the property.

This is all negotiable, and there is no right or wrong way to address the repairs. For deals I have facilitated, I usually ask for money off the purchase price because I would prefer to have the work done by a contractor I know. If you are asking the sellers to make the repairs, make sure you specify that the work is to be completed by a licensed contractor. This will help ensure that the repairs are done right and with quality materials, preventing you from having future problems with them down the road.

When you are negotiating during the inspection period, make sure that the numbers still make sense for you. Just like when you were negotiating the purchase price at the beginning of the process, you want to make sure that you don't turn the property into a bad deal. Even if you spent $300 on an inspection and time on the purchase of the property and you end up not buying it, you can't get into the mindset that the time and money is lost. Think of that $300 as an opportunity cost that kept you from getting into a bad deal. That $300 could have saved you thousands of dollars if you hadn't done the inspection and instead found out about the expensive repairs after closing. Perhaps that $300 just saved your entire investment career!

Once you have passed the inspection and put in your earnest money deposit, a lot of the legwork is left in the hands of the title company to close on the property. Again, the title company and/or your attorney will make sure the title is clear, meaning it does not have anyone else who is claiming to own the property or have an interest in the property. This is the time to start working on the other details of owning a property.

## Insurance

It is a very good idea to have insurance on your property. In order to have the coverage effective on the day of closing, you should start working on this now. Your insurance agent or broker will need information on you and the property to properly insure the building.

As I mentioned earlier, I decided a couple of years ago to get my insurance license to help another investor open an insurance agency. I will be completely honest again: I hated it. I don't think I'm alone in detesting everything even remotely related to insurance! If you feel the same, you will want to find an agent who can help you understand what insurance coverage you need. There are so many different options and choices. Some insurance companies will require an inspection of the property, which usually just involves checking the exterior of the property. They will take pictures and verify the data you submitted is accurate. This can be done after closing. The insurance company will give you a deadline as to when you need to have the inspection complete. If there are issues that they want corrected or mediated, you will receive notice that you have so many days to make the repairs.

> This inspection is completely separate from the one mentioned earlier in the chapter. Not all insurance companies will do an inspection, but some will, and, most likely, it will just be the exterior. It is not as in-depth as paying for a third-party inspector during your due diligence period. Their main interest is in verifying that the property and structure are what you say.

An insurance company I used on the cheapest property I ever purchased required some exterior repairs within thirty days of the inspection. I had to have areas of the house repainted where there was peeling paint (on the exterior), replace a window where there was plywood covering it, and have the tenants clear their belongings (blocking an exit, and a fire hazard) from the back porch. These are all things we would have done anyway but weren't planning to do within the first thirty days of ownership. We had purchased a portfolio of twelve units and there was work on other properties that felt more immediate. Oftentimes, an insurance agent will be aware of some of the things that the inspector calls out. For this property, we had the issues addressed and sent photos to the insurance company to show the improvements. This kept the insurance in place and prevented it from being canceled.

> If your insurance lapses, banks will also get insurance on your behalf and include it in the cost of your next loan payment or add it to your escrow. Most often, this option is a lot more expensive than if you went out and quoted it.

Another tip on insurance is to talk with your insurance agent beforehand to find out if there are certain things that may increase your premium or items that would prevent coverage at all.

Here are a few examples that I have come across.

- Pools with tenants in the property
- Trampolines with tenants in place
- Row houses

- Tenant dogs that are locally restricted breeds
- Galvanized pipes coming out of the building for plumbing

These are just a few examples. You should consult an agent or broker in your area. Some of these expense-increasing items can be eliminated (goodbye, trampoline!), while others cannot (good luck separating a row house from its neighbors). It's good to know about these premium increasers not only to see where you can find savings within a deal but also so that you know what kinds of things to avoid as you look at future properties.

While you are working on getting insurance on the property, you can simultaneously set up the utilities in your name. Even if there are tenants in the property that have utilities in their names, you may have to set up a landlord account with that utility company. If a tenant moves out, the utility provider may automatically revert the utilities back into the name of the landlord. If the current owner has the utilities in their name, you will have to have the utilities in yours effective the day of closing. This is also something you don't want to forget. If the current owner calls to cancel the utilities in their name and you haven't called to put the utilities in yours, then the utility company will shut the utilities off! This just becomes a pain. You now have to have everything turned back on, which can sometimes be more difficult than a phone call. For example, if the gas gets shut off to a property, you may have to wait around between 8:00 a.m. and 4:00 p.m. for a tech to show up to turn the gas back on. They must have interior access (to check the stove or another gas appliance to make sure there are no leaks) and someone must be there to let them in. Talk about a day wasted! You can avoid all of this if you create a landlord account before you close.

## Closing Day

Okay! It's the big day! You've made it! Closing day. I constantly annoy my business partner's with the song "Closing Time" by Semisonic each time we close. I mean, what's more celebratory than spontaneous karaoke?

I know it might feel a little nerve-racking . . . especially the first time around as a rookie.

The day of closing and what it involves will depend on if you are using a title company or an attorney. It will also depend on if you are using a lender and if you are physically located where the closing is taking place. There are a lot of variables, but in most circumstances, you will go to an actual "closing table." (So official!)

If you are working with an agent, they will usually ask if you want to do a final walk-through of the property right before closing. This is to make sure the property is in the same condition it was when you first saw it and put an offer on it. You don't want to close and then find out afterward that all the pipes burst a week ago because the current owner shut the heat off too soon which caused the water to freeze in the pipes.

Then you'll meet at the title company office, an attorney's office, or even downtown at the county clerk's office. The title company or the attorney will walk you through the documentation that needs to be signed. If you are using a lender, they may have a representative (such as their attorney) present to have you sign the mortgage documents. If all goes well, you sign and get the keys. Hooray!

If you are not in the area, you can close using a notary. A notary will come to you and have you sign. This could happen at your house, at a Tim Hortons (if you know, you know), or on the beach. There will of course be additional fees for having the notary come to you. The notary is sent all the required documentation ahead of time and will have it ready for you to sign. They then get the necessary papers back to the title company, attorney, or mortgage company (usually by overnighting the signed documents). Documents can be signed prior to closing. Then, on the actual closing day, the documents are filed with the county and the title of the property is transferred to you.

Don't feel uncomfortable asking questions or wanting things explained to you during the closing process. You are paying everyone in some way (or the seller is). Use every experience you encounter as an opportunity to learn. Someone once told me you always want to be the dumbest person in the room. While that might not sound like great advice, you learn and grow best by surrounding yourself with people who are knowledgeable.

## Closing Statement

The closing statement will be provided by the title company or your attorney. This document will show how much you owe and where your money is going. You will need this for your bookkeeping to properly allocate your funds.

You can see a sample closing statement below. By taking time to familiarize yourself with the look and wording of these documents now, you'll be able to feel more confident when sitting at that deal-closing table!

**Sample:**

---

### LAW OFFICE OF ROBERT D. STRASSEL

### REAL ESTATE CLOSING STATEMENT SELLER

Seller(s) Remington James
Purchaser(s) Development, LLC
Address: 2255 Oliver Road
Centerville, New York 14024
Closing date 24-Jan-22
Adjustment date 24-Jan-22

| | |
|---|---|
| **PURCHASE PRICE** | **$49,900.00** |
| Additions to purchase price | |
| 2021–2022 School Tax $440.32 / 365 days × 158 days | $190.60 |
| 2022 T/C $853.16 / 365 days × 342 days | $799.40 |
| **SUBTOTAL** | **$50,890.00** |
| Subtractions from purchase price | |
| Down Payment (held by Metro Roberts) | $2,000.00 |
| Balance due seller at closing | $48,890.00 |
| Payable to Robert D. Strassel, Attorney | $48,626.50 |
| Payable to Allegany County Clerk (transfer tax, TP, Notice & Mtg discharge) | $263.50 |
| **SALE DISBURSEMENTS** | |
| Search continuation | $461.16 |
| Survey | $0.00 |
| Realtor Comm. (balance) | $994.00 |

---

| | |
|---|---|
| Notice to Seller | $10.00 |
| TP-584 | $5.00 |
| Transfer tax | $200.00 |
| 2022 T/C | $853.16 |
| Mortgage Payoff Record | $48.50 |
| Postage & Courier | $150.00 |
| Wire charges | $0.00 |
| Legal Services (balance) | $0.00 |
| Total disbursements | $2,721.82 |
| **BALANCE DUE SELLER AT CLOSING:** | **$48,890.00** |
| Disbursements: | |
| Proceeds to seller on 12/31/2022: | |

## Beginning Rehab

Once you've signed the papers, it's time to hit the ground running and get that rehab rolling! You will want to line up contractors for work that needs to be done, get bids, create contracts, and hire contractors. As a refresher, refer back to the scope of work template I've provided. Later on in chapter 12 I will reference software you can use to track the rehab and assist in project management.

Think about the property you have purchased and which items on the list need to be done first, which can wait, and which you can remove completely. Then get to work . . . even if that just means picking up the phone.

## Rental Property Considerations

If you are using this house as a rental, you may need to handle inherited tenants. What do you do if there are already people living in your units who plan to stay with you as the new management?

One of my friends used to drive around the first Sunday of every month and collect rent from his tenants in person. Stopping at each house one by one. Yeah, no thank you. Gas is expensive enough, and the last thing I want to do on a Sunday is see or talk to people who aren't one of my only five friends that live near me.

There are multiple ways to accept payment: Venmo, money orders, cash, checks, or electronic transfer. In your lease agreement, state how you want rent paid. Do you want it mailed to your house? Maybe a PO box? That's what I did. I set up a PO box to receive rent checks in addition to the bills for my properties. This box costs me $79 a year to rent. There are different sizes of varying prices, so you can pick what works for your needs and budget. I liked the idea of all my business mail being in one location and not getting tossed around in all the junk mail that comes to my actual house.

When you are receiving the security deposit and first month's rent at move in—or prior—I recommend not taking personal checks. Money orders, cashier's checks, or electronic funds transfers are going to guarantee you will actually get the money. There is too much risk that a personal check will bounce, and if it does bounce but you have already handed off the keys, you might have just given someone a rent-free unit to stay in until the eviction goes through. This might feel like thinking through the "worst-case scenario" lens, but I want you to protect yourself and your investment . . . so take these precautions.

My favorite way (and a less time-consuming way) for tenants to pay is by electronic funds transfer through property management software. There are lots of options out there, and you should consider setting something up while under contract. My recommendation for your first few units is to use Avail or RentRedi, but there is new software coming out all the time, so make sure you do a demo of several and see what features you like. As you start to build your number of units, there are more complex softwares available. The ones I have used and like are Buildium and AppFolio. We'll talk more about software and automation in Chapter 12, so stay tuned!

If the property you are purchasing already has tenants in place and they are going to stay and continue to rent from you, you need to create an estoppel agreement. With the current owner's permission, you can contact the current tenants in the property to gather information and compare what the tenant is saying to the current lease agreement provided by the landlord. If there is no lease agreement, you can compare whether the landlord and tenant are saying the same thing. You can also find out repairs and maintenance that need to be done on the property while you're at it. I like gathering the tenants' information ahead of time so I can enter it into my property management software and give them a heads-up on how they will pay their rent once the property closes and becomes mine. If a landlord doesn't want the tenants to know they are selling, you can give the forms to the current landlord to give to the tenants and just have them let the tenants know they are updating their records (or something along those lines). Of course, once you close on the property the tenants will need to be notified of the change of ownership because you will want the rent payments to come to you! There is no reason for the seller to have to disclose to the tenants that he is selling until it is actually closed. It can be common for the seller to not want to tell his tenants for various reasons until the deal is finalized. If the property is listed on the MLS, then the tenants already know the property is for sale and this shouldn't be an issue.

Here is a sample estoppel agreement for you to take a look at. You can find it along with the other materials at **www.biggerpockets.com/rookiebonus**.

---

### ESTOPPEL AGREEMENT

Tenant Name(s): _____

Tenant Address & Unit Number: _____

Mailing Address: _____

Phone Number: _____

Email: _____

Do you have a written lease for this apartment? _____

If not, did you have a verbal lease agreement? _____

When did your lease begin? _____ / _____ / _____ (date).

When does your lease end? _____ / _____ / _____ (date).

Are you currently on a month-to-month lease? _____

---

Please list the legal names of all people living in your property.

_____

_____

How much is your monthly rent? _____

When is your rent due? _____

Have you paid a security deposit? _____

If so, how much did you pay for a deposit? _____

Did you pay for "the last month's rent" when you moved in? _____

If so, how much did you pay for "the last month's rent"? _____

When was the last time you paid rent? ____ / ____ / ____ (date)

For what month? _____

How much did you pay then? _____

What utilities do you pay for, if any? _____

Do you take care of snowplowing or lawn care?
If no, do you reimburse landlord? _____

Did you pay any other deposits or prepayments when you moved in?

_____

If so, how much—and for what? _____

Do you own any of the appliances in your unit? _____

If so, what? _____

Do you have a pet? _____

If yes, how many? _____

If yes, what breeds? _____

Do you have any other written or verbal agreements
with the landlord? _____

If yes, what are they? _____

Are there any problems related to your tenancy or any repairs needed for your unit?

_____

## SIGNATURE
*I certify that the above answers are true and correct to the best of my knowledge.*

Signed by tenant _____ Date: _____

Signed by tenant _____ Date: _____

I have reviewed the answers given above and agree with the tenants' statements regarding their payments, agreements, and deposits.

Owner: _____ Date: _____

Manager: _____ Date: _____

## Setting Up Property Management

A final consideration you'll want to think about is property management. We've talked about this topic a few times already, but it's finally time to make your decision and follow through. Are you going to hire a property manager or a third-party property management company, or are you going to do it yourself?

I've already babbled on long enough about the pros and cons of each option. I'm not going to rehash those thoughts here. But what I am going to do is tell you the next steps for each, so you can dive right in, no matter which option you choose.

For rookies, hiring a property manager and a third-party manager will be the same. If you only have a couple of units, it doesn't make sense to take on a W-2 employee as a property manager. To cut confusion, let's just say your choices are to hire a property management company or to self-manage.

Your first step is to call several property managers in the area. You can get recommendations by attending meetups, checking Facebook groups, or posting in the BiggerPockets forums. You can also check out apartment complexes in your area to see if they have third-party property management in place. If all else fails, a simple Google search will pull up a couple of leads.

Take your time interviewing potential property managers. I like to ask what their fee schedule is. There are so many fees beyond the percentage they charge on rent. Make sure you understand every circumstance in which they will charge you. Next, understand their processes. What happens when a tenant has a maintenance request? How do they put in a request? How long until someone gets back to them? Do they have a time frame of when maintenance should be completed after a request is submitted? Get an understanding of the leasing process as well. In order to feel comfortable hiring someone, you should feel comfortable with the system and process they plan to put in place.

Finally, if property management is something you want to tackle on your own, then make sure you are willing to know your state laws and regulations. A great resource is www.avail.co/education/laws. You will also want to familiarize yourself with fair housing laws.

## HOMEWORK

**1.** Line up each key player (title company, attorney, agent, inspector, appraiser, contractor) in your closing process and make sure you have a plan to communicate with each.

**2.** Draw up a closing and post-closing timeline so you can hit the ground running once closing day is complete.

**3.** Decide on and take the first step on your property management plan.

# Chapter 11

# AFTER CLOSING

## Vocabulary You'll Need to Know

**ARV (AFTER-REPAIR VALUE):** Estimates the potential value of a property after all repairs have been made.

**HOLDING COSTS:** Costs associated with storing/holding inventory—such as a property—that remains unsold. This is the interest payments on loans, utilities, insurance, property taxes and other expenses incurred until the property is sold or rented.

**LEASE:** A contract between a tenant and a landlord allowing the tenant to live in a property for a set period of time for a certain cost. The lease will state the conditions and terms to this agreement as well as the costs and responsibilities for each party to the lease.

**TENANT:** Someone who occupies a property and pays rent to have use of the property. This could apply to many different asset classes of property, including a single-family home, a multifamily home, an apartment, a storage facility, or more.

**REFINANCE:** To finance something (such as a piece of property) again, putting a new mortgage on the property that typically has a new loan amount and terms.

**Y**ou have a property! Congratulations! I knew you could do it. I am so excited for you!

You've probably guessed what I'm going to say next: As exciting as this is, the work isn't done. Let's go over what you can get a jump on once you close on the property.

## Take Before Pictures

I don't know about you, but I love those before and after pictures I see on Instagram. With a simple swipe of my finger, I get to see the dramatic changes people have made to their properties, whether it's through full-gut remodels or the perfect color of paint. It isn't as easy when you are the one doing the work, but the results feel even better. It would be a shame if you were the only person to be able to see the difference.

When you take before pictures, you get to compare them to the after pictures. These are great images to share with any social following you have, as well as future renters or buyers, depending on your plans for the property. Having before and after photos can also help you build out a great portfolio and demonstrate value to future potential business partners. You have proof in hand of the great work you are capable of doing. Plus, I won't lie. It's super fun. Before. After. Before. After. It never gets old!

If you are furnishing a space for a short-term or medium-term rental, I highly recommend using a professional photographer, especially one with experience doing real estate photography. You want clear, crisp pictures that will force people to, as the Real Estate Robinsons like to call it, "Stop the scroll." Make people pause, pay attention, and think, "I *have* to stay there!" because the photos are so amazing.

> Did you know Airbnb will send out a photographer for you (for a charge) if that's a platform you'll be relying on? (Importantly, these pics can ONLY be used on Airbnb.)

## Refinance Process

If your plan is to keep the property but you bought it with some kind of short-term financing (hard money, a private money lender who needs to be paid back, or maybe cash from your line of credit you want to pay back), then you need to put some long-term financing on it. This could also be the case if you rehabbed the property and increased its value, and you want to capitalize on that by pulling money out of it and putting a new mortgage on it. In fact, refinancing is a crucial part of the BRRRR strategy—you need to refinance to pull your capital out of the deal and put it into another property.

When you are close to finishing your rehab and ready to rent out your property, contact the loan officer you want to get long-term financing with. You will need your property finished when the appraiser comes out to the property to find the new market value. It is rare that an appraiser will get out to your property right when you start the refinance process with the bank, so I always like to at least get the paperwork flowing with the loan officer first to expedite the process.

Once the appraisal is done, the bank will let you know the amount they will lend you based on the results (new property value). Your goal is to have it appraise higher than what you bought it for and what you put into it for the rehab. It is typical for the bank to lend you 70–80 percent of the appraised price. When you are shopping banks, they will be able to tell you what that percentage is and then when the appraisal is done you will know the exact amount they will lend you.

If you had another mortgage on the property, the bank will use your new loan money to pay off that other mortgage. If you didn't have a mortgage but used borrowed cash (like hard money or a line of credit on your primary house), it is your responsibility to pay that off and not just blow all that dough on new kicks and cars. Your property may even appraise higher than you expected, but if you pull out 80 percent of that amount with a new loan, then there is the possibility your rental income won't cover the mortgage payment. At this point, you may decide to only draw 70 percent of the appraised value to keep your payment lower.

Refinancing is a great way to grow and scale because it provides you with cash to invest in additional properties!

As a reminder for those BRRRR investors out there: Many banks will require a "seasoning period" (around six to twelve months) before you can refinance a property using its new ARV and rental income. Ask this upfront before deciding on a lender!

# Renting It Out

I'm guessing that you got into this investment real estate game to make some money! If you let your property sit vacant and empty, that is not going to happen. The longer you wait on this step, the more money you stand to lose.

## Setting Rent

As the landlord, you need to familiarize yourself with market rent so you know the appropriate rent to charge for your property. You can find market rent through current listings on Facebook Marketplace, Zillow rent, and Apartments.com, as well as with the BiggerPockets rent estimator. You can also call local property managers and ask what they currently charge for units even if they are not available for rent.

You will want to compare your properties finishes to the units you see listed and find comparable properties. Do an apples-to-apples comparison. If your unit has medium-quality laminate and finishes, it wouldn't be accurate to compare it to a luxury penthouse, and you'll be sorely disappointed when no one wants to pay what you're asking. Once you have established what the market rent is (what people will pay to live there), then you can set that as your monthly rent. Additionally, you may have other fees associated such as pet fees, water fees, or garage fees. The amount of rent and fees you charge will determine the income you are producing from this property. Remember I said income, not profit. You still have your expenses to pay!

On the expense side of things, you will need to decide what fees and tasks will be included in rent and what will be the responsibility of the resident. For example, who will take care of the lawn or pay for utilities? This should all be laid out in writing in the lease agreement. This is also a great opportunity to use comparable properties as your guide.

## Preparing the Property

Before we get into the lease agreement, let's talk about preparing for renters. Just because you have purchased the property, that doesn't mean you are ready for renters to move in. There are many things you need to get ready and tasks you must first complete, such as:

- Changing locks and making keys for you and residents.
- Cleaning.
- Landscaping.

- Testing appliances, plumbing, and heating.
- Touching up paint.
- Making repairs.

You will want to put the time and money into getting the property repairs done now, during the vacancy, rather than waiting until the tenants are in place. Once they are living in the property, it is much more difficult to complete these tasks. Plus, wouldn't you rather have your tenants blissfully unaware of the property's past problems? Why worry them with something that is no longer an issue? Instead of saying, "Oh, that sink leaks and drips, but I'll fix it," you'll get to say, "We just put a brand-new faucet in the kitchen." Much better, right? Remember, you can lean on your team to help you complete these tasks. That's what you found them for!

If you have decided not to hire out property management, these are duties you can take on yourself, but make sure you have the time and are informed enough to take on that responsibility. There are many laws and regulations for property managers, and you must know them all. Even on the contractor side, you must know when and what permits to pull—not just how to lay tile.

Even if you aren't actively managing your property, it is still important to be familiar with laws and regulations as a landlord. When you hire a property manager, ask to be on the property management company's email list for important updates regarding changes in laws. They oftentimes will send newsletters out to clients or potential clients. There are also free or low-cost landlord training classes offered by nonprofit organizations that can be good sources for this kind of information. Google your local market to see what is available. In Buffalo, for example, the local nonprofits that offer training are Belmont Housing and HOME (Housing Opportunities Made Equal).

I know we've already talked about insurance, but make sure you have liability protection and property coverage in place. Some insurance carriers have specific policies for landlords that can even include loss of income coverage. Along with landlord insurance, there is also renter's insurance. This is what your tenants will have in place for their personal property. As the landlord, you are not responsible for the contents they bring into the home. Some landlords require renter's insurance before the tenant moves in. It is very inexpensive and, in my opinion, worth it for a tenant to get the policy.

## Drawing Up the Lease

Now for the decision-making part. You will have to decide what policies and procedures you want in your lease. For example, will you allow pets? What are the late fees? (Be careful with this one, as your state law could limit the amount you charge for late fees.) Will you have annual property inspections? What happens if the tenant breaks the lease? Can they sublet? How are repairs handled? Where should tenants park? The list goes on.

An attorney will be helpful to draft a sample lease for you and then you can add or expand to include your specific policies. Be aware that you can start with a template, but most leases will have to be tailored for each specific property. For example, some of the policies for a single-family home will vary from those of a duplex.

> If you don't have an attorney yet and want a head start on creating a lease, you can access attorney-approved state-specific leases at **www.bigger pockets.com/landlord-forms**. This is free if you have a Pro membership or you can pay for them individually if you don't. Such a great resource! Take advantage of it!

One tool I've created to help streamline the introduction of new tenants into a property is the New Tenant Handbook, which you can find and customize at **www.biggerpockets.com/rookiebonus**. A tenant handbook is a great resource because you can lay out all sorts of important information for your new tenant  to help them feel welcome and comfortable, as well as teach them how to "do business with you." Meaning, you can explain how and when payments should be made, how to make maintenance requests, and other pertinent procedures to follow. You can obviously edit this document to fit your needs, personality, and specific property, but it's a great place to start!

As a landlord, you can tailor the lease however you want, but know that you have to follow laws and know your responsibilities as a landlord. Your job is more than collecting rent. You are required to provide an implied "warranty of habitability." Take this job seriously and be aware that code enforcement can be called if there is anything not to code! These are the basic needs you have to meet.

- Clean water

- Heat (not necessarily pay for the utility that provides the heat, but there must be some HVAC system in place)
- Working bathroom
- Local building codes (which includes making sure it's a fire-safe environment)

When you market the unit, you will have to state your policies in the listing, such as no pets, tenant pays electric, etc. You will also have to state what security deposit is required to move in. This also varies from state to state as to how much you can charge. For example, in New York State, you can only charge up to one month's rent and cannot ask for last month's rent in advance. But each state is different, so check yours! When you create your lease, I suggest adding an attachment with your state's guidelines for what is considered normal wear and tear and what charges can be deducted from the deposit at move out. Your state may also give guidance as to when the security deposit must be returned (e.g., thirty days, fourteen days, "within a reasonable time").

## Marketing Your Unit

Speaking of marketing your unit, here are some tips on spreading the word about your property!
- Take and post clear, nice pictures of the unit showing each room.
- List an accurate description of the unit and any highlights of the neighborhood. For example, "This unit is in the Summerdale School District, which is highly rated."
- Clearly state the lease terms, such as rent, security deposit, tenant responsibilities, and lease length.
- Have a link to the application or prescreening form.

## Tenant Screening

Before we move on to the next topic, let's button up this renting portion of the chapter and take a quick minute to think about tenant screening.

One thing you can do before a showing or even during or after a showing is a prescreening application. This can significantly reduce the number of applications you need to read and showings you have to do. This can be created in your property management software or in Google Forms, and the responses will be sent to you. You would be amazed at the number of people who read in the application that you don't allow pets and still try to apply.

Again, if you are self-managing it's crucial you familiarize yourself with fair housing laws in tenant screening (and even if you aren't self-managing it's still a good idea). This is important when creating your listing. You can't say in the listing, for example, "This would not be a good unit for children because the carpet is white." When you screen tenants, you can only reject them for reasons that do not go against fair housing laws. For example, if you don't want a tenant because they are eighty years old and think they will call you to change light bulbs, that is not a valid reason. You can't deny a tenant housing because of age; unless they can't legally sign a lease agreement because they are not old enough or don't even have a government ID for proof of identity, age cannot be a factor in your decision.

You will need to decide if you want to learn fair housing or if you want to outsource your property management. Education is key. Take the time to learn and understand. Don't be careless. Having an attorney who knows fair housing law can be a great resource to run questions by as well.

My investor friend Ashley Wilson (@badashinvestor on Instagram) told me she takes a fair housing law class for landlords once a year. If you are reported for not complying with fair housing laws, having the record of taking the class to educate yourself can come to your defense. Check out your local housing organizations to learn about fair housing laws for free or low cost. Each county usually has one or several nonprofits that offer these kinds of programs.

One way to safeguard your compliance is to have criteria that apply to everyone. Set standards as to what is acceptable.

## LET'S GO THROUGH SOME ITEMS THAT CAN BE ON YOUR CHECKLIST.

☐ Credit score
☐ Clean background check
☐ Clean eviction history (This is actually illegal in some states, so know your state laws!)
☐ Debt-to-income ratio
☐ Current employment and past employment history, with reference checks
☐ Income
☐ Positive landlord reference checks

Sometimes, there will be instances where you may waver from sticking to your criteria. For example, if someone has a lot of debt but it is mostly medical bills, I may not hold that against them. If someone has student loans, I may weigh that differently than if they have the same amount in credit card debt. Or if they are an investor and have a lot of mortgages on rentals, obviously I'd understand that debt.

For each criterion, you will need to understand your market before you set that criteria. Typically, there are different classes of real estate: A, B, C, or D neighborhoods. If you are investing in a C or D neighborhood, it may be more difficult to find renters who have an income that is 3.5 times the amount of rent. If you are investing in an A-class neighborhood, this may be more achievable. If you have student housing, some of the young renters might not even have any credit built yet to meet your minimum credit score.

## LET'S GO OVER AN EXAMPLE OF WHAT YOU MIGHT ASK IN AN A-CLASS NEIGHBORHOOD SINGLE-FAMILY HOME OR MULTIFAMILY UNIT.

☐ Credit score of at least 600
☐ Proof of income that is at least 3.5 times rent (must be verifiable)
☐ Proof of identity through government-issued ID
☐ No criminal offenses within the past seven years that caused harm or danger to others including [then you could list murder, armed robbery, etc.]
☐ No judgments against them for more than $1,000
☐ Reference from previous landlords or verification of housing history if they owned it
☐ No bankruptcy within the past six months

Your criteria can change, but keep it consistent per unit. Don't all of a sudden change the criteria from one applicant to another when they are applying for the same unit. That's shady and could get you in trouble.

As much as we want to trust everyone, you can't always. That is why we run credit, background, and eviction checks. A little fun fact: Not all states allow you to use eviction as a screening criterion. You can run the check, but it's not a sufficient reason to not rent to someone. There must be another reason. Fortunately, there is once again software to make our lives easier on this. I personally prefer software that has it all integrated. One example is TenantReports.com and another is RentRedi, both of which have automatic screening software built right into their program. When the tenant fills out the application, they will be able to enter their information to complete the screening process, which will eventually give you the information you need to understand their background and credit score. The tenant pays for the report directly and it is no cost to you.

> One more thing to note: You can't run someone's credit without their permission. You need to have their authorization and approval. That's why I like using software that has the tenant process their information for the screening, then the report is sent directly to you on the processing side. There could always be that tenant who says, "Yes I gave you my social security number, but I didn't know you were going to run my credit!"

Tenant screening is just one piece of the application process. There is also the application itself, where you collect data from the tenant. Once again, trust but verify. As exciting as it is to receive applications and as much as you want to just pick who looks good on paper or even the first applicant just to get it rented, you need to do the work to reduce the risk of getting a bad tenant. There is no way to 100 percent protect yourself from damage or an eviction, but you can take steps in the application process (background check, calling references, etc.) to mitigate it.

You also want to get your property rented!

Go through the applications in a timely manner, because the perfect applicant could be applying for different rentals too. If you take too long, they might choose to live somewhere else. Once you have decided who you are going to accept, message them first before denying others. There is a chance they no longer want the apartment and you don't want to dismiss your other applicants until you know for sure that you have a commitment from your chosen one. Take a deposit from them to reserve the unit while you create the lease and get their move-in date set. The deposit I usually charge is $200. This $200 will go toward their security deposit when they move in. If they do not move in by a certain date, then the $200 is kept for nonperformance on their part. (You could have rented to someone else, and all that time was wasted; now you have to start over finding another tenant!) After the deposit is received, you will ask for their move-in date and start creating their lease and charges.

> When you collect the deposit to hold the unit, make sure you have them sign a letter stating they are reserving the unit and how the deposit works (when it will be applied to their security deposit or first month's rent and reasons they would not get the deposit back). You always want to be clear and up front with the applicants and tenants. The more you can get in writing, the better.

Send the applicants you did not choose a letter denying their application. There are many examples online that you can use as templates. You may also have adverse action letters too. These tell the applicant why they were denied. That's why it's a great idea to have your rental criteria listed on your website or in the listing or on the application. It will save everyone time and prevent some unpleasant surprises for potential renters.

## Flip

We talked a bit about flipping houses back in Chapter 2 when I laid out all the different investment strategies available. If you have decided on the fix-and-flip model, now is the time to roll up your sleeves and get your work boots on (or hire a contractor!).

Every day your project isn't sold costs you money. Every day it sits unsold, you are paying holding costs. Every day you wait for contractors to start or delayed materials to arrive . . . I think you get the idea.

> Holding costs are the payments you must make on the property during the period in which you hold it but haven't sold it, such as your insurance on the property, utilities, property taxes, lawn care, and so on, plus any interest you may be paying on a loan for the property.

That said, even though you want to complete your project as fast as possible, don't cut corners. That will just end up costing you when the inspection is done and additional work is requested or when someone backs out of the deal and you have to re-list the unit.

As you are designing your flip, look at properties in the area that have sold. What kind of finishes do they have? Does almost every house have granite countertops and hardwood floors? That could indicate that laminate countertops and carpet flooring aren't going to go over well. If you choose finishes outside of the norm of the area (which are likely less in demand), you are more likely to get a lower return on your investment or no one may even want it. This isn't to say that you have to go high-end each time you do a flip. Middle-grade flips that make affordable housing out of distressed housing are important for the health of a housing market and are usually in high demand. You just need to figure out what other houses in the area are doing and use their choices as a guide.

When you initially purchased the property and ran your numbers, you should have figured out what your desired ARV (after-repair value) was for the property. Revisit these numbers to see what finishes make sense. If you are only going to get $5,000 from the sale of the house and putting in granite countertops will cost you $5,000, is it even worth doing? If you are able to get $12,000 more and they cost $5,000, then yes, it's probably worth it to do the upgrade. But in some neighborhoods, people aren't willing to pay for those upgrades. Some people would rather save money than pay for a higher finish; while in a different part of town or in the next city over, people may swoon for those fancy finishes. Know your market and be careful to not over-upgrade or under-upgrade your property to the point that it doesn't make sense. It's easy to go overboard and lose sight of the actual numbers, so as you are going through the rehab, stick to your plan. New ideas will come up, but keep an eye on the budget. I recommend having a good bookkeeping system in place so you know each week where you are with the project budget.

If things start to go over budget, have an open conversation with your contractor. Look at other places you could save if you need to spend in another category. One time, my partner and I hired a crew of three contractors. The project started off great! After three months, progress just dropped, and then became nonexistent. They were billing us for work that seemed to drag on and never finish. There is a saying that goes, "Hire slow and fire fast." We made the decision to let them go. But finding a contractor at the last minute is hard, especially a good one. We ended up taking tasks we needed done and outsourcing to several different contractors who could fit us in for a day or two. This did cost us more than we originally planned. My business partner is currently finishing up the last-minute items on the project himself. Even though our goal is to be as passive as possible and we don't love to be hands-on in flips anymore, being handy when you are in a bind can be a project-saver.

As I've continued to harp on during this book, make a checklist and document what you have to do for your rehabs. What's the process going to be?

Have a look at the template I created on Monday.com at ***www.bigger pockets.com/rookiebonus***. Use this as inspiration to see how organizing the tasks can make them feel more manageable.

Once the rehab is done, it's time to stage the property! While this step isn't mandatory, a well-staged home can really sell the property. The end buyer is looking at a well-used space instead of an empty space. It's difficult to imagine life in an empty home. Staging can spur your future buyers' imaginations and help them already see themselves "at home" in the property. Be sure to vet your stager and choose one that has an eye for design and not just a storage unit full of miscellaneous furniture that they throw together.

If you see photos online of houses that are beautifully staged, reach out to the listing agent to ask who the stager is. You can usually tell if a house is being flipped and staged by viewing the sales history. If the house just sold six months ago for $200,000 and now is renovated, furnished, and being sold for $320,000, then it's most likely a flip. You can also see in the photos that there are no personal pictures, no clothes in closets, no kids' toys, and not much of anything in the house besides furnishings. Even if you end up being wrong and it's not a staged house, all it took was five minutes of your time to call or email the listing agent.

On the MLS listing, it will tell you who the agent is and you can search their brokerage to get their information. Sometimes they will provide you with their information directly on the listing.

You can choose to list your property with a real estate agent or for sale by owner. Whether you are deciding on staging or using an agent, the cost should all be included in your numbers. You don't want to forget to add the cost of commission from the sale or the cost of staging and hurt the profit you were expecting.

Finally, do a home inspection with a third-party, licensed inspector before you sell. This will give you a final check to see if there was anything that was missed. You can let your prospective buyers know you have already done an inspection, of which you are happy to provide a report, saving them several hundred dollars by not having to pay someone to do it themselves. If there are things that come up in the inspection, you can fix them before you show the house and have it all taken care of.

## Responsibilities of a Property Owner

As the adage goes, "With great power comes great responsibility."

Is it great to be a property owner? Absolutely! Does it come with a lot of perks and opportunities? Yes! As a property owner, are you also obligated and responsible for maintaining that property? Another yes.

I used to love snowstorms and rainstorms. I could sit on the front porch for hours watching the rain fall and the lightning strike. Then I had my first incident where a tenant called in a panic that the basement was flooding and the sump pump wasn't working. A sump pump typically pumps out any water that collects in the basement, and it's a common fixture in the northeast. After that incident, any time a storm blew in, I would cringe and watch the sky with a panicked eye, hoping a tree wasn't about to fall on any of my properties.

I'm not telling you that these things will never happen to you. But fortunately, you can account for the unexpected and unwanted by having reserves, proper insurance, and even a property manager to handle these situations while you continue to sleep soundly through the night. Proper insurance is key for liability too.

Remember way back at the beginning of this book when I said that my one fear was getting sued? If you neglect your properties and they do become a hazard, then, yes, you could get sued. And they could win. Basically, keep up on your maintenance and don't let your property get into disrepair. You don't need to have top-of-the-line upgrades and beautiful finishes (depending on your area), but make sure it's at least safe. You could have the ugliest house on the block that is also completely habitable and safe. Meanwhile, the house down the block with brand-new siding may have rotted wood underneath causing mold to form.

Now you guys are all going to have property nightmares! I'm sorry! I get it. And while that nervousness can take a bit of getting used to, I want to warn you not to get too comfortable. I took a motorcycle safety course once, and they always said that if you feel comfortable as a rider, then you're more at risk of an accident. Stay uncomfortable so you are always aware and alert. The same lesson can be applied to real estate investing and your business too.

It is your responsibility as a property owner to be one of the good ones. If you have a rental property, you are providing a service—buying, operating, and maintaining a property—and in exchange for that service, your tenants pay you more than your mortgage. The same is true for a fix-and-flip—you are orchestrating the headache of renovating a house so that someone can pay more than you did in exchange for a beautiful, move-in-ready home. Never forget that!

Okay, time to roll up your sleeves and get to work. Take what you've learned in this chapter and put it into action with this homework.

# HOMEWORK

**1.** If you are going to immediately resell your property, set up an appointment with the bank to begin your refinancing process.

**2.** If you are planning to rent out your properties, create your own tenant handbook, using the template provided at **www.biggerpockets .com/rookiebonus**.

**3.** If you are going to hire a property manager, begin your search by making a list of potential people/companies, and then start making some calls!

**4.** If you are going to do rehab, create a plan and list the necessary people you'll need to get on board/hire to help with the project.

# Chapter 12

# AUTOMATION AND SOFTWARE

## Vocabulary You'll Need to Know

**AUTOMATION:** The use of technology to execute recurring tasks or processes in an organization where manual effort can be replaced. The goal of automation is to minimize costs while also increasing efficiency and streamlining processes.

**VIRTUAL ASSISTANT:** A remote employee who offers administrative support, usually part-time. This person can do tasks that an executive assistant would typically handle, such as scheduling appointments, making phone calls, arranging travel, and organizing emails.

I know this topic may feel like it's coming too soon, even at nearly the end of the book. You just learned how to do *all the things* for a single property and we are already talking about growing and scaling? Not only that but also the role of automation?

Yes we are.

Successful entrepreneurs look way down the road for what's ahead and how they can most effectively face it. David J. Schwartz, author of *The Magic of Thinking Big*, puts it this way: "Success doesn't demand a price. Every step forward pays dividends."

What do you want? Going forward, what are your hopes and dreams for this real estate investment journey you've started? Take a moment and ask yourself these questions. Write the answers down or talk them through with your accountability partner or group—remember them from Chapter 1? That wasn't just a one-and-done thing!

- Do you want to stop at one property?
- Do you want to grow and scale your investments?
- Do you want to outsource tasks and become more passive?
- Do you want to create a property management company?

As a rookie investor, you have an advantage. You can build your systems, processes, and automation now while you have a handful of properties instead of waiting until you are overwhelmed with a large number of them.

As you decide what areas of your investment business you'd like to automate and which apps you'd like to fill those roles, ask yourself, "What is most important to me?" Perhaps think about tasks you don't enjoy doing, areas that could use improvement, or things that just take too long.

I want you to keep in mind that you don't have to automate everything all at once. In this chapter, I will lay out many possible options. You don't have to do all of them. In fact, you don't have to do any of them if you don't want to. This is a choose your own adventure, remember? Right now, just commit to seeing what's out there. Then, afterward, pick and choose what feels right for you right now. And remember that you can always add more later.

## Property Analysis and Management

As you're working through the information in this book, you might find yourself searching for the most effective and efficient way to run a process in your business. Or, at the very least, you might be asking, "Is there an app for that?" In fact, there are several. I have apps that help me analyze deals, apps that help me store and organize files, and apps that help me make sense of my schedule and to-do lists. There are a million apps out there, some better than others. Let me save you some search time and tell you about my favorites.

## Property Analysis

These first few apps are ones I use on the go, while out and about looking at properties. They help me decide if it's worth running a "deep dive" analysis on a property. I still follow the steps we talked about in Chapter 7 (Deal Analysis). But these apps are a starting point.

- **Zillow** is my app of choice for looking at listings, but there is also Realtor.com, Trulia, and many others. Each one has similar features but displays information in a different layout. Play around with them to figure out which one feels best for you. There really isn't a wrong choice, since the information these sites feed out is the same—it's more about finding an interface that is user-friendly to you.

- **LandGlide** and **OnX Hunt** are very similar. You only need a paid subscription to one. (Both have free trials if you want to try them out before committing to one or the other.) Both show the parcel lines and even satellite images of the lot. I find it beneficial to be able to see the visual image of the whole property and where the lot lines go. I have found that the satellite images in OnX Hunt are more recent than what's on Google Maps or another search engine, which is why I prefer checking the app over using the good old world wide web in general.

- **DealCheck** acts similar to the BiggerPockets calculators. You input your numbers to receive a quick analysis. There are pro features you can purchase, but the basic is all you need. The advantage of DealCheck is that it's an app, so it's easy to use on the go. Deal analysis tools will vary depending on your strategy and your end goal (e.g., appreciation versus cash flow), so try as many out as you like. Ultimately, I think you should build out your own system with all the features that you like (from different calculators); but as far as choosing one single go-to app, DealCheck is the one I like best.

- **Homesnap** is a new one for me. The app uses GPS to locate the property you are taking a picture of. It gives you information on the property and shows you the most recent picture that was taken of the property (besides yours). The app will also guide you to walk the parcel lines by using the phone on your camera. It can be very useful to see where lot lines start and end. So far, I have found it pretty close to accurate when playing around with it on my own properties.

I love being able to work from my phone while I am out and about as well as having systems in place to run a deal quickly. Using these apps helps me quickly eliminate deals that don't meet the buy box criteria without losing too much time running the numbers and researching the properties.

## Property Management Software

If you are going to take on the task of property management, know that there are a ton of apps out there that can make your tasks easier and more efficient. Here are a few of my favorites.

- Avail
- Buildium
- RentRedi[13]
- AppFolio
- Apartments.com

Each of these apps varies but offers roughly the same capabilities, features, and options. I would recommend taking advantage of the free demos as an opportunity to figure out which one will work best for your business. As you are vetting each one, consider if the features they offer would make your job and life easier. Which app has the best combination of features for your situation, property, and preferences? Here are some of the amenities I look for and how they benefit me.

- **Electronic lease signing**. Electronic lease signing makes bringing new tenants on board so much easier! Instead of making an appointment time that works for both parties and showing up at a designated place at a specific time, you can simply send your new tenant an electronic form through the app to sign. This is a must for out-of-state investors but I recommend it for everyone.
- **Tenant electronic payments**. Check to see if the app you are trying has a payment portal that allows tenants to pay their rent electronically. Submitting a payment through a phone that automatically goes to your bank is way better than having to pick up checks at a PO box and drive them to the bank. Plus, the app will likely have a bookkeeping feature as well, allowing you to skip that task too.

---

**13** My fellow BiggerPockets lovers will be happy to know that RentRedi is a complimentary feature for Pro members.

When I managed a forty-unit apartment building, there wasn't a system like this. Every month the tenants had to mail in or drop off their checks, which I then had to deposit and record in the book-keeping records. It was so time-consuming! Imagine getting all of that money but skipping all of that work!

- **Online maintenance requests**. You can save yourself a lot of time on the phone if you have a place for tenants to submit their maintenance requests online. Instead of your phone constantly ringing and pinging, you can get an email notification about work that needs to be done. You can then handle the request on your own or forward it to a contractor.

- **Other amenities**. Another amenity I use frequently and would suggest you look for is the communication capabilities. Can you send a mass email to everyone in your units letting them know about a new building policy, a maintenance project affecting the whole building, or a note outlining a new city ordinance about street parking? Having an app that allows you to communicate with everyone all at once is a lot faster than sending dozens of individual emails. A few other features I have enjoyed accessing are bookkeeping helpers, profit and loss statements, leasing schedulers, additional property onboarding, and rent roll reports.

Each app is different. It is important to find one that works for you and your needs. Like I said, play around with the free trials before committing to a paid subscription so you can be 100 percent happy with your choice and what it has to offer you.

## Task Management Software

A real estate investor, by nature, wears a lot of hats and does a lot of things. It can be difficult to manage all that needs to be handled. I know I couldn't do it without some sort of system to keep me organized and on the ball. Below is a list of apps you can use to help keep control of your calendar and to-do list.

- Monday.com
- Asana
- ClickUp
- Trello

The task management software from this list that I use most frequently is Monday, but I have used each of these. I use Monday to create lists of tasks and procedures. It helps keep me and my team organized and on track. Once I create a checklist—say, for acquiring insurance on a property—I can use it as a template and repeat the process each and every time that task needs to be completed. This increases the ease and efficiency of the task and allows me to delegate tasks (or even portions of larger tasks) to others on my team seamlessly.

I would recommend using checklists like the ones featured in these task management software programs even if you are a solopreneur. If and when you do bring on more people, you'll be able to more easily explain what needs to be done, allowing you to confidently hand off tasks.

Here is an example that I created in Asana. In this screenshot of an Asana board, you can see a rehab template, including the different phases and tasks that need to be completed.

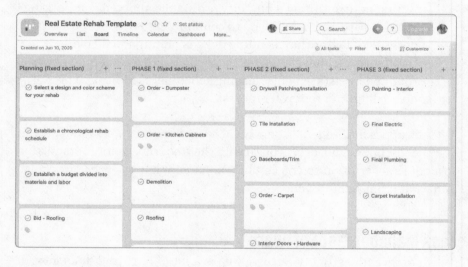

Some of what you may like or dislike about these different task management programs is their visual aesthetic. Also know that every strategy, be it turnkey or fix-and-flip, commercial or residential, necessitates its own to-do lists. Every investor will also prefer different methods and layouts of organization, and there's nothing wrong with that.

# Document Storage and Organization

A lot of the property management softwares have great storage capabilities, allowing you to attach a receipt right to the payable or a lease right to the tenant. The problem with this is that if you decide to no longer use the software, it is almost impossible, or at least very time-consuming, to pull the documents from the software. I recommend you also store documents in a cloud storage option, such as Google Drive, OneDrive, Dropbox, or iCloud. I personally use Google Drive because of how it integrates with Google Docs and Sheets, but all serve the same purpose.

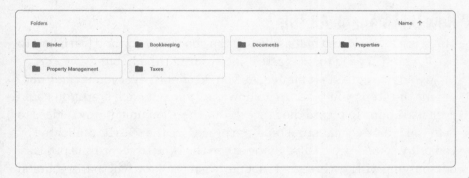

# Asset Management and Bookkeeping

Another area of your investment business that can be benefited by apps is asset management and bookkeeping. Here are a few that I've found to work well.

- Stessa
- Quickbooks
- Autobooks
- Excel

Personally, I recommend Stessa. This app allows you to keep information about a property (such as the purchase contract and insurance info) right in the app. It also lets you link directly to a bank account. How cool is that? If you are unfamiliar with bookkeeping, Stessa is a great app to start with because it is tailored specifically to real estate investors. And remember, if you are really stressing about this aspect of your business, you can always hire a team member to take care of it or outsource it to a virtual assistant.

## How Do I Manage All This?

There is a lot to do and manage. Once you choose an app and learn how to use it, you still need to integrate it into your life and habits.

My advice is to start simple. As you do simple, everyday tasks, document the steps you take. Write down or type out each step. You could even use **Loom** to record the process. Use these documents and videos to help you create checklists—steps and processes that can be replicated by you or by someone else. By having taken the time to record the process, outsourcing will be a breeze. Trust me when I say you will thank yourself later!

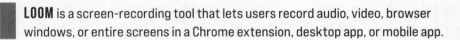

**LOOM** is a screen-recording tool that lets users record audio, video, browser windows, or entire screens in a Chrome extension, desktop app, or mobile app.

Need a little help and advice about creating checklists? Check out this BiggerPockets podcast episode with Shelby Osborne. (*BiggerPockets Real Estate Podcast* episode 406)

Here's the beauty of having a document and list like this: No matter who is completing the task, you can be sure it is being completed—and in the way you want too. You do want the person accomplishing the task to know exactly what needs to be done and how to accomplish it.

Here are a few of my checklists, some of which I complete on my own, others of which I hand off to team members and partners. Sometimes we learn better by seeing how others get it done. It doesn't mean we have to replicate what we see, but it gives us a place to start building our own models and systems. (Again, you can download these to reference or modify at *www.biggerpockets.com/rookiebonus*!)

## Sample Operating Procedure for Monthly Bookkeeping

Bookkeeping for Rental Property, LLC

### Visit www.Bank.com
- Select Login
- Enter username and password
- Select Account Name
- Select Statements
- Download Statement for Month to be reconciled

### Visit www.managebuilding.com
- Select sign in—upper right-hand corner
- When login appears, select Sign in here for a rental owner at the bottom of page
- Enter username and password
- Select Reports in top right corner
- Under Financial Category select Rental Owner Statement
- Under Date Range select Period Ending for month to be reconciled
- Income Statement should be checked
- Select Run Report
- Download Reports—Owner Statement and Income Statement

### Open Quickbooks for Property, LLC
- Enter password
- Select Banking at Top Task Bar
- Select Make General Journal Entries
- Enter Date of Owner Statement
- For entry number "pm month.year," e.g., pm 11.20
- Enter the following:

| ACCOUNT | DEBIT | CREDIT | MEMO | NAME | BILLABLE | CLASS |
|---|---|---|---|---|---|---|
| Rent Income | | Amount from Income on Owner Stmt | | | | Property House Number and Street |
| Expense Account *could be multiple of these to enter<br><br>e.g., repairs and maintenance (labor, sales tax, and materials all go under repairs account) | Amount from Income Stmt under expenses | | e.g., sales tax, labor, or materials | | | Property House Number and Street |
| Bank Checking Account | Amount from Owner Draws on Owner Stmt | | | | | Property House Number and Street |
| "House Number Street Name" Main Reserve Account | Amount left in this account | | | | | Property House Number and Street |

- Select Save in bottom right corner

## Enter Bank Account Transactions

- Select Banking at Top Task Bar
- Select Use Register
- Select Community Bank Checking Register
- Enter Transactions from Checkbook register or Bank Statement
- When entering the transactions, add a class to each transaction for the property the expense was for. House number and street name.

## Company-Specific Entries

| COMPANY | ACCOUNT | DOCUMENT | LOGIN | PASSWORD | SAVE DOCUMENT HERE |
|---|---|---|---|---|---|
| Company ABC— Enter Credit Card Charges | Chase Credit Card Class: House # | Link to credit card stmts | | | |
| Company ABC— Adjust interest for loan payment | Loan Payable— XXX Class: House # | Link Amortization Table | | | |
| Company MMM— Adjust interest for loan payment | Loan Payable— AAA Class: House # | Link Amortization Table | | | |
| Company BPB— Enter monthly pymt assign principal & interest | Bank Mortgage And Interest Expense Class: House # | Link Amortization Table—click on payment to view breakdown of principal and interest | | | |
| Company XXY | Loan Payable— CYD | Link Amortization Table | | | |

| | | |
|---|---|---|
| Company DFH | Loan Payable—XXX | Link Amortization Table |
| Company ABC | Bank Account XXXX | |

## Reconcile Bank Accounts

- Select Banking at Top Task Bar
- Select Reconcile
- Select Account
- Confirm Statement Date
- Confirm Statement Beginning Balance
- Enter Statement Ending Balance
- To Reconcile the Reserve Account Use the Ending Cash Balance on the Owner's Statement
- Select OK
- Select Transactions that match Statement
- Select Reconcile

## Email Reports and Backup File

- Select File on the Top Task Bar
- Select Export
- Select To Quickbooks for Mac
- Save File and label it: month.year llc name
  - E.g., 11.20 remington place llc
- Upload File to Google Drive (Link Folder)
  - Select QKBK Backup File Folder for that entity
  - Select File Upload
  - Select backup file and upload
- Email File to accountant@taxmagic.com

Let me show you my Move-In Checklist for new tenants (including directions I use to integrate it with Buildium).

# Move-In Checklist

*Tenant Name:*

*Property Address:*

*Date of Move In:*

| DATE COMPLETE | TASK | BUILDIUM |
|---|---|---|
| ☐ | Application Accepted | |
| ☐ | Enter applicant info into Buildium | Add applicant in Buildium |
| ☐ | Send Hold Deposit email. Template in Buildium | |
| ☐ | Tenant Hold Deposit received of <$XXX> | |
| ☐ | Create tenant Google Drive folder. Labeled <Last Name. Unit#> Saved in Property folder in tenants folder | |
| ☐ | Save Template into Tenant Folder in Google Drive. Labeled <move in checklist. tenant last name> | |
| ☐ | Tenant Move-in Process activated in Buildium | Buildium Applicant Move in |
| ☐ | Enter Tenant Move-in Date from application | |
| ☐ | Enter Tenant Move-in charges and recurring charges from application and unit listing | |
| ☐ | Generate lease | |
| ☐ | Verify data and information in lease; update as necessary | |

| | | |
|---|---|---|
| ☐ | Send lease to tenants to sign electronically | |
| ☐ | Countersign lease | |
| ☐ | Replace cylinder locks with new unit cylinder locks | |
| ☐ | Place old unit cylinders/showing cylinder in storage and tag keys with key code | Buildium End Lease |
| ☐ | Label new keys with unit name and key code | |
| ☐ | | Buildium List Unit |
| ☐ | | Buildium Withhold Tenant Deposit |
| ☐ | | Buildium Move Out Tenant Steps |

## Assistants Can Save the Day!

We can't work 24-7. Even though we may want to sometimes, it just isn't possible, nor is it sustainable. When you think about automation, it might look like hiring someone else to complete a task—a task that will then *feel* automatic because the work is being done without expended effort on your part. Pretty great, right? But where do you find these people and how do you know you can trust them? Good questions. Before I answer them, I want to present you with one of my own. What is one of the first things you can outsource?

Your answer will likely depend on your strategy and passivity goals. But common first responsibilities that you, as an investor, can outsource include: property management, bookkeeping, and even someone to source deals (listen to *Real Estate Rookie* episode #57 for more on using virtual assistants to source deals).

Some tasks can be easily outsourced to virtual assistants (VAs) or even interns who want to be mentored. The first step in getting a VA is to ask yourself what you'd like them to do. To figure that out, I'm going to ask you even more questions.

- What is the task you dislike doing the most?
- What is giving you the lowest return on your time?
- What should you be doing now to get that task off your plate?

Two places I have found virtual assistants are Fiverr and Upwork. Before hiring a virtual assistant, put together a job description and budget, and have a process in place for them to follow (aka those checklists we just talked about). Know exactly what you want them to do. Also, be prepared to do several training calls. Those checklists are great but likely can't stand on their own during the infancy of your new VA's life on your team. But don't worry. That little VA will be off and running (and doing all sorts of great things for you) sooner than you think!

 If you want more advice and expertise about hiring a virtual assistant, check out this *Goal Digger* podcast episode from Jenna Kutcher.

The value of outsourcing isn't just virtual; bringing in assistance can be about freeing up tasks that aren't virtual or even directly related to your business. Let me give you a personal example.

One person I brought on board was a house cleaner for my personal home. Cleaning my house was a task that took up a chunk of my time that I'd rather spend doing something else. Whether that time was used for making money through real estate investing or spent hanging out with my friends and family, both had more value to me than time spent cleaning. So I hired it out. Perhaps for you, this time-sucking activity is grocery shopping and meal prep. You don't need to limit this delegation conversation strictly to your business. Hiring an assistant or someone to take over that role is about reclaiming time and energy you can put into something else. At first it might feel lazy, but if you reframe it, it can be incredibly empowering.

Before we move on to the rest of the chapter, I want to make a quick note that interns are also an option for completing some of this automated work. What's the difference between an intern and a VA? Not a whole lot, but it is a distinction worth noting. Typically, VAs work remotely, thus the whole "virtual" part of their title. They do not take up office space and should be able to walk in ready to complete the jobs you've assigned. An intern is typically a person new to the field, present to learn as much as they are to work. According to Chris Ducker, serial entrepreneur and expert mentor, interns(ships) tend to focus on "the experience" and "learning" rather than "performing." VAs are paid and interns can be too; internships don't have to be unpaid positions. You will probably get a better output from the intern if there is some kind of compensation or possibly even a mentorship opportunity.

## General Apps

In addition to the apps listed earlier in this chapter, here are some of the apps I use on the daily!

- **Personal Capital**. I have all my assets and liabilities listed on this app. I can also link my investment, bank, and mortgage accounts directly, including credit card balances and any other loans. This app makes it easy to check all of your account balances at once! I manually update my Fixed Assets (e.g., properties, farm equipment, herd and vehicle values) every quarter. There is also an option to link your property to Zillow, but I don't recommend relying on the Zestimate.
- **EZ Calculators**. I run different scenarios through my head almost every day. I'm always thinking about how I can improve my financing or my investing. Or if I see a new deal, I want to know what my mortgage payment would be. With this app, I can usually get a rough estimate and decide if it's worth digging into things further. This app has lots of different calculators at your fingertips.
- **Google Tasks**. This app is basically an online to-do list that syncs with your Google Calendar, letting you know what you need to get done. I know I can't be the only one who finds it super satisfying to mark a task complete! Plus, you can keep multiple lists—perfect for people with many projects or multifaceted lives.
- **HoursTracker**. I know we touched on this strategy way back in Chapter 1 when we talked about goal setting, but I want to talk about

it again here because this app is such a powerful tool. I started using this several years ago for my full-time job. Whenever I am not feeling productive, I track where all of my time is going. At the end of the day/week it's interesting to see where it's going, where I can improve, and what needs to be cut out!

Like I said earlier, start simple. Try out one program at a time, and once you have it fully integrated and it feels automatic, add in another one. Soon, you'll be able to use all the time you saved from automated tasks to grow and scale even further.

# HOMEWORK

**1.** Create a checklist for one task. It can be as simple as one of these.

☐ How you pay the water bill for a property

☐ How you search for deals on Realtor.com

☐ How you drive for dollars

☐ How you enter a transaction into bookkeeping

☐ How you list a property for rent

**2.** Download and play around with a few of the apps mentioned above. Choose one that feels like a good fit and try integrating it into your daily routine.

# Chapter 13

# MOTIVATION AND INSPIRATION

The people who make the most from real estate investing don't just have one property—they have a portfolio of properties. Right now, the idea of creating your own portfolio might feel like an Everest too big for you to climb.

For some of you, that may be one property. Good for you. That's what the majority of this book was all about. Finding and making money from one property.

But if you want more—if you want to extend your journey—that's great too. It might mean that you are unable to see your final destination from where you currently stand. It might mean that you need to fuel up for the road ahead. That's what this chapter is all about—motivation and inspiration to carry you through.

There are two wells I visit to draw these important components of my business from: myself and others. I find motivation in seeing what others have achieved. Rather than feeling jealous or competitive, I feel grateful because they have shown me what's possible. Even if they don't tell me how they arrived successfully at their elevated position, I am grateful because through their example, I know that if they can do it, I can too.

As a rookie, it might feel like you don't (yet) have a lot to offer yourself as you stand in this new-to-you arena. Let's look to some others first.

# ALEX ST. MARTIN

**Market:** Hilton Head Island, South Carolina
**Units:** 2
**Strategy:** Seller financing, flipping, buy-and-hold, MTR, STR, and BRRRR (when/if rates go down)
**Years investing:** 2
**Years following BiggerPockets:** 3

I started working for a real estate investor when I was fresh out of college in 2013. I'd never even considered getting into real estate previously, but the longer I had the job, the more I learned and the more I realized how powerful of a tool real estate investing is. I loved the idea of having the freedom and flexibility to spend time with my family and work on my own terms.

In time, I was promoted to property manager and eventually to manager of the entire portfolio. In 2019, my boss had some major, unexpected health problems, so I stepped up and began running the entire company.

My fiancé, Cameron, had expressed interest in investing in real estate. I told him that if he was serious, he needed to do his homework. I pointed him in the direction of BiggerPockets, and the *Real Estate Rookie* podcast premiered that same week! Fast forward only two weeks and Cameron was laid off at the start of the pandemic. He made the best out of a not-ideal situation and spent his newfound free time to really dig into BiggerPockets books and podcasts to learn as much as possible about different investing strategies.

In February 2021, Cameron and I made an offer on one of my boss's properties. We financed the deal with seller financing and ended up flipping the property, selling in December 2021 during excellent market conditions. We used the profits from the first deal to buy two more properties in May 2022, again using seller financing. We're currently renovating both properties and will rent them as short-term rentals in the summer and medium-term rentals in the winter. We have forced a lot of equity with our renovations and will one day BRRRR when/if rates improve.

We've learned so much in the process of doing three full rehabs. We felt like we really went through the ringer on our first deal, since 2021 was such a difficult time in terms of hiring contractors and sourcing materials. That project was such a challenge that all we could do was tell ourselves, "It should never be this hard again!"

Our goal is to buy more of my boss's holdings over the next two years. We want to have the freedom to live lives of our own design, being able to spend time with family and travel as much as we want to. Our philosophy is to create spaces where we could spend time making memories with our families—in turn, others will want to do the same.

# ROSS BOESCH

**Market: North Central Ohio**
**Units: 12**
**Strategy: STR, small multifamily, single-family rentals, flipping**
**Years investing: 6**
**Years following BiggerPockets: 3**

Deep down, I've always known real estate made the most sense to me. I did not have great exposure to REI growing up, but I was always trying to convince my debt-averse mother to make moves. In 2011, at 25, I finally convinced my parents to get a HELOC I could use to buy my first live-in flip. When my wife and I sold that in 2016, we moved into our second live-in flip. After a year of living/working there, we bought our first house hack: a century home in Sandusky, Ohio, with a basement apartment, just when some friends were talking about this new-ish thing called Airbnb. We set up the apartment as a short-term rental and it doubled our expectations.

In 2018, we added a waterfront condo short-term rental to our portfolio, and then took another under management in the spring of 2019. Later that year, while we were renovating the original house hack Airbnb, I was looking for some books to listen to and stumbled across *The Book on Investing in Real Estate with No (and Low) Money Down* by Brandon Turner. As the book started, I recall thinking that this had to be a sales pitch—but I was completely wrong. This is when things started really clicking for me. I purchased pretty much every BiggerPockets title available, signed up for a Pro membership, and immersed myself in the podcasts.

In February 2020, we bought our first BRRRR single-family from a sheriff auction, finished the BRRRR in July, and then bought a fourplex in October. The building was fully rented by spring of 2021, so we grabbed another short-term rental condo later that year, closing on my 35th birthday. But when it rains, it pours (in a good way); the day we got the keys to new the condo, our Realtor told us one of the buildings we'd been chasing—a 10,000-square-foot mixed-used building—fell out of contract. We didn't know how we'd purchase it, but we put it in contract and lined up private financing, closing in January of 2022! We gutted 3,000 square feet to add three more short-term rentals, going live for Memorial Day that year. Currently, we're working on flipping an eight-property single-family portfolio.

Our family goals are to be independent and financially free. Without having stumbled upon one little book, it's unlikely we would have been equipped with enough confidence to pursue the passion hidden inside.

# JACQUELINE BURCH

**Market:** Southeast Michigan
**Units:** 3
**Strategy:** Buy-and-hold, live-in flip, soon venturing into BRRRR
**Years investing:** 7
**Years following BiggerPockets:** 7

My husband and I ventured into real estate just a few months after our fourth son was born. We bought two long-term rentals in a market near our home. They had long-term tenants and cash flowed modestly. Those initial investments took up most of our savings at the time, so we took a break to replenish our reserves (plus, we were pretty busy with full-time jobs and four kids!). Flash forward to 2019, we had the crazy idea to renovate our single-family, bungalow-style home (900 square feet in a high-appreciating market) into a two-and-a-half story colonial to generate massive returns on sale to fund our next investments.

In 2020, we moved our family to the other side of the state and visited the property on the weekends to continue with our renovations. My husband has his builders' license so has been able to do a lot of the work himself. A few months later, we found ourselves pregnant. Surprise! With twins. (We both almost fainted.)

We moved the family back to town into our home with little more than drywall and one working bathroom. My husband laid the floors, tiled all the bathrooms, set all the cabinets, did the trim work and built-ins, finished the closets, hung the doors, installed the hardware, and painted the entire home. Our twins were born in March 2021, and we finished renovations in 2022.

We purchased the home in 2009 for $132,000, put $450,000 into renovations, and recently appraised the home for a whopping $885,000. We're still living in it, with plans to do another live-in flip once we recover and find a property with a bit of land that is large enough for our family of eight.

We have overcome having to sacrifice in the short-term for the sake of our long-term goals and dreams. One image I have is of our twins snuggled up in baby carriers, strapped to our chests while we nail filled trim! We wouldn't trade this experience for anything. It has grown us as investors, as craftspeople, and it's genuinely brought our family together in a unique way. We invest because home is our passion.

Our plan is to turn our sweat equity into BRRRR buy-and-holds over the next few years in order to create spaces that a future tenant can be proud of, raise a family in, and rest in after a long day. We love doing quality work and improving the community around us.

# BRIAN KEITH FOSTER JR.

**Market:** East Texas
**Units:** 3
**Strategy:** Single-family buy-and-hold, BRRRR
**Years investing:** 5
**Years following BiggerPockets:** 2

I first came across the idea to invest in real estate during my high school years. My dream was to live on a boat and travel the world, but I knew in order to do this, I was going to have to save some money. The idea of owning multiple homes resonated with me a lot. I only had one family member who owned a home, and I thought just getting my first house would be an amazing accomplishment in and of itself, not to mention owning enough to live off the income.

In 2013, I finally qualified for my first home using an FHA loan, a two-bed, one-bath house on five acres in Morongo Valley, California. Being young and impatient, though, I moved onto a couple of other business ventures before deciding it was time to get that boat.

I moved to Texas and bought a boat to live on in 2014. It was at that time I realized I could fulfill my need to learn more about real estate while making money by, you guessed it, getting a job in real estate. I took a self-paced course and got my real estate license in a few short weeks. Next, I came across a company that did wholesaling and hard-money loans, and I got a job there (despite having never heard of either industry before). My first month there, I was sales associate of the month; my second month there, I sold five homes in one week alone! I quickly moved into the acquisition side of the company and learned so much. By 2016, my first home had appreciated $100,000, so I sold it and pocketed a great return.

The story isn't all great, though. I was searching for a property to BRRRR and finally found a great property; the plan was that a local credit union would qualify me for a 75 percent cash-out refinance after I bought the property for cash and rehabbed it. But a day before my option was up on the property, my credit dropped severely due to an electric bill going to collections that was under my name despite being for my parents. I had to back out because I was afraid of locking up all my capital without an exit plan. This discouraged me a lot, and I switched my investing strategy completely in 2017—out of real estate.

After a four-year hiatus, I was finally ready to get myself back into real estate. After listening to BiggerPockets podcasts and learning many new techniques, I felt I could take control of my investments. I bought my first rental property in cash for $66,000 in east Texas; by buying in cash, I felt I had less to fear if I couldn't get it rented or had other issues. After getting property management in place, I qualified for an investment loan with my wife, and we bought our second rental property later that year—it needed $30,000 in rehab and took longer than expected, but it was so worth it.

A referral from my property manager got me a great recommendation for a credit union to do a cash-out refinance with the first rental for 80 percent of the value, and I used the money to buy a much better-quality house with higher rents for my third rental. I'm even in the process of refinancing my second rental, and I'll use that money plus the money I have saved to buy a small multifamily closer to where I live.

My next goal is to get my rental portfolio over the $1 million threshold, which I'm a little over halfway to. From there, I'll focus on steady growth until I'm ready to trade my single-family rentals into small multifamily rentals. My loftier goal is to one day own a hotel—I love to travel and have always dreamed of the idea of owning a part of that side of the real estate industry!

I am at a huge advantage when it comes to being inspired by others because I'm the cohost of the *Real Estate Rookie Podcast*. I'm motivated each time we interview a guest. Every time someone talks about one actionable item they did to reach their goal or get their first deal or the next, it makes me realize I can do that thing too! Hearing how others accomplished their goals makes it feel like a possibility for me, and my guests always provide a road map that I—and any listener—can follow or take inspiration from. The great news for you is that this experience isn't one that only I can have. Every one of the interviews I have done (not to mention BiggerPockets as a larger organization) is free and available to you![14]

I also surround myself with like-minded individuals, which for me mostly consists of other real estate investors. I spend time with these people by attending meetups and events, and traveling to visit these real estate friends. Be willing to make that up-front investment in the form of your event ticket. You could pay $900 to attend a two-day event, which might feel like a lot, but during that event, one conversation could pay dividends on your investment in yourself.

At BPCon 2021, at 2:00 a.m. in a pizza place on Bourbon Street in New Orleans, my friends and fellow investors Tyler and Zosia Madden asked me a couple of questions that made me realize exactly what I needed to do with my business. That one conversation propelled me. Without it, I might still be spinning my wheels. Sometimes you know what you should do but still feel stuck, and it's not until someone else asks you questions

---

**14** www.biggerpockets.com/podcasts/real-estate-rookie

that has it just register differently. Sometimes it's not easy knowing your next move, and getting a different perspective or point of view somehow makes the answer obvious. And then there are the people you meet and the connections you make. All this is to say: Buy the ticket. Attend the event. Show up. You'll be happy you did!

## Looking to Yourself

Throughout this book, I've called you a rookie. I probably should have said this earlier, but I view that word "rookie" positively. It's a status. A status that can change.

By definition a rookie is a new recruit, a person in their first season. Look at the attention (and money!) we shower on rookies in the sports world! These players are new and exciting! They are full of promise and potential. That is you!

Just because you are a rookie, don't discount yourself and what you bring to the table. Look at how far you have already come. Look at the knowledge and experiences you have gained. Don't believe me? Ask your accountability partner or group. At your next meeting, take a moment and ask: What is one way you have seen me grow, improve, or level up since we first started meeting? What is one thing you think I do well? When it comes to investing, what do you think is my strongest attribute or skill? And then sit back and listen. You'll be amazed what your community sees in you, how they see you, and, perhaps, how their vision differs from yours. Let their answers lift you up, inspire you, and motivate you to do even more.

Try asking yourself the following questions. Reflect on your answers. See if you can find bits and pieces that motivate and inspire you. Then lean on those words, experiences, and feelings to lift you up to the next level.

- What was your biggest accomplishment in the last ninety days?
- How will you use what you learned going forward?
- What is the biggest change in your life since you started your real estate investment journey?
- What action items are you going to continue?
- What is your next goal?
- How are you going to celebrate your wins?

Let's look at it another way. What if another person in your life suddenly became interested in real estate investment? They have no idea what it all entails and are looking for some information to dip their toes in the proverbial investment waters. They have seen you working in this field and have come to you for advice on getting started. What would you say?

My point is that you would have things to say. You would have advice to give and stories to share. You would have resources and people you could recommend. Look at you go, rookie! Look. At. You.

Remember that woman I said I was in my twenties? A complete Real Estate Rookie. If I can make it, why can't you? The answer is simple: There is no reason. You can do this. You already are. I am still a Rookie at many different investing strategies, and that's one of the great parts of real estate investing. It never gets boring; there is always more to learn and room to grow.

Take off that rookie jersey and slide into a uniform more appropriate to your current status. I'm proud to say that you've graduated.

We could stop here. It would be a nice ending. But I want to go just a little further on down your real estate journey road. Yes, this book has been mostly about purchasing your first property. Hopefully through the advice and knowledge I've shared with you on these pages, you've been able to accomplish that goal. But what if you want more?

## Pull a Ross Geller and PIVOT!

We have talked about building a strong foundation with a single strategy when you start out. Can you do that strategy forever? Yes, probably. Are there factors that affect that strategy's continued success? Yes again. If markets change, laws or regulations change, or even funding changes, you may need to pivot.

Pivoting means readjusting your goals and possibly your business plan to something that is more opportune. Let me be clear: This is different from shiny-object syndrome. This is not chasing different strategies and methods and seeing what sticks. This is coming up with a game plan to reassess what you are currently doing and deciding if you need to restructure to better accommodate other variables that are affecting your business.

Remember in Chapter 2 when we discussed the short-term rental regulations changing in Joshua Tree? This is a prime example of a reason to realign, and pivot if necessary. This is just one example, but I share it in the hopes of showing you how situations can change. Do regular check-ins with yourself and your business to be sure you are still on the best path. And if not, PIVOT!

## Preparing for What Comes Next

You are an investor. Buying that first property may be the first step, but it's a huge step. It propels you into your journey. There are a lot of people who never take that first step. If you don't ever start, you'll never get your next property. My favorite thing about real estate is that there are so many opportunities—opportunities that are absolutely achievable. You don't have to attend college; you don't have to have a lot of experience or money. Real estate investing really does have a low barrier to entry. You are fully capable of doing lots of cool stuff, and buying that first property is just the beginning.

Now that you have done that, stay focused on your strategy. Become an expert on that strategy and in your market. Honestly, after a while, it may get boring. It may not feel sexy enough to be clickbait on YouTube. But do you know what's *not* boring? Becoming a millionaire, retiring from your W-2 job twenty years earlier than planned, and having peace of mind that you can afford those emergency expenditures that occasionally pop up. No matter the path you choose to start with, stick with it. If you do, you'll be able to move more efficiently and effectively than you could if you wandered all over the real estate map.

Have you ever heard the saying "Money can't buy you happiness"? I believe that's 100 percent correct. But have you ever heard the song "Buy Me a Boat" by Chris Janson? Despite the first popular saying, I believe that song holds some truth as well. Chris talks about how money can't buy happiness, but it *can* buy him a boat, and a boat will make him happy. The way I see it, unhappiness can be caused by not having money. Money can't guarantee that you will be happy, but I do think it can help relieve a lot of stress and give you the opportunity to be happy. In my opinion and experiences, creating wealth increases a person's ability to be happy and have peace of mind. Just remember, as you pursue wealth and independence, to not lose sight of your "why."

There were three people in my life who recently told me that they were proud of me. It was extremely meaningful because these people don't throw that word around lightly. It was tremendously motivating and validating to know, through their compliments, that I was on the right path. I felt like I was walking on air knowing that people cared and recognized that I was trying to make a difference. The feeling these three people instilled in me had nothing to do with money. It was all about my work ethic, my endurance, and what I was accomplishing. I'm going to tell you right now to surround yourself with those types of people. Maybe it's one person, or maybe it's a group of people. But you need to have people in your life who won't be jealous, who won't hold you back, who won't judge you, but who will instead push you to be better while simultaneously supporting you. Whether that person is your spouse, your business partner, or a fellow investor, find the connection. Having someone who actually recognizes the wins and celebrates with you to hold you accountable will make this journey a lot more impactful (and also more fun!).

I do honestly believe that most people crave a sense of belonging. But it's not just a desire to belong to any old thing. What people really crave is a sense of belonging to a community that is like-minded or has a similar interest. Real estate investors attend conferences and masterminds to be with like-minded individuals, people join churches to be around others with similar beliefs, and outdoorsy people join conservation clubs to shoot trap and 3D archery. The examples are endless.

My point is this: *Find your people.* Whether you start your own community or you join one, find the people who will inspire you, motivate you, push you, and understand what you are trying to do. Even if those people aren't in your town, you can make it happen. Our ability to connect online and through videoconferencing and social media is greater than ever. Don't let proximity or geography keep you from finding or spending time with your people. The real estate people I met at a real estate mastermind in March of 2021 are now *my people.* We are scattered across the country and yet, somehow, we still end up seeing one another at least every other month. You can make this happen. It is important that you do.

And that's it. We've reached the end of the rookie road. Thank you for taking the time to read and learn with me. While your real estate education will be a lifelong journey, by reading this book you are equipped to make your first investment and take the first step to an independent, entrepreneurial life. Now head on out there and show the world the pro I know you are capable of becoming. Make sure you do these final homework assignments, but also know that I am so proud of you!

# HOMEWORK

**1.** Check in with your accountability partner or group. Share your wins as well as your new goals! Remember to cheer them on and offer support as well. In these groups, you should be giving as much (or more!) than you get.

**2.** Place notes in your calendar three, six, nine, and twelve months out to check in on your investments and pivot as necessary.

**3.** Find at least two online mentors (like me!) to follow and learn from. Just because we've reached the end of the book doesn't mean you should stop learning!

# ACKNOWLEDGMENTS

**H**ave you ever succeeded or accomplished anything all by yourself—without the help of even one person? I doubt it. Teachers, coaches, mentors, friends, family, vendors, contractors, accountants, attorneys . . . the list goes on. So many people have influenced and provided value to the accomplishments and achievements of others, whether directly or indirectly. Ever since Pace Morby brought this idea to my attention, it's stayed with me. I can't think of one time I did something without the help of others. In some way or form, I've always leaned on other people. This book is a product of all those people who have touched my life and helped to build what is in this book.

The idea of writing a book was a dream it never occurred to me to have. It took a lot of people to guide me into what that actual process was and most importantly motivated me that I could do this. There is nothing more I dislike than sitting down at a computer for hours and hours. Let's just say the "high" of writing a book wore off quickly as I learned how difficult it is to do! Thank you to the BiggerPockets Publishing team, especially Savannah Wood, who pushed me, supported me, had a ton of patience, and was my biggest advocate. Katie Miller and Kaylee Walterbach, I want to thank you both for believing in me, even if this took way longer to write than planned! Thank you to Peri Eryigit for the marketing magic. And I'm grateful to the editors and designers who made this book beautiful— Wendy Dunning, Peter Kranitz, and Janice Bryant. Also, so many thanks to Amanda Zieba for helping me find the words to my thoughts.

When I first started writing this book, my friend Brian Murray was a wealth of knowledge and insight on what to expect during the process. I'm forever thankful for his friendship and those initial conversations not only on writing a book but also on investing in general.

This book would never have come into fruition if it weren't for my *Real Estate Rookie* podcast co-host, Tony Robinson, along with my handler,

Eric Knutson. Every recording is a blessing, and we are so lucky to have the honor of leading the rookie community, which motivates us more than anything. Every time we get to record with a guest, we learn something new. A huge thank-you to every guest who has taken the time to appear on the show, giving their experience and knowledge to us all. The podcast wouldn't have been possible without Kevin Leahy—I say that he "discovered me" and I'll always be grateful for the opportunity and how he changed my life overnight.

Finally, to the rookie community . . . you all are rockstars. Taking the initiative to change your lives is something a lot of people are scared to do. Every day, it blows my mind to see what you all are capable of doing. For those of you just getting started—thank you for beginning with this book. I hope it creates the start of a whole new life.

# More from
# BiggerPockets Publishing

If you enjoyed this book, we hope you'll take a moment to check out some of the other great material BiggerPockets offers. Whether you crave freedom or stability, a backup plan, or passive income, BiggerPockets empowers you to live life on your own terms through real estate investing. Find the information, inspiration, and tools you need to dive right into the world of real estate investing with confidence.

**Sign up today—it's free! Visit www.BiggerPockets.com
Find our books at www.BiggerPockets.com/store**

### The Book on Tax Strategies for the Savvy Real Estate Investor

Taxes! Boring and irritating, right? Perhaps. But if you want to succeed in real estate, your tax strategy will play a huge role in how fast you grow. A great tax strategy can save you thousands of dollars a year. A bad strategy could land you in legal trouble. With *The Book on Tax Strategies for the Savvy Real Estate Investor,* you'll find ways to deduct more, invest smarter, and pay far less to the IRS!

### Buy, Rehab, Rent, Refinance, Repeat

Invest in real estate and never run out of money! In *Buy, Rehab, Rent, Refinance, Repeat*, you'll discover the incredible strategy known as BRRRR—a long-hidden secret of the ultra-rich and those with decades of experience. Author and investor David Greene holds nothing back, sharing the exact systems and processes he used to scale his business from buying two houses per year to buying two houses per *month* using the BRRRR strategy.

### The Intention Journal

Some people can achieve great wealth, rock-solid relationships, age-defying health, and remarkable happiness—and so many others struggle, fail, and give up on their dreams, goals, and ambitions. Could it simply be that those who find success are more intentional about it? Once you build intentionality into your daily routine, you can achieve the incredible success that sometimes seems out of reach. Backed by the latest research in psychology, this daily planner offers an effective framework to set, review, and accomplish your goals.

### First-Time Home Buyer

Everything you need to buy your first home, from initial decisions all the way to the closing table! Scott Trench and Mindy Jensen of the *BiggerPockets Money Podcast* have been buying and selling houses for a collective thirty years. In this book, they'll give you a comprehensive overview of the home-buying process so you can consider all of your options and avoid pitfalls while jumping into the big, bad role of homeowner.

### The Book on Flipping Houses

Written by active real estate investor and fix-and-flipper J Scott, this book contains more than 300 pages of step-by-step training, perfect for both the complete newbie and the seasoned pro looking to build a house-flipping business. Whatever your skill level, this book will teach you everything you need to know to build a profitable business and start living the life of your dreams.

### The Book on Rental Property Investing

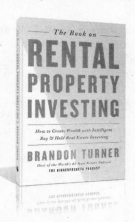

With nearly 400 pages of in-depth advice for building wealth through rental properties, this evergreen best-seller imparts the practical and exciting strategies that investors across the world are using to build significant cash flow through real estate investing. Investor, best-selling author, and co-host of *The BiggerPockets Podcast,* Brandon Turner has one goal in mind: to give you every strategy, tool, tip, and technique you need to become a millionaire rental property investor!

### *The Book on Managing Rental Properties*

From the top-selling author of *The Book on Rental Property Investing*, this companion book will be your comprehensive guide to effectively managing tenants in your rental properties. Being a landlord doesn't have to mean middle-of-the-night phone calls, costly evictions, or daily frustrations with ungrateful tenants. With this book, you'll learn every trick, tool, and system you need to manage your rentals—leading to more freedom, less drama, and higher profits from your real estate business.

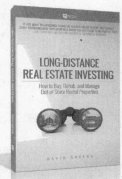

### *Long-Distance Real Estate Investing*

Don't let your location dictate your financial freedom: Live where you want, and invest anywhere it makes sense! The rules, technology, and markets have changed: No longer are you forced to invest only in your backyard. In *Long-Distance Real Estate Investing*, learn an in-depth strategy to build profitable rental portfolios through buying, managing, and flipping out-of-state properties from real estate investor and agent David Greene.

### *Short-Term Rental, Long-Term Wealth*

From analyzing potential properties to effectively managing your listings, this book is your one-stop resource for making a profit with short-term rentals! Airbnb, Vrbo, and other listing services have become massively popular in recent years—why not tap into the gold mine? Avery Carl will show you how to choose, acquire, and manage a short-term rental from anywhere in the country, plus how to avoid common pitfalls and overcome obstacles that keep many would-be investors from ever getting started.

### *The House Hacking Strategy*

Don't pay for your home. Hack it and live for free! When mastered, house hacking can save you thousands of dollars in monthly expenses, build tens of thousands of dollars in equity each year, and provide the financial means to retire early. Discover why so many successful investors support their investment careers with house hacking—and learn from a frugality expert who has "hacked" his way toward financial freedom.

# CONNECT WITH BIGGERPOCKETS

## Live Life on Your Terms Through Real Estate Investing!

Facebook
/BiggerPockets

Instagram
@BiggerPockets

Twitter
@BiggerPockets

LinkedIn
/company/Bigger
Pockets

Website
BiggerPockets.com